The Amistad Revolt

MEMORY, SLAVERY,
AND THE POLITICS
OF IDENTITY IN
THE UNITED STATES
AND SIERRA LEONE

The Amistad Revolt

Iyunolu Folayan Osagie

UNIVERSITY OF GEORGIA PRESS

ATHENS AND LONDON

© 2000 by the University of Georgia Press
Athens, Georgia 30602
All rights reserved
Designed by Erin Kirk New
Set in 10 on 13 Sabon by G & S Typesetters
Printed and bound by Thomson-Shore
The paper in this book meets the guidelines for
permanence and durability of the Committee on
Production Guidelines for Book Longevity of the
Council on Library Resources.

Printed in the United States of America

04 03 02 01 00 C 5 4 3 2 1

Library of Congress Cataloging-in-Publication Data

Osagie, Iyunolu Folayan, 1960–
The Amistad revolt : memory, slavery, and the politics of
identity in the United States and Sierra Leone /
Iyunolu Folayan Osagie.
p. cm.
Includes bibliographical references and index.
ISBN 0-8203-2224-5 (alk. paper)
1. Slave insurrections—United States.   2. Amistad (Schooner)
3. Afro-Americans—Ethnic identity.   4. Group identity—
Political aspects—United States.   5. Memory—Social
aspects—United States.   6. Memory—social aspects—
Sierra Leone.   7. Freedmen—Sierra Leone—History—
19th century—Case studies.   8. Group identity—Political
aspects—Sierra Leone.   I. Title.
E447 .O73   2000
326'.0973—dc21   99-087625

British Library Cataloging-in-Publication Data available

To God be the Glory

Shuttles in the rocking loom of history,

the dark ships move, the dark ships move,

their bright ironical names

like jests of kindness on a murderer's mouth;

plough through thrashing glister toward

fata morgana's luscent melting shore,

weave toward New World littorals that are

mirage and myth and actual shore.

Voyage through death,

    voyage whose chartings are unlove.

"MIDDLE PASSAGE," BY ROBERT HAYDEN

Contents

Acknowledgments ix

Introduction xi

PART ONE. REMEMBERING THE PAST

Chapter One. The Amistad Story in the American Context 3

Chapter Two. Slave Revolts and the Production of Identity 24

Chapter Three. The Amistad Returnees and the Mende Mission 53

PART TWO. REINVENTING THE PRESENT

Chapter Four. Sculpting History: African American
Burdens of Memory 71

Chapter Five. National Identity: The Dramatic Return
of Memory in Sierra Leone 98

Chapter Six. Hollywood Images, African Memories:
Spielberg's *Amistad* and Sierra Leone Culture and Politics 119

Afterword 136

Notes 139

Works Cited 161

Index 175

Acknowledgments

This research was generously supported by grants from the Research and Graduate Studies Office, College of Liberal Arts, and the Minority Faculty Development Office at the Pennsylvania State University.

The helpful comments offered by the University of Georgia Press readers have guided me through the revision of this book. I thank especially Kristine Blakeslee of the University of Georgia Press and Jayne Plymale for their editorial help. I also want to thank my English department colleagues for both professional and personal support. I am grateful for the valuable suggestions on parts of the manuscript received from Bernard Bell, Cary Fraser, and Deborah Clarke. I am indebted to Carla Mulford who read the entire manuscript and offered helpful criticism and advice. Family and friends also offered their unfailing support throughout this project. Let me especially thank my sisters, Octavia, Kashope, Susan, Michele, and Deborah, and my children, Iviose, Osaze, and Ebinose. Finally, I thank my husband Sylvester for his helpful criticism and infinite patience.

I am also deeply grateful to the following people for granting me interviews: Alfred Marder, Ed Hamilton, Charlie Haffner, Raymond Desouza George, and Samuel Pieh. I also thank the staff of the Amistad Research Center at Tulane and the Beneicke Rare Books Library at Yale.

I gratefully acknowlege permission to reprint from the following source: Iyunolu Osagie, "Historical Memory and a New National Consciousness: The Amistad Revolt Revisited in Sierra Leone," *Massachusetts Review* 38, no. 1 (Spring 1997): 63–83.

Introduction

The many stories surrounding the Amistad revolt and its aftermath are compelling arguments in the nineteenth-century arena of identity politics and in twentieth-century discourse on the formation of political conscious-ness. The revolt and the subsequent trial cases in the United States are relevant to people living in both the United States and Sierra Leone, even to this day. Analysis of the social and political factors that precipitated the debate on slavery and the question of human rights, first in the United States and more recently in Sierra Leone, shows that the Amistad revolt of 1839 initiated key dialogues about race, culture, and the law. The Amistad case helped to ground abstract debates about the constitutional rights of American slaves through the corporeal reality of the Amistad Africans, whose rhetorical insistence throughout the trial focused the debate on the defendants' identity rather than on their actions.

The Amistad case also produced a major paradigm shift in the ap-proach of the U.S. North to the problem of slavery. The politics of aboli-tionism was effective at two levels: although the battle against slavery was necessarily fought in the American justice system, its success depended on the grassroots involvement of a sympathetic public. The implications of the Amistad event in the arena of identity politics are manifest in a specific body of commemorative processes in both the United States and Sierra Leone. These processes engage individual and collective "re-memory" of resistance in slavery.

The Amistad story revolves around events that began in 1839 just off the waters of Cuba. African captives onboard an American-built schooner, named *La Amistad* ("friendship" in English), revolted against their Spanish captors with the hope of freeing themselves and returning to Africa. In the ensuing struggle, the captain and his cook were killed; two of the Africans also lost their lives. The Africans spared the lives of the Spanish shipmasters, believing that the mariners would help navigate the ship to Africa. However, the Spanish crew tricked them by sailing east toward Africa during the day but at night sailing westward, following the North Star in an effort to reach the United States. Captured by an American naval crew two months later, the schooner ended its meandering route near Culloden Point, Long Island, New York. The ship was towed to New London, Connecticut. Charged with murder and piracy, the Africans were jailed in New Haven.

Three major Western powers—the United States, England, and Spain— and two American presidents, President Martin Van Buren and former president John Quincy Adams, were involved in the diplomatic and legal battles that followed. With the support of American abolitionists, the Africans took their case to the Supreme Court and won their freedom. In November 1841 they boarded another ship, the *Gentleman,* along with black and white American missionaries, to return to Sierra Leone, the land from which they had been stolen. Today, the State of Connecticut, the city of New Haven in particular, takes pride in the legacy of the Amistad affair. Connecticut's 1992 celebration of the 150th anniversary of the Amistad event and the state's $2 million commission for a model of *La Amistad,* designed as a floating museum, are part of the institutional attempts to memorialize the Amistad story in America.

Although the Amistad case is well documented and was widely known in the nineteenth century, it has until recently been largely ignored. Even though the Amistad rebellion is credited with being one of the first notable civil rights events in the United States, the somewhat arbitrary and inadequate commemoration of the Amistad story mirrored the extent to which most Americans were unaware of the Amistad case in American history. Individual historians, literary artists, and fine artists have, from time to time, returned to the event, but it is only in the last decade that corporate effort, both in the United States and Sierra Leone, has institutionalized the event. In the United States in particular, Steven Spielberg's film *Amistad,* released in December 1997, has precipitated much interest in the history of the Amistad and the legacy of America's slave past.

In Sierra Leone, the event went unheralded for one hundred fifty years. Most Sierra Leoneans were ignorant of the grand events of the Amistad victory, but commemorative processes now in place have ignited the nation's imagination and engendered a sense of national identity. The portrait of the Amistad hero, Sengbe Pieh (known in America as Joseph Cinque), now graces the highest denomination of currency in Sierra Leone. Through other iconographic forms, such as wall murals and stamps, the nation has succeeded in commemorating the event.

My interest in the Amistad incident began in 1993 when I stumbled on the story in Charles Johnson's *Middle Passage* and Robert Hayden's poem of the same name, both of which I subsequently assigned as required reading in a class I taught on African American writers at Pennsylvania State University. Researching the Amistad story as part of the background plot to Johnson's *Middle Passage,* I was stunned to discover the citizenship of the Amistad revolters. Although I was born and raised in Sierra Leone, I never once heard the story told in the community, nor did I encounter the story as a part of the school curriculum. In fact, like most Sierra Leoneans, I was totally unaware of the story's existence. This discovery has since led me to wonder about my ignorance of other significant stories that have been erased from the cultural memory in Sierra Leone. Having been nurtured in the settler community of Sierra Leone's capital city, Freetown, I now wonder why slavery's resonance has been muted. How could we have forgotten such hallmarks in our history? Why did we forget the Amistad story? More important, why have we chosen to remember this story now, at the close of the twentieth century?

These questions led me in 1994 on a month-long field trip to Sierra Leone. Supported by grants from the Research and Graduate Studies Office of the College of Liberal Arts and the Office of Minority Faculty Development at Pennsylvania State University, I conducted interviews in Freetown and observed the performative discourses (such as theater) related to the Amistad story in particular and the slave past in general. Since 1995 I have worked with the American Missionary Association archival documents housed at the Amistad Research Center at Tulane University. I have also traveled to New Haven, Connecticut, the site of many of the Amistad court trials. On the site where the Amistad slaves once were jailed, a commemorative sculpture now stands. I have had the opportunity to study this sculpture and to interview the artist who created it. Excitement continues to build on both sides of the Atlantic over ways to commemorate the Amistad saga. It is not at all coincidental that a filmmaker of Steven Spielberg's stature chose to depict this classic narrative.

In *The Amistad Revolt,* I take up the story of the Amistad by focusing on how its reappearance as a collective act of memory is influencing and revitalizing nation-building and cultural identity. Other scholars have mainly focused on the legal and historical aspects covering the twenty-seven-month incarceration of the Amistad Africans. Interestingly, apart from an occasional paragraph or two, the narratives of most authors conclude with the departure of the Africans from the United States. Some fictional works, such as Blair Niles's *East By Day* (1941), have attempted to reconstruct later events. But these works imagine rather than account for the historical facts of the Amistad story, which continued to unfold in Sierra Leone. Part of my goal is to reconstruct the events that took place after the captives returned to Africa. This search for the missing pieces in the Amistad story, I believe, is only a part of our mission as contemporary scholars. Sierra Leoneans such as myself must also examine the ways in which we have taken for granted our cultural past, even as we come to terms with more current representations that assist in creating a national identity.

How should we relate to a victory that is found in medias res in the Amistad story? I attempt to answer this question by approaching the Amistad story as an interdisciplinary text. My goal is to analyze the multiple registers at work in the nineteenth-century world of the Amistad event and to consider the differing cultural acts of production of the Amistad narrative today. *The Amistad Revolt* is an attempt to bridge the gap between past and present, to establish the ongoing relevance of the Amistad event to the identity politics of our day.

Part one of this book offers narrative and analytical accounts of the configuration of African bodies—slaves, captives, the colonized—in nineteenth-century encounters with the West. The first chapter presents the Amistad case in the American context and reviews the existing literature on it. Although the Amistad story has attracted a select community of writers in disciplines such as history, law, anthropology, literature, and the fine arts, the narrative facts of the case still need to appeal more broadly to the American public. Therefore, in addition to recounting the Amistad revolt and the subsequent trials, I also attempt a metanalysis of the universe of materials relating to the Amistad case. Part of my goal is to reveal the wealth of information available and to acknowledge the gaps that still need to be addressed, especially now that the Amistad saga is becoming a popular subject.

Chapter 2 explores historical antecedents to contextualize the Amistad narrative with other slave revolts in the Western Hemisphere. Because the Saint Domingue revolution was the rallying symbol for several major slave revolts in the United States during the first half of the nineteenth century, this chapter explores the centrality of this symbol through the impact it had in the public arena of politics and in the private desires of both masters and slaves. The Saint Domingue resistance provided an unparalleled heroic affirmation of the humanity of Africans consigned to life in bondage as chattel slaves. The terror this resistance created in the slaveholding world climaxed in the outcome of the Amistad trials. My reading of this cultural narrative of terror is assisted by Erving Goffman's suggestions about the dramatic model in *The Presentation of Self in Everyday Life*. Although the Saint Domingue story and the Amistad event were almost half a century apart, their symbolic potency for the discourse of slave revolts resonates in the copious literary material they have inspired.

The third chapter focuses on the early years of the Mende mission in Sierra Leone and the ways in which the Amistad returnees negotiated their new status as "recaptives" within the colonial context of an emerging nation. The American missionaries who accompanied the Amistad returnees became significant players in the production of new African identities. The collision of cultural ideologies and the subsequent effects of the colonial process on the missionaries and their African "flock" is reflected in letters from missionaries to their sponsors in the United States. This chapter also explores the responses—the complicities and resistances— of the Africans and the missionaries to the pressures of colonization. The political, spiritual, and social processes set in motion by the initial revolt of the Africans in the Americas demonstrate that Africans were historical agents who actively engaged the colonial project of modernity.

Part two of *The Amistad Revolt* examines the relevance of the Amistad revolt in contemporary society. Through a number of artistic and political interpretations, contemporary artists reveal the many dynamic ways in which the historical past can become usable in the present.

Chapter 4 shows how African American artists have interrogated the politics of identity through the themes of exile and return. Foregrounding the revolt rather than the court trials (the latter is common in American narratives on the subject), Owen Dodson's 1939 centennial dramatic production, *Amistad*, inscribes the historical challenges of the Great Depression years in the struggles of Africans onboard *La Amistad*. John Thorpe's

Amistad play titled *Chap Am So* (1996) equally illustrates the significance of interpreting the past from the vantage point of the present. His postmodern style reflects the fluid, multidiscourse approach of the 1990s and uses the Middle Passage experience to examine issues of race, nationality, cultural memory, and identity.

This chapter also reviews the iconographic influences of the Amistad Memorial, designed by artist Ed Hamilton of Louisville, Kentucky. Hamilton has shaped the historical event of 1839 in the context of his own African American reality. For example, he interprets the Amistad experience more in terms of captivity than in terms of the Africans' return to the homeland. By emphasizing the Atlantic crossing to the Americas, symbolized in the droplets of water that form the surface texture of the monument, Hamilton focuses attention on African Americans' state of exile in the United States. The Amistad memorial is a testament to the slaves who died in the incident, even as it recalls those who reversed the situation and returned to Africa. Hamilton's tripartite sculpture is the only known public monument in America that is clearly dedicated to continental Africans. As a symbol of unity between Africans and their diasporic relatives, and between black peoples and their new relationship with the West, this monument both commemorates and helps fashion the debate on diasporic identities.

In chapter 5, I address the issue of collective memory by examining the intersections between the Amistad incident and current social and political engagement of the episode in Sierra Leone. For over one hundred fifty years, Sierra Leoneans knew little or nothing about the Amistad incident or its dramatic unfolding in the Americas from 1839 to 1842. Only recently, after a century and a half, has the nation "suddenly" remembered the event and claimed it as part of its heritage. Just as a specific set of circumstances prevented this event from taking its proper place in history, so too have certain social, political, and performative discourses been responsible for the reinscription of the Amistad in the psyche of the nation. Specifically, the literal intervention of Charlie Haffner's play, *Amistad Kata Kata,* helped to awaken the cultural and political consciousness of the Sierra Leonean people during the military coup of 1992. Playwright Raymond Desouza George, a professor of theater arts at the University of Sierra Leone, has also used the Amistad narrative as a means to revive the nation's interest in Sierra Leonean heroes of the past; his play *The Broken Handcuff* explores the broader historical and social implications of cultural memory.

In the final chapter, Steven Spielberg's movie, *Amistad,* is read against the cultural memory of the Amistad revolt, which Sierra Leoneans now see as a dynamic historical force in their lives. Meditating on the controversies surrounding the movie and the ambivalent responses from audiences and film critics, this chapter locates the politics of representation in the movie within the context of the opposing cultural memories of Sierra Leoneans.

My goal in *The Amistad Revolt* is twofold, then. I seek to map the story of the Amistad revolt while also examining the links between the past and current revivalist interpretations. Part of my project, however, is to explore specific connections between the perceptions of the event in the United States and those I have gleaned in Sierra Leone. As a transatlantic project that engages history, dramatic literature, plastic arts, sociology, and film, this work analyzes identity politics from within the specific historical and cultural environment. It also considers the concepts of memory and identity that are necessary to the cultural negotiations with which black peoples around the world today are engaged and, perhaps more important, that they seek to understand.

PART ONE

Remembering the Past

The song is over, but words remain in excess.

SIERRA LEONEAN PROVERB

CHAPTER ONE

The Amistad Story in the American Context

By the nineteenth century, when the Amistad[1] tragedy unfolded, the traumatic realities of pillage, death, and enslavement were lived experiences in most of Africa. To mention one particular instance, many Africans from around the Vai-Mende country were taken captive to Dombokoro, or Lomboroko or Lomboko,[2] and sold to Laigo and Luiz, two notorious Spanish slave dealers.[3] Dombokoro was on the western coast in the Gallinas country, what today is the border area between Sierra Leone and Liberia. In Lomboko, Spanish and Portuguese slave dealers built several forts where captured Africans were imprisoned for months at a time, as circumstances demanded, to await slave buyers who made lucrative wholesale purchases for even more profitable retail markets in the New World. The captives' stories were often similar. Many had been kidnapped, overpowered by several African slave catchers, while on a journey to their farms, on a trip to another village to buy goods, or while running some simple errand in the vicinity of home. Some were taken, in a putatively legal subterfuge, as prisoners of war, while they were trying to escape from their villages that were being pillaged.[4]

Throughout most of the eighteenth century, and increasingly in the early and mid–nineteenth century, both intertribal and intratribal wars in Africa were incited by the high demand for slaves in the West.[5] In the attempt either to protect their villages or to participate in the principal market economy that slavery had become, many chiefs and their people went on the "war path" or "war road."[6] The economic and social instability evoked by these wars in the entire Senegambia region made the acquisition of slaves extremely easy. The situation ensnared many families into pawning their children for unpaid debts. In some cases, children were kid-napped, or the parents themselves were forcibly taken and pressed into slavery. Whatever their individual stories, African captives from the south-ern part of Sierra Leone and the northern part of Liberia, and even as far as the southeastern part of present-day Guinea, often met a similar fate once they arrived at a slave-trading center such as that in Dombokoro.

The Spanish dealers at Dombokoro, Laigo and Luiz, might have been agents in the service of the infamous Pedro Blanco, a Spanish slave trader who owned a large part of the slave industry and whose formidable trade in human flesh was an established fact in the Western world. Blanco ser-viced many slave-trading ports in the Americas. Accounts by some of the Amistad captives who had been among the dispossessed Africans in Laigo and Luiz's establishment and by other sources reveal that Blanco had purchased about six hundred slaves from both Spanish and Portuguese establishments. These slaves were transported onboard the Portuguese slaver *Tecora* in the spring of 1839 to a barracoon just outside Havana, Cuba, then a Spanish colony.[7]

Spain had signed a treaty with Great Britain in 1817, agreeing to com-ply with the suppression of the African slave trade; this treaty took effect in 1820. It was common knowledge, however, that Spanish peoples in the colonies consistently allowed the ongoing trade in the territories. Indeed, Spanish territories in the Caribbean depended heavily on slave labor for cultivation of plantations. Because their arduous tasks literally killed slaves by the thousands, the system was dependent on the African slave markets to replenish the continually depleted workforce. In the Cuban markets, a bureaucratic veneer was all that was needed to grant safe pas-sage to slave traders and their human cargo. Through false documenta-tion, slaves were quickly dispersed under Blanco throughout the island as *ladinos,* resident slaves before 1820 (when the treaty took effect), rather than according to their true status as *bozales,* slaves illegally imported after 1820.[8] Blanco's advertised sale drew many investors, among them Pedro Montes, who bought three girls and one boy, all under twelve years of age, and Jose Ruiz, who purchased forty-nine men. Though mostly un-related to each other, this particular set of captives generally came from the interior part of the Mende country in the southern area of present-day Sierra Leone.

Their new owners were headed for Guanaja, en route to Puerto Príncipe, now called Camagüey, about three hundred miles east-southeast of Havana, their final destination. Along with the slaves, Montes and Ruiz had boarded *La Amistad,* the Baltimore-based vessel originally named *Friendship* prior to being transferred to its Spanish owner, Captain Ramon Ferrer. Built for speed, the long, low, black schooner was about six years old, a veteran of the horrendous trade even before its adventure with the Amistad captives, as this particular set of slaves came to be known.

On June 28, 1839, Captain Ferrer, his cook Celestino, his cabin boy Antonio, Montes, Ruiz, and their fifty-three Africans and two Spanish crewmembers left Havana for a seemingly uneventful trip to Puerto Príncipe. The journey should have ended within three days, but contrary winds kept them at sea on the third night, when the captives revolted against their captors.[9] Although the captives' bondage onboard *La Amistad* was, relatively speaking, less horrendous than their Middle Passage trip from Africa to the Americas on the *Tecora,* the slaves reacted violently because Celestino had taunted them that they were to be killed, salted, and cooked as meat for their Spanish owners.[10] The troubled captives believed the story, and Sengbe Pieh (commonly known as Joseph Cinque or Cingue in most Amistad accounts),[11] who was looked upon as a leader, finally decided that they should defend themselves: "We may as well die trying to be free, as to be killed and eaten," he had concluded.[12]

The Revolt

That night, Sengbe, with the help of Grabeau, broke the padlock and the chains of the iron collars around their necks. Wasting no time, Sengbe and the forty-eight men secured some cane knives they had found in the hold of the ship. In the ensuing struggle between captors and captives, the captain and his mulatto cook were killed. Montes sustained a gash on the head but survived. Two of the African captives were killed. The two Spanish seamen escaped overboard in a small boat. Closely aided by Grabeau, Sengbe emerged as the charismatic leader. With the full support of the other captives, Sengbe wrested control from his captors.

Lacking navigational skills, however, the Africans required the help of Ruiz and Montes, their new prisoners. Antonio, Captain Ferrer's cabin boy, was installed as an interpreter for them and their Spanish prisoners. Invoking many threats, they commanded Ruiz and Montes to sail back to Africa. Montes had been master of a vessel once, so was skilled in manning the schooner. Unbeknownst to the Africans, however, he intended to use his navigational skills to his and Ruiz's advantage. During the day, he complied with Sengbe's demand to sail east in the direction of the rising sun. But at night, Montes navigated by the stars, heading north and west, hoping for help from some other ship that might rightly assess their situation.

While they zigzagged along, eastward then westward, their food and water ran out. The Amistad Africans took the risk of occasionally buying these essentials from other ships and from a few islands. According to Montes, in his testimony onboard the *Washington* brig, which eventually came to their rescue: "We anchored at least thirty times, and lost an anchor at New Providence." During their two-month-long journey along the American coastline, eight more died of various diseases. With death in their midst, the Africans' most immediate need was to survive as best they could in the deteriorating circumstances at sea. They eventually realized that the Spanish prisoners had indeed tricked them, but their immediate concern with replacing vanishing food supplies forestalled all punitive measures against their Spanish deceivers. Thus, after lingering near Long Island, New York, for three days, they decided to berth at Culloden Point, near Montauk, on August 26, 1839.[13]

The American Experience

Weeks before *La Amistad* berthed, stories about a piratical-looking schooner manned by blacks had been circulating in the newspapers, causing much excitement among New England residents. Several ships had sighted *La Amistad,* and two pilot boats had actually made contact with the Africans, but none could decipher the schooner's strange orientation or its destination. Eventually, Sengbe and a few other men disembarked to buy much-needed supplies. On learning that Long Island was not slave territory, the Africans finally negotiated with local residents Captain Henry Green, Captain Peletiah Fordham, and a few of their associates, and offered to pay the Americans if they took them back to Africa. Green and Fordham appeared interested, although their focus was on Sengbe's doubloons, and their thoughts strayed to the possibility of claiming salvage rights if they turned over the schooner to the U.S. government.[14]

While the Africans bartered with the whites, Lieutenant Gedney and his men stationed on the U.S. brig *Washington* lowered a boat to investigate. On seeing the naval patrol near their ship, the Africans abandoned

Green and Fordham and attempted to row back to the ship, but were cap-tured by the heavily armed naval boat and taken prisoner under Gedney's command. The remaining Africans on the *Amistad* schooner were also taken into custody and kept below deck while Gedney heard the story of the revolt from the two Spanish "prisoners," one of whom spoke good English. In spite of their arrest, Sengbe remained the impassioned leader to whom the Africans looked for support and assistance. Expecting the worst from their arrest, he attempted to incite his comrades to resist their new captors. Sengbe was so unmanageable to the naval crew that, in the end, he had to be separated from the other captives and manacled aboard the *Washington*.[15]

On August 27, the *Amistad* was towed into New London, Connecticut, where the U.S. District Attorney for Connecticut, William Holabird, de-termined the immediate fate of the Amistad affair. Since the ship and its human cargo were estimated at nearly $70,000 in the Havana market, and Gedney and his crew were complicating matters by asking for salvage rights, Holabird decided that the proper place for deciding matters of such legal proportion was the court. Andrew Judson, the judge of the Dis-trict Court of Connecticut, who, like Holabird, was an appointee of the Van Buren administration, presided.

Like President Martin Van Buren, Judson and Holabird had strong pro-slavery sentiments. The fate of the Amistad captives was, by all ac-counts, dismal. Not only did the captives expect a merciless verdict, they also expected to die with their version of the events unheard. Two days later, on the morning of August 29, Judson held judicial hearings aboard the *Washington* in New London harbor. Ruiz and Montes supported their testimonies with the ship's documents and the records of ownership of the Africans. The Africans had been assigned Spanish names (to pass them off as *ladinos* rather than as *bozales*) so that their owners could eas-ily pass through security checks in Cuba. The Africans (minus the four children) were indicted on charges of murder and piracy.

It seemed likely at this point that Judson might easily have handed over the ship with its human cargo to the Spanish consul at Boston, but both Gedney and Lieutenant Meade (who was first mate under Gedney and who was also serving as interpreter for the Spanish slavers) insisted on compensation, and so the matter was referred to the Circuit Court at Hartford. In the meantime, the thirty-nine Africans in custody were taken to the larger New Haven county jail. The four children and Antonio, who were considered material witnesses for the State, were also retained at the New Haven county jail, since they could not realistically post bond for themselves.

Meanwhile, Dwight Janes, an abolitionist who had attended the August 29 hearing and learned from Judge Judson's hearing that the Africans had been brought illegally into Cuba, saw before him an opportunity to bring the issue of slavery before a national audience.[16] The wealthy New York businessman and abolitionist, Lewis Tappan, had also been intrigued by newspaper accounts. A week later he, Reverend Joshua Leavitt (who was editor of the *Emancipator*, an abolitionist newsletter in New York City), and Simeon Jocelyn, white minister to the first black church in New Haven, formed the Amistad committee, a formidable team that was able to rally the support of other abolitionists. The committee's intent was to meet the legal defense needs of the Africans and, through awareness raised by the Amistad case, to rally public support for abolitionist causes. Abolitionism was diminishing in political successes but became increasingly effective as a tool for the discussion of morality and human rights. This paradox best underscored the escalating tensions between the North and the South. Thus, the Amistad case was heaven-sent to Northern abolitionists who were interested in having moral rectitude influence legal justice.

Many Americans considered abolitionists to be fanatics bent on tearing the Union apart with their radical beliefs about immediate emancipation for slaves. Some in the free states believed in gradual emancipation, while others were disinterested and indifferent to the fate of the slaves. The South, of course, was generally opposed to abolition and did, at various times, put prices on the heads of prominent abolitionists like William Lloyd Garrison, founder of the abolitionist newsletter the *Liberator* in Boston, Massachusetts,[17] and the Tappan brothers, Arthur and Lewis, who had financed a number of notable abolitionist causes.[18] Prudence Crandall, a Quaker activist for black education, also encountered stiff opposition when she admitted black girls into her school in Canterbury, Connecticut, in 1833. She and her students were almost killed when angry mobs attempted to set fire to the school building in 1834.[19] Like Elijah Lovejoy of Illinois, who was killed by a mob in 1837, some abolitionists did in fact die for their beliefs.[20]

The unpopular sentiments which abolitionism provoked created many setbacks and added to the confusion among both black and white aboli-

tionists who employed contrasting strategies in the face of mounting public hostility. The moral strategy adopted by some approximated the religious argument that slavery was a sin. However, the "gag rule" of 1836
that was introduced into Congress by proponents of slavery prevented pe-
titioning for the abolition of domestic slavery. Moreover, antislavery
newsletters, intended to awaken the conscience of the South, were banned
in many of the slave states. Other abolitionists believed that the institutionalized misery of slavery called for more radical political action, but
aggressiveness on their part further justified the public's image of them as
fanatics. Regardless of the abolitionists' factional beliefs, however, the
Amistad case was an opportunity for all to unite under a single banner. In
the face of a compelling call for action, abstract arguments were put aside.

The Amistad Africans' most immediate need was for an interpreter who
could give voice to their side of the story. To this end, Dr. Josiah Willard
Gibbs, a Yale professor and notable scholar of Hebrew whose specialty
was philology, determined that the language spoken by the Africans was
Mende, a language group in the British colony of Sierra Leone.[21] Gibbs
learned to count to ten in the Mende language and using these rudimentary skills, traveled to the New York waterfronts in search of anyone who
could speak the language. He located John Ferry, a free Negro and Mende
by birth, who had lived outside Mendeland from an early age. Ferry's
Mende had not been put to use for many years, so he was limited as an
interpreter. Nevertheless, he was able to deliver the main points of the
Africans' story at the September 17 trial in Hartford.

The trial was presided over by Associate Justice Smith Thompson of the
U.S. Supreme Court and by Justice Andrew Judson, who was administer-
ing on behalf of the district court. Counsel for the defense included New
Haven attorney Roger Sherman Baldwin (the grandson of Declaration of
Independence signer Roger Sherman Baldwin), Theodore Sedwick, and
Seth Staples of New Haven (who later became the founder of Yale Law
School). These highly qualified men were selected because it was impor-
tant to the abolitionists that in the face of obvious threats from the gov-
ernment, they muster all of their legal strength.

The pro-slavery government perceived the potential for political gain in
the Amistad crisis. With elections drawing near, Van Buren's vested interest in the case increased. The Spanish minister in Washington, Angel
Calderón de la Barca, was also putting pressure on Secretary of State John

Forsyth to work in the interest of the Spanish government. Citing the 1795 Pinckney treaty between the United States and Spain, Calderón stressed three articles that he believed favored Ruiz and Montes:[22]

> Article 8: In case the subjects and inhabitants of either party, with their shipping, whether public and of war, or private and of merchants, be forced, through stress of weather, *pursuit of pirates or enemies, or any other urgent necessity* for seeking shelter and harbor, to retreat and enter into any of the rivers, bays, roads, or ports, belonging to the other party, they shall be received and treated with all humanity, and enjoy all favor, protection and help; and they shall be permitted to refresh and provide themselves, *at reasonable rates,* with victuals and all things needful for the subsistence of their persons, or reparation of their ships, and prosecution of their voyage; and *they shall no ways be hindered from returning out of said ports* or roads, but may remove and depart when and whither they please without any let or hindrance.

> Article 9: *All ships and merchandise, of what nature soever, which shall be rescued out of the hands of any pirates* or robbers on the high seas, shall be brought into some port of either State, and shall be delivered to the custody of the officers of that port, in order *to be taken care of, and restored entire* to the true proprietor, as soon as due and sufficient proof shall be made concerning the property thereof.

> Article 10: When any vessel of either party shall be wrecked, foundered, or otherwise damaged, on the coasts or within the dominion of the other, their respective subjects or citizens shall receive as well for themselves as for their vessels and effects, *the same assistance which would be due to the inhabitants of the country where the damage happens, and shall pay the same charges and dues only as the said inhabitant would be subject to pay in a like case;* and if the operations of repair should require that the whole or any part of the cargo be unladen, they shall pay no duties, charges, or fees, on the part which they shall relade and carry away.[23]

Reminding the U.S. government of both its territorial and economic investments in Cuba, Calderón also stressed that the Amistad case, if ruled otherwise, would set a bad precedent, encouraging further slave revolts in Cuba. The effect of such a precedent in the U.S. territory was certainly not lost on Forsyth, who employed many questionable tactics to bypass judicial process of law.

Taking his lead from Judge Thompson's ruling that any crimes committed by the Africans in Spanish territory could not be determined under U.S. law, Judge Judson decided that while questions of property rights were being further investigated, the Africans were no longer to be held as "criminals" by the United States. They were, thus, legally "released," but the Africans continued to be housed in the New Haven jail because the abolitionists did not want to post bail. This was a political maneuver: bail was equivalent to the Africans' price as slaves in the Havana markets, and it seems the abolitionists thought that posting bail at "slave" prices would be counterproductive to their case. They appointed a New Haven committee, which included Leonard Bacon, Henry Ludlow, and Amos Townsend, to attend to the Africans and to supply religious and educational instruction. The committee members invited George E. Day, a former professor at the New York Institution for the Deaf and Dumb, to assist them with the adult Africans. The committee also employed a woman to teach the four children, Margru (or Margue), Teme, Kagne, and Kali (or Kale).

While they awaited the next trial, slated for mid-November, the abolitionists mounted another search for a more fluent Mende speaker. In October, Gibbs succeeded in locating a seaman, James Covey, a young man about twenty years old who was Mende by birth but had grown up in Freetown, Sierra Leone, after he had been liberated from a slaver by a British patrol boat. His Mende was imperfect, but he was more adept than the first interpreter and remained the interpreter of choice throughout the legal proceedings. Through Covey, the details of the revolt were divulged to the world. Moreover, Yale students and their professors who had taken an interest in the welfare of the Amistad Africans were able to teach them English with Covey's help. However, Covey became ill, and the November hearing was later adjourned to January.

In the interim, several events transpired. Dr. Richard R. Madden, an Irishman who served on behalf of the British commission to suppress the African slave trade in Havana, had heard about the Amistad case and had come to the United States to testify as an eyewitness to slave matters in Cuba. His deposition that some twenty-five thousand slaves were brought into Cuba every year—with the wrongful compliance of, and personal profit by, Spanish officials—strengthened the defense's case. Madden also told the court that his examinations revealed that the defendants were brought directly from Africa and could not have been residents of Cuba.[24] Madden's visit clarified England's position on the matter, which was already attracting international attention. After communing with

Madden, the British minister in Washington, D.C., Henry Fox, wrote Secretary of State John Forsyth expressing Her Majesty's personal interest in the case.[25] Madden later had an audience with Queen Victoria regarding the Amistad case.

Around the same period, the abolitionists, somewhat misjudging public sympathy, filed suit on behalf of two of the Africans against Ruiz and Montes. The abolitionists charged the two Spanish litigants with assault, kidnapping, and false imprisonment of the Africans. Both Spanish citizens were jailed, and there was a public outcry against the abolitionists. Montes posted bail and left for Cuba. Ruiz, more comfortable in a New England setting (and entitled to many amenities not available to the Africans), hoped to garner further public support by staying in jail.

Needless to say, correspondence between the Spanish minister's office and the executive office of the President of the United States increased. Shortly after the September hearings, Spanish minister Calderón was replaced by Cavallero Pedro Alcántara Argaiz, who continued Calderón's caustic accusations against America's judicial system and continued to condemn the abolitionist affront. Ruiz's imprisonment only added to Argaiz's anger, and he pressured Forsyth to seek ways to throw out the case altogether. Ruiz, however, soon tired of his martyred lifestyle in jail and posted bond. Like Montes, he returned to Cuba and was not present at the district court hearing when it reconvened on January 8, 1840.

During five days of testimonies, counsel for the defense argued that the Amistad Africans were never slaves but rather kidnap victims who had a right to defend themselves. Madden's deposition had helped to clarify their status as *bozales*, slaves that had been brought illegally into Cuba. As free men asserting their human rights, Baldwin argued, they could not be claimed by the prosecuting team as Spanish property. The defense counsel buttressed its argument by citing Spain's 1817 treaty with England. By denying the de facto slave trade, Spain conferred on all *bozale* Africans the status of freedom.

Moreover, Sengbe's testimony, which was confirmed by both Grabeau and Fuliwa, dramatically conveyed the events before, during, and after the revolt.[26] His graphic demonstration of the Middle Passage experience electrified the packed courtroom. Representing the Spanish Crown, Holabird argued that on the basis of advice given earlier by U.S. attorney Felix Grundy, the United States had no jurisdiction over the Amistad case and that all should be restored to the Spanish government in Cuba for prosecution under its own laws. Contrary to the hopes of the executive branch, however, Judge Judson ruled that the Africans were free men under the "law of Spain itself." All salvage claims that had also been heard during the proceedings were ruled upon. Gedney and his crew were entitled to salvage rights to the vessel but not to the Africans, who had no property value in the State of Connecticut.[27] Green and his men did not board the vessel and therefore had no salvage rights.

As expected, Holabird followed the directive of the executive branch by immediately filing an appeal against Judson's verdict. Had Holabird won the case, Van Buren's orders to immediately relinquish the Africans to Spanish authorities could have obstructed defense lawyers' attempts to file an appeal. In anticipation of a favorable verdict, Forsyth had written a letter to the Secretary of the Navy, with a confidential request to prepare a ship that would take the Africans back to Cuba. The USS *Grampus* was readied for such an eventuality.[28] Rumors surrounding the clandestine mission alerted the abolitionists, who in turn made preparations to ship the Africans to Canada if they lost their case. In fact, after the Supreme Court hearing, the abolitionists helped Antonio, a material witness for the Spanish accusers and the U.S. government, to escape to Canada.[29] In a letter written in Montreal to the Reverend Joshua Leavitt, John Dougall reported that "the lad Antonio of Amistad celebrity came in here safely two or three days ago and is consequently beyond the reach of all the slaveholders in the world." [30]

The seeming victory was only temporary. Awaiting additional representation before the U.S. Supreme Court, the Amistad Africans were confused by the fact that they had been set free but were still not allowed to return to Africa. By the time they were moved from New Haven to more comfortable quarters in Farmington, Connecticut, where a large house had been prepared for them, there were only thirty-six surviving Africans. Their longing to go home could not be assuaged. Many who empathized with the Amistad Africans were eager to see the long judicial process come to a successful end in the form of release.

Lewis Tappan and the Amistad committee believed that they needed a nationally known lawyer to fight their case at the Supreme Court level. Many of the justices on the Supreme Court bench were either from the South and had strong pro-slavery sentiments, or like Chief Justice Roger B. Taney, they had a reputation for protecting individual property rights in the interest of the Union and sympathized with the South.[31] Seven of the nine Supreme Court Justices had strong pro-slavery sentiments, so an unbiased hearing was not likely.

Only a lawyer of John Quincy Adams's caliber could evoke any hope of winning the Africans' case. Adams had been the sixth American President (1825–1829) and was still a politician to be reckoned with in the House of Representatives. Although initially hesitant because of his age (he was seventy-four) and because he had not argued a case before the Supreme Court in thirty years, Adams accepted the challenge. Sympathetic to the Africans' case, he had meticulously followed earlier trials from his home in Quincy, Massachusetts.[32]

In January 1840, Adams received two letters handwritten by Kali and Kinna (or Kenna), one of the adult captives. Both letters pleaded with Adams to fight valiantly on their behalf, because, as both Kali and Kinna pointed out, Adams would have done as much if Americans were in a similar plight. Insisting on their freeborn status, Kali used the rhetoric of equality as a premise for his argument in the letter. "Dear Friend Mr. Adams," he wrote: "We all born in Mendi. . . . Some people say Mendi people crazy; Mendi people dolt; because we no talk American language. Merica people no talk Mendi language; Merica people dolt? . . . Dear Friend Mr. Adams, you have children, you have friends, you love them, you feel sorry if Mendi people come and carry them all to Africa." Kali's claim to both humanity and freedom were inscribed, not on the discourse of race or color but on the discourse of thought and the revelation of the inner-self. "If American people give us free we glad, if they no give us free we sorry—we sorry for Mendi people little, we sorry for American people great deal, because God punish liars. . . . Dear Friend, we want you to know how we feel. Mendi people think, think, think. Nobody know what we think; the teacher he know, we tell him some. Mendi people have got souls. . . . All we want is make us free."[33] Adams had much to ponder as he waited for the Supreme Court trial that opened after delay on February 20, 1841.

Henry Gilpin, the U.S. Attorney General who had replaced Grundy, argued in much the same vein as Holabird had done earlier. If Spanish law defined the Africans as slaves, then they were property under Spanish law. He presented the captives' Spanish passports as evidence to support his claims and restated Holabird's argument that the case should be tried on Spanish territory and under Spanish law.

Gilpin also cited the case of the *Antelope* as a precedent for the Amistad trial. In 1820, the U.S. Coast Guard brig *Dallas* captured the *Antelope*, a Spanish slaver, off the northern coast of Florida. The *Antelope*, also known as *Ramirez*, had some two hundred eighty Africans onboard when it was recaptured. Although it flew the colors of *La Plata* of Venezuela, at that time revolting against Spain, the *Antelope* was in fact the piratical prize of the American captain of the *Arraganta*, who had drowned in a shipwreck near Brazil, and his mate, Captain Smith. Smith's claim to the *Antelope* and its human cargo was the beginning of an eight-year trial in the United States (during James Monroe's and John Quincy Adams's terms in office). Other claimants were Spain, which cited article 8 of the Pinckney Treaty of 1795 (reference to acts of piracy), and Portugal, which filed specifically for the Africans who had been captured off a Portuguese slaver by the *Arraganta*.

It was a complicated legal process, but in the end, the Spanish and Portuguese representatives successfully asserted that the Africans were indeed property. Although the United States ruled that the Africans legally were free persons under the suppression of the African slave trade act, it followed "due process of law" in granting the rights of the two foreign governments. Gilpin saw "due process of law" as supportive of the rights of the Spanish government and as favorable to his case against the Africans.[34]

Roger Baldwin eloquently refuted Gilpin's argument. In his opening statement in defense of the Africans, he reminded the justices of Judge Judson's earlier ruling in favor of his clients and immediately outlined the principle issue in the case: "the question of freedom or property, which lies at the foundation of all jurisdiction over the Africans."[35] Baldwin was meticulous and thorough in his presentation, but like Attorney General Gilpin, he added nothing new to the case.

The tempo changed, however, when John Quincy Adams began his argument on February 24, 1841. His defense was laid out in two days, and his pungent arguments were the highlights of the case. Adams accused the executive branch of employing many obstructive measures to bypass justice mandated by the Constitution. He had earlier examined the correspondence between the Spanish government and the United States and felt justified in questioning the intentions of an executive administration that subjected itself to coercion from a foreign government. He criticized the Spanish ministers' letters and the suspicious role of the *Grampus*, which lay in wait at New London harbor to snatch the Africans back to Cuba. Living up to his reputation as an eloquent speaker in the House of Representatives, Adams presented an emotional argument about respect for the constitutional authority vested in the judicial arm of government.

Using his rhetorical prowess, Adams garnered sympathy for the Africans by declaring the judicial system itself to be a victim of the conspiracies of what he called "executive tyranny." Like the Amistad Africans, the entire judicial system was in a state of abject helplessness. Questioning Calderón's demands on the presidential office, Adams concluded that the Spanish representative's letter demanded that "the Chief Magistrate of this nation" turn himself "into a jailer." Further the Chief Magistrate should become:

> a tipstaff to take them away for trial among the slave traders of the baracoons. Was ever such a demand made upon any government? He must seize these people and keep them safely, and carry them, at the expense of the United States, to another country to be tried for their lives! Where in the law of nations is there a warrant for such a demand?
>
> May it please your Honors—If the President of the United States had arbitrary and unqualified power, he could not satisfy these demands. He must keep them as a jailer; he must then send them beyond seas to be tried for their lives. I will not recur to the Declaration of Independence—your Honors have it implanted in your hearts—but one of the grievous charges brought against George III was, that he had made laws for sending men beyond seas for trial. That was one of the most odious of those acts of tyranny which occasioned the American revolution. The whole of the reasoning is not applicable to this case, but I submit to your Honors that, if the President has the power to do it in the case of Africans, and send them beyond seas for trial, he could do it by the same authority in the case of American citizens.[36]

Thus, the captivity of the Africans became a metaphor for the executive branch's dangerous precedents—precedents that, if allowed to continue, could very well stifle the personal freedoms of white Americans. Adams showed how the executive branch undermined the authority of the courts and, by implication, how the courts could snatch away the freedom of the blacks. In this way, Adams sublimated the question of color to the question of freedom.

Recalling Gilpin's reference to the Antelope case, Adams argued that if the case served as a precedent at all, it was in demonstrating that due process of law had to be followed in the Amistad case as well. In a sense,

Adams saw an opportunity in the Amistad case to right the wrongs of the Antelope case. He regretted that the Africans in the Antelope case had not been sent back to their homeland. Nevertheless, he defended his record by insisting on his consistency in defending the constitutional process of law—a process evidently under duress in the Amistad case. After a rather haunting presentation in which Adams conjured up the legacy of the founding fathers as his ultimate witness that right was on his side, he left for his home state of Massachusetts.

The Supreme Court decision, which was delivered on March 9, upheld Judge Judson's earlier ruling—the Africans were not slaves or fugitives but free men. The Africans' safe passage back to Africa, ruled as the responsibility of the U.S. government by the earlier verdict, was a point declined by the Supreme Court. Baldwin hastily wrote a letter to Adams declaring that "the captives are now free."[37] Lewis Tappan had also written Adams on the same day, thanking him "in the name of humanity and justice."[38] The decree of the Supreme Court was published in the *National Intelligencer,* and the release of the Africans from the Marshall of the District of Connecticut was secured. Antislavery advocates had reason to rejoice. The Amistad committee trumpeted their victory by widely publicizing it. The Africans, too, were relieved that their battle was over.

After the trials, the government absolved itself of responsibility, essentially abandoning the Africans to their fate. To ensure that the initial victories were not marred by such inaction, the Amistad committee, with the cooperation of the Amistad Africans, began raising funds for the trip back to the Africans' homeland. Responses to public appeal for funds extended beyond New England's borders. Common farmers, individual citizens, people of color, the Female Emancipation Society—all contributed.[39] The Africans helped by making and selling handicrafts and by going on speaking tours at both black and white churches to raise awareness. In testimonies of their captivity, descriptions of the social and political life of their country, displays of their improved English skills, and demonstrations of their grasp of basic biblical truths, the Africans endeared themselves to the crowds and in the process, ennobled the abolitionist cause.

The funds needed for the trip back to Africa were, however, far greater than the revenues received. The abolitionists needed to outfit a ship for the voyage and to provide about three years worth of provisions for the Africans and the missionaries who were to accompany them to the Mende-speaking area of Sierra Leone. The abolitionists' dream of Christianizing

Africa through the window of opportunity afforded them in the Africans' eventual return was ambitious. They wanted to build houses and schools in Sengbe's village and from there, expand the ministry to other places in Sierra Leone. Thus, the funds were to serve a much larger purpose than merely a return trip to Africa. Moreover, time was a factor: a few more years spent in the United States would better prepare the Africans to become missionaries to their own people. In this way, the Africans could better serve the purposes of the American Missionary Association (AMA), established at the behest of the Amistad committee.

Restlessly yearning for their native land, the Africans became less cooperative and increasingly despondent as their apparent victory stretched into endless months of waiting. Another New England winter was unacceptable. A pivotal moment came when one of the remaining Africans who lived at the Farmington house drowned in a nearby pond. Foone was reputed to be an excellent swimmer, and many observers believed that he had committed suicide. He had despaired of ever seeing his homeland again, and the hope of reuniting with his people in the spiritual world, according to Mende traditional belief, might have prompted his actions. Foone's death forced the Amistad committee to reconsider the expediency of retaining the Africans longer than was financially necessary.[40] At this point, only thirty-five of the original fifty-three captives were still alive.

To prevent another tragedy, the Amistad committee curtailed the campaign for funds and hastily organized a departure. On November 27, 1841, the Africans sailed with Covey and five missionaries (William and Elizabeth Raymond, James Steele, and the African American couple Henry and Tamar Wilson) on the vessel *Gentleman* back to Africa.

Historical and Literary Scholarship Reconsidered

In retrospect, from August 1839, when the first rumors of "pirate" sightings appeared in New England newspapers, to the Amistad Africans' departure in November 1841, the Amistad story was a constant feature in the press. The Supreme Court victory had precipitated further marketing of the Amistad story's public status. Abolitionist defenders, who had staked their future and credibility on the meaning and outcome of the case, published thousands of copies of the verdict. The Amistad success was a sign to them that the cause should continue with vigor and purpose. The cooperative spirit in which abolitionists of differing persuasion had allied themselves provided structure and incentive for combating advancing pro-slavery forces.

The public's vital interest in the Amistad case certainly was responsible for the copious literature produced during and after the trial. Newspapers throughout New England and the nation's capital provided daily briefing on the progress of the case. In May 1840, shortly after the circuit court and district court proceedings on the Amistad case ended, John W. Barber compiled a "correct statement of the facts" of the case, availing himself of the privilege of his "personal conversation" with the Africans. His *History of the Amistad Captives* is fundamental to scholarly references to the case. Court and congressional records and the AMA archival collection are the major sources used by scholars to retell the Amistad case. John Quincy Adams's family papers and diaries are also useful in understanding some of the particulars relating to the Supreme Court trial. For the continued drama of the Amistad incident, which naturally went far beyond the documentation of official proceedings in the American legal system, the Adams papers and the AMA archives have helped contemporary readers recall the temper of the past.

Although widespread public interest in the Amistad trial climaxed with the Supreme Court verdict and died down with the subsequent departure of the Africans, the AMA antislavery collection remains a gold mine of information. It has enabled contemporary scholars to glimpse "life" after the American saga. Letters from the mission base in Kaw Mende, Sierra Leone, to the Amistad committee offer insight into the welfare of the mission, the state of the Amistad Africans, the cultural texture of Mende society, the social and political upheavals of the day, and missionary efforts to convert the Mende people. The letters were selectively published in antislavery organs such as the *Herald,* the *Emancipator,* and the *American and Foreign Anti-Slavery Reporter.* Thus, dissemination of information on mission work in Africa was limited. However, contemporary readers have the advantages of posterity on their side: scholars have access not only to the letters meant for publication but also the private correspondence that transpired at the time.

The AMA's founding in September 1846 helped to strengthen the fledgling Mende mission, which was then under the directorship of William Raymond. The AMA had been established with the goals of expanding the base of the Mende mission, founding schools in Sierra Leone, and working among the poor of Haiti, British Guiana, the slave states in the American Union, and the indigenous population of the Americas. The AMA's global vision included destitute blacks in Canada and foreign nations "where an abolition doctrine was not preached."[41] The onerous task of helping the downtrodden accelerated at the conclusion of the American Civil War in 1865. The burden of integrating recently freed slaves into American society fell mostly in the lap of benevolent institutions such as the AMA. Missionary energies being expended in foreign lands were needed back home. Thus, the AMA diversified its resources beyond its Amistad vision.

Of course, the Mende mission continued to receive support from the AMA. It expanded its work further in the colony, the effect of which is on-going in present-day Sierra Leone. Nonetheless, the narrative singularity of the Amistad case was now competing with the excitement of the Civil War, the challenge of Reconstruction, and the restructuring of America's national identity.[42] As a result, even though correspondence between the mission in Sierra Leone and the AMA continued well into the twentieth century, few scholars of late nineteenth- and early twentieth-century American history have deliberated on its significance.

To be sure, historians such as Joshua Coffin, Thomas Wentworth Higginson, E. J. Hobsbawn, and David Brion Davis have, in their discussions of the influences of slave revolts on American politics, mentioned the Amistad incident in their work. But their interest has been confined to the drama of the revolt and the outcome of the U.S. court trials. One could perhaps argue that, given the purview of their subject matter, these historians could not have done otherwise.

However, the wider significance of the story's global impact, and particularly the continuing effect in Africa, has rarely been considered. The general silence about the events that occurred beyond the shores of America illustrates a general tendency by American historians to dismiss the particularities of African history. The tendency to categorize black *history* as a footnote to *History* has certainly plagued the narrative contextualization of the unfolding story in Sierra Leone.

In the literary sphere, the mid–nineteenth century publication of Herman Melville's short story "Benito Cereno" makes extensive reference to the Amistad incident. Melville's use epitomizes the general characterization of the Amistad story as historical backdrop to other narratives in the latter half of the nineteenth century. Melville employs the incident to embellish his version of a suppressed slave revolt recounted in Amasa Delano's *A Narrative of Voyages and Travels in the Northern and Southern Hemispheres*. Nonetheless, the Amistad story's powerful dramatic nature retains its resilience in the works of Melville and other scholars and artists. As reference or inspiration, the Amistad has become an uncanny presence in the American literary imagination.

Around the middle of the twentieth century, historians, artists, playwrights, and fiction writers reawakened the relative dormancy of the Amistad corpus. A number of scholars have written what might be called quasi-historical accounts that have accorded adequate respect to the Amistad story. Such accounts often are faithful to the historical record but are embellished with imaginary dialogue and reconstructed landscape in an attempt to redress gaps in documented accounts. Employing the characteristics of historical fiction, this new genre exemplifies by far the most typical use of the Amistad story.

The following writers can be categorized as quasi-historical in their interpretation of the Amistad story: William Owens in *Black Mutiny*, Christopher Martin in *The Amistad Affair*, Helen Kromer in *The Amistad Revolt*, Bernice Kohn in *The Amistad Mutiny*, Mary Cable in *Black Odyssey*, Howard Jones in *Mutiny on the Amistad*, and Karen Zeinert in *The Amistad Slave Revolt*. Those whose work can be classified as fictional (with heavy use of fictional characters and events) are Blair Niles in *East by Day*, Emma Gelders Sterne in *The Long Black Schooner*, Mary Dahl in *Free Souls*, and Barbara Chase-Riboud in *Echo of Lions*. A recent addition is David Pesci's *Amistad*. All of these writers, with their own peculiar idiosyncrasies, vary in terms of narrative texture, style, emphasis, and audience. Some address adult versus teenage readers, and others consider academic versus lay readers. Nevertheless, the goal of these writers is the same: to engage our collective memories of the past.

Steven Spielberg adopts a similar stylistic approach in the movie *Amistad*: he privileges dramatic and narrative cohesiveness over historical accuracy. Although the movie heightened public awareness of the Amistad story, it inadvertently contributed to a misreading of key events. Alex Pate's *Amistad*, based on the screenplay by David Franzoni and Steven Zaillian, is equally limited in its vision because, as a project commissioned by Spielberg's company, DreamWorks, it follows the movie very closely. Those of us who have found the Amistad case compelling lament the fact that while in a sense, it is a story already told, it remains to be truly heard.

Most of the existing published works on the subject are documented compilations of the Amistad proceedings and quasi-historical narratives. Currently, there are few analytical essays on the Amistad subject. The "Occasional Papers" of the Connecticut Humanities Council published in *The Connecticut Scholar,* commemorating the 150th anniversary of the capture of the *Amistad,* is a promising example of the kind of analytical study that might occur in the future. In the collection of the Connecticut Humanities Council, the four perspectives on the Amistad story offered by Howard Jones, John Blassingame, Gladdis Smith, and Frank Kirpatrick defy the tendency to repeat only the story without adequate analysis. In addition, Clara Merritt DeBoer's *Be Jubilant my Feet,* while focusing mainly on the activities of African American abolitionists in the AMA, broadens our knowledge of the events that transpired after the Amistad Africans returned to Sierra Leone. DeBoer's analysis and interpretation, reconstructed mainly from the letters in the AMA collection at the Amistad Research Center, are helpful to Amistad scholars. Unlike the fictionalized "endings" of the quasi-historical accounts, DeBoer's painstaking examination of the Amistad letters from Sierra Leone has produced some realistic specifics of the Amistad story.

Whereas many writers prematurely end their investigation of the Amistad story with the American phase of the Africans' journey, Howard Jones's "American ending" in *Black Mutiny* is justified. In a rhetorical analysis of the legal proceedings in the Amistad case Jones concludes as Cable does in *Black Odyssey:* by tidying up affairs left unfinished at the Africans' departure. Unlike Jones, however, Cable details events in Sierra Leone. Another text, Sterne's *Long Black Schooner,* ends with the sighting of land as the *Gentleman* barque draws near the Freetown coast. Sterne's fairy-tale ending, although tastefully rendered, leaves out the victories and failures encountered in Sierra Leone.

Particularly troubling are those texts that end with the Africans disembarking and "melting" into the jungle. Both Owens and Martin offer racist rhetoric as a satisfactory conclusion to the Africans' return to Africa. Toward the end of *Black Mutiny,* Owen states that the missionaries "watched the *Amistad* Africans serve faithfully awhile and then turn to paganism and disappear into the jungle."[43] Martin seems to rely somewhat on Owens's account: "nearly all the *Amistad* Negroes had . . . disappeared into the wilds of the African bush."[44] Although it is true that due to missing letters and inconclusive documentation, the African phase of the Amistad story is somewhat "hazy," there is nothing in the existing literature that accounts for Owens's and Martin's descriptions. The information available in the AMA archives at the Amistad Research Center calls for more serious reconstructions of the Sierra Leone phase.

Among the quasi-historical narratives of the Amistad story, the accounts by Helen Kromer and Mary Cable are by far the most accomplished attempts to define later events. Like Kohn who saw the *end* of the Amistad case as only the *beginning* of a new struggle in Africa, Kromer's sensitive reading puts the Amistad phase in Africa "straight into history." [45] While she does not offer an analysis of the experiences she chronicles, her insight is at least balanced. Cable's account attempts to analyze the events in the Sierra Leone phase within the geopolitical context of events in Sierra Leone. Still, there remains much work to be done on the Sierra Leone experiences. It is not at all surprising that the vague, confused, and sometimes fictionalized accounts have been misleading.

The suggestion that Sengbe became a slave trader after his return to Sierra Leone is also misleading. Many quasi-historical accounts have reported the rumor without any proper investigation. A careful reading of arguments in the New Haven District Court proceedings indicates that there are grounds for this unproven though widely held suspicion. [46] During the trials, there had been some confusion in the translations of Sengbe's conversations by the interpreter, Covey. Norris Wilcox, the Marshal, erroneously believed that Sengbe had been a slave dealer in Africa, information he allegedly received from Covey. When Wilcox appeared in court to testify on behalf of Gedney that he had witnessed the conversation, both Covey and Sengbe individually denied ever giving such testimony. After lengthy deliberation and much confusion, the testimony was excluded from court records.

In John Barber's compilation of the facts of the case and his personal conversations with the Africans, he stated that Sengbe was "a planter of rice and never owned or sold slaves"—an important qualifying statement. [47] Unfortunately, it had been reported in a local newspaper that Sengbe had been a slave trader in Africa. We can conjecture that this troubling rumor plagued him on his return to Africa. This initial rumor also may have been fodder for twentieth-century reports that Sengbe entered the trade after he left the mission house at Kaw Mende, even though missionary letters in the AMA collection do not verify this information. Nevertheless, since much remains to be "discovered" in the Sierra Leone phase of the story, lingering questions on this and other issues still need to be addressed.

CHAPTER TWO

Slave Revolts and the Production of Identity

Confusion about how we view the Amistad story can in part be resolved by examining it in the context of its Sierra Leone experience. Just as important, however, are the slave revolt contexts of the Americas from which the Amistad emerged in the first place. The historical specificity of slavery in the Western Hemisphere produced its own framework of inter-group relationships. Recent studies in social psychology speak to the centrality of interpersonal relations in the formation of the individual's self-concept. Such studies suggest that group identity is fundamental to the construction of self-identity.[1] Thus, "interdependent or relational self-concept is defined in terms of relationships with others in specific contexts, and self-worth is derived from appropriate role behavior"[2] Slaves exhibited certain levels of self-evaluation in relation to each other, and they shared in-group characteristics which they projected onto the dominant out-group community of whites. The identity of the slaves was therefore a function of membership both within the in-group and equally by exclusion from the out-group. Given the protracted conflicts engendered by slavery as both an enterprise and an institution, slaveholders and the slaves themselves were seen as embodiments of the institution, thus rendering divergent practices, by both black and white individuals, invisible in the entrenched and sanctioned structures of the institution. For example, the classic struggle between masters and captives in the Amistad revolt, an expression of both black and white collectivities, was censored in the South where institutionalized slavery demanded that the only sanctioned narrative be that of master over slave.

Consequently, the slaves' desire to shift their collective identity from the level of a demoralizing status quo to self-assertive social relations with the out-group demanded a high level of cooperation. Attempts to recategorize their social identity, whether through discrete forms of protest, strike, or open rebellion, usually occurred in concert with other in-group members.

Because self-worth and other motivational factors often are circumscribed by defined limitations of the group as a whole, the search for individual self-emancipation is realized effectively only at the level of collective emancipation. This does not suggest that individual and collective identities and desires are always congruent; rather, the convergence between identities suggests that the goals of a collective identity reflect, at least in part, the desires of individual members. Thus, in my discussion of the relationship between slaves and their masters, between in-group and out-group identities, the term *identity* is understood to be a collective entity.

The institutionalized superiority of whites over blacks can be explored using a method adapted from Erving Goffman's *The Presentation of Self in Everyday Life*. Goffman's theater analogy of self-identity in relation to social space is one way to describe the intergroup relations between masters and slaves in the Western Hemisphere. Although Goffman uses dramaturgical performances to describe specifically the selective presentation of self in contemporary society, his conceptualization is a useful rhetorical tool in analyzing the production of identities in slave revolts. According to Goffman's model, human performance is an attempt to sustain a particular impression or "sell" a specific identity package to others.[3]

Goffman shows that our multiple identity roles are based on our interpretation of our relationships with others.[4] Using the performative models of dramatic action and dramatic interaction, Goffman suggests that assumptions about the "other" always affect and determine behavior patterns and social definitions of interaction. Goffman defines dramatic action as the social dynamic between performers on stage and the audience; each group has a defined role. Using the exchange between two football teams as an example, he defines dramatic interaction as the intense interdependence between actors and audience.[5] Similarly, the structural relationship between master and slave is circumscribed by predetermined characteristics or behavior patterns; this relationship constitutes a role play. The interdependence of the protagonists' actions underscores the representations available to both communities.

Many historical, sociological, and literary documents on slavery attest to an affinity between the theater and the psycho-dramatic structures of the plantation household. It is common knowledge, for instance, that slaves affected various roles of servitude-with-contentment to "fit" the part slaveholders assigned them. In turn, slaveholders played the roles of masters or mistresses, complementing the overall performance of plantation life. When slaves rebelled, they violated (and thereby revised) intergroup relations with their masters. The latter, in turn, transgressed the constructed role of "kind master" (if such a veneer existed in the first place) to put down the rebellion and to re-contain relations within more predictable levels of interaction. Indeed, both dramatic action and dramatic interaction between in-group and out-group identities in the slaveholding world provided the text through which both power and recognition of the "other" were mediated.[6]

David Brion Davis, in *The Slave Power Conspiracy and the Paranoid Style*, illustrates the significance of Goffman's model by elaborating on its "conspiratorial" relevance to the master-slave social structure. Discussing the symbolic use of conspiracy, Davis explores the identity constructs that have been used not only to conceptualize certain paranoid views of segments of the American society, such as those held by Southern Slave Power, religious bodies, and abolitionists, but particularly to define national identity. He observes that after the American and French revolutions, conspiracies or imagined threats from foreign forces, such as the British government and the French illuminati, often were used to galvanize internal political interests as well as to define America's identity.

The same paranoia was employed in defining the role of slavery by the dominant white culture. The South, for instance, assured unity by promulgating fear-based allegations that black colluders bent on revolt were threatening the established social structure. Davis states, "It does not seem overly fanciful to see such a cultural ritualization in the slavery controversy, or to suggest that *Americans increasingly used slavery as the primary symbol for defining the values and roles that would constitute their social identity.*"[7]

It is in this context of an inter-textual production of identity that several slave revolts that contributed to the national agenda of identity formation are examined. As these conspiratorial dramaturgies intensified, they precipitated the shifting of boundaries and the renegotiation of identity relations between in-group and out-group communities. The symbolic trope of the Saint Domingue (modern-day Haiti) slave resistance was a central image in white paranoia, and it contextualizes three major American episodes involving efforts by slaves to redefine their relationship with slaveholders: the Gabriel Prosser and the Denmark Vesey conspiracies as well as the Nat Turner revolt. These episodes preceded the Amistad event and offer a context for understanding the milieu in which the Amistad incident unfolded. Thus this chapter opens with a discussion of Saint Domingue as a symbol of paranoia that informed America's national identity in that era. The Saint Domingue resistance was such an entrenched symbol in American politics that as a precursor to the Amistad story, reactions to the former served to explain reactions to the latter.

In both literal and symbolic terms, the significance of Saint Domingue in the discourse of slave revolts in the United States should not be underestimated. Eugene Genovese's persuasive critique of the "Age of Revolution" establishes Saint Domingue as a significant influence in shaping the role of the United States in world history.[8] In the wake of America's secession from Britain and as a result of the volatility of slavery as an economically viable enterprise, the balance of power in Europe at the turn of the nineteenth century had changed. Spain's imperial decline accelerated. France, having lost Saint Domingue, surrendered its claim to colonial power in the New World. The withdrawal of France opened the door for American westward expansion, and the purchase of the Louisiana territories and surrounding areas epitomized the U.S. rhetoric of Manifest Destiny.[9] The revolt in Saint Domingue enabled Britain to reassert its claim to dominant colonial power in the Western Hemisphere, although fears of a Saint Domingue–like uprising in its territories precipitated its offer of emancipation to Caribbean slaves. Just as the French Revolution had redefined the structure of power within and across European society, the revolt in Saint Domingue struck a mortal blow to the continuation of slavery and European colonial authority. Saint Domingue became the raison d'être in arguments for and against slavery.[10]

To American abolitionists, the revolt in Saint Domingue was cited as the reason why it was necessary to extend constitutional rights to the slaves. Only immediate abolition could avert the bloodshed that would descend upon the land.[11] To southern pro-slavery forces, it was the reason why freedom should *not* be offered to the slaves; they were, in the slaveholders' opinion, "unfit" to handle power. Slaveholders' cries for American territorial expansion reached a fever pitch as the specter of Saint Domingue manifested itself in increased unrest among the slaves. Slaveholders generally believed that southwestern territorial expansion would lead to widespread acceptance of the "peculiar institution" of slavery.[12] Thus, while Saint Domingue was a catalyst in the debate over slavery, it also prompted the enactment of repressive laws against the slave populations of the South. Saint Domingue's narrative of terror was reflected in the laws of the master classes, laws that sometimes resulted in further rebellion by slaves.[13]

Nonetheless, since southerners believed their livelihood was tied to the prosperity of the institution of slavery, they continued to deny their common humanity with the slaves while seeking to maintain the sanctity of freedom as a fundamental tenet of their ideology. Ironically, when slaveholders asserted their "inalienable rights," they were in the double bind of voicing the grievances of their slaves. This innate claim led many slaves to choose the path of death as the only meaningful road to achieving freedom. Historically, death and the risk of failure have never stopped slaves from taking chances at gaining their freedom when such opportunities appeared.[14]

The composite sketches of slave revolts offered in this chapter do not attempt to rewrite the history of any of the documented slave revolts under discussion. Rather, they map out the landscape of resistance that had, at certain contested levels, produced moments of recognition between masters and slaves. From its origins in a slave revolt to the establishment of independence as a black nation, the 1791–1804 Haitian Revolution was central in redefining the ideology of slavery and the sustainability of a slave-based social order in the Americas. Years later, the Amistad case would in part impel this change in the social order. The Supreme Court, with seven staunch pro-slavery supporters among its nine judges, would deliver a verdict of "not guilty" to black men who had not only revolted openly against the institution of slavery but had obstinately insisted on their right to freedom. Thus, a compelling argument can be made that the final outcome of the Amistad trials should be understood within the historical processes that produced it. Saint Domingue is one such significant revolutionary trope in American politics of the nineteenth century.

Saint Domingue as Trope of Reality

Michel-Rolph Trouillot has noted in his path-breaking essay, "From Planters' Journals to Academia: the Haitian Revolution as Unthinkable History," that before the Saint Domingue revolt, slaveholders in the Americas tended to explain slave rebellion as a biological or pathological aberration. To slaveholders, "[r]esistance did not exist as a global phenomenon. Rather, each case of unmistakable defiance, each possible instance of resistance, was treated separately and drained of its political content."[15] However, the success of the bloody revolt in Saint Domingue and the revolutionary changes that followed forced slaveholders in the United States and elsewhere to reconceptualize their responses to the fact of violent resistance. They were forced to rethink their strategies when unrest sprang up in their own backyards. It is true, as Trouillot has further argued, that Saint Domingue's classic restructuring of its society— power wrested from the slaveholders by the slaves—was, until recent years, unthinkable as "revolution" to the dominant white society. Yet the force of the Saint Domingue revolt (which came to be known as the Haitian Revolution) and its very historicity shattered the notion of European control over the New World and the assumptions of imperial dominance that underlay that control.

Because the Saint Domingue revolt symbolized the vigor of slave resistance in the New World, the institution of slavery was permeated with the fear of "another" potential Saint Domingue. Thus, Saint Domingue produced two narrative paradigms—that of terror among the slaveholders and of liberation among the slaves. Coexisting independently of each other, these paradigms nourished volatile race conflicts in the New World. As Trouillot has noted, both proponents and opponents of abolitionism used San Domingue as "pretext" to engage their varied agendas.[16] Even though San Domingue mattered to all parties involved in the discourse of slavery, and it served the West as a tool in a variety of ways, the West never considered it to be important historically in and of itself. San Domingue was marginalized in Western narratives. Although Trouillot discusses the West's response to San Domingue, I focus on the slaves, who were both inside and outside Western discourse. I make the argument that to other slaves outside the island who got wind of the Saint Domingue narrative, the revolt was not *pretext* but *text,* not merely drama but dramatic interaction, one in which the slaves were major players in its continued production. The theatrical arena of the Saint Domingue revolt extended beyond the island to eager actors in America and on the world stage.

Saint Domingue remains significant to the Amistad story and other slave revolts because it was an event that provoked and precipitated the debate on slavery—a debate that from its ambiguous beginnings in the 1500s had crystallized into an almost categorical assurance of the slave's inhumanity by the 1800s. Given the ways in which the new United States emerged, it would seem that the American War of Independence sealed the fate of those who did not fall within the sphere of humanity. The declaration of the constitutional rights of "Man" did not include the slaves, even though in hopes of receiving their freedom, slaves had fought under the revolutionary flag as much as others had done under the British flag. The revolutionary discourse of the late eighteenth century ignored the contributions that slaves made to the revolutionary process because to be revolutionary was to create history and therefore to assert one's humanity. Such deeply held beliefs about the nature of humanity also precipitated the 1789 revolutionary class struggles in France. However, the two events differed in that the American Revolution ensured only a narrow application of the term "freedom," whereas the French Revolution broadened the basis of political participation for every French citizen. In wresting leadership from the hands of the nobility, the Jacobins created sociopolitical access to power.[17]

These ideological transformations of the late eighteenth century did not, however, translate automatically into universal application within or across societies. While Europeans sought to confront the internal contradictions posed by the French Revolution and its redefinition of political identity, the barbarous actions undergirding Europe's civilizing mission in the world remained largely uncontested. Critiquing the assumed superiority of the Western world, in which Man was "undeniably Western at the end of the eighteenth century," Trouillot has noted further that proponents of the Enlightenment "never fully questioned the ontological principles behind the colonialist enterprise, namely that the differences between forms of humanity were not of degree but of kind, not historical but primordial."

Trouillot further elaborates that the revolutionary significance of Saint Domingue was considered unthinkable history, both as it was happening and as it came to be interpreted even after the fact: "the Haitian Revolution did challenge the ontological assumptions of the most radical writers of the Enlightenment. The events that shook up Saint Domingue from 1791 to 1804 constituted a sequence for which not even the extreme political left in France or in England had a conceptual frame of reference. They were 'unthinkable' facts in the framework of Western thought." [18]

A major tendency in Western thought was the assumption of racialized vocabulary in conceptualizing Man, which actually meant *European Man*. Thus, a term such as "revolution" was imbued with an ethnocentric coloring which elided subjugated races from its sphere of reference. It is for that reason that Saint Domingue—one of the great events to occur during the "Age of Revolution," as the 1776–1848 era is now known— has often been appended as a footnote of history, rather than ascribed the centrality it warrants.[19] Yet, some two centuries ago, Saint Domingue was central to the colonial enterprise in the Western Hemisphere. Toussaint L'Ouverture, Jean Jacques Dessalines, and other Haitian players were well-known actors on the world stage. Although their collective activities helped to end French and, in general, European preeminence, their influence has received marginal consideration in the conventional historiography of Europe.

The Haitian Revolution

In the late eighteenth century, as France was unleashing its cataclysmic rebellion against its nobility, the nation's revolutionary themes of liberty, equality, and fraternity resounded on the island of Saint Domingue. Saint Domingue itself was well known in the colonial world, the site where the complexities of Europe's encounter with the New World developed. It was Columbus's treasured island, the one he had suppressed and renamed Hispaniola—"little Spain."

Years later, the French conquered the Spanish, thereby acquiring the more fertile region, the western half of the island, and becoming the envy of the world by successfully cultivating half of the world's sugar. Although France was losing ground to other colonial powers elsewhere, its waning glory and treasury were brightened by its economic prospects in Saint Domingue. Thousands of young Frenchmen availed themselves of the new opportunities. They emigrated to Saint Domingue, where personal wealth and political power were readily available. Also, African slave labor was cheap and immensely profitable. Regardless of the slaves' high mortality rate, business boomed. Slaves were eagerly exchanged for much-needed sugar by other European and American interests, and they were never in short supply. Consequently, an annual supply of about 30,000 slaves quickly outnumbered their French landlords by at least two to one. Still, the French presence remained dominant.[20]

By the turn of the eighteenth century, Saint Domingue had some 30,000 French residents, besides its army base and colonial administrative personnel. Its mulatto population of some 25,000 were born free, although they lacked full citizenship. The intricacies of power and freedom gave rise to a complex definition of humanity, both visually and psychologically. Not all black peoples were slaves. Many slave women became free through concubinage. The children born under such circumstances were not only free but could inherit property, own slaves, and become educated. Besides the planter class, "high" born mulattoes had more access to power and wealth than "lesser" born whites. This dialogic of identity was played out in front of enslaved blacks who had no access to power, but who were witnesses to power's versatility.

The French Revolutionary tribune of 1789 would provide the "props" needed in this theater of power. One of the influential societies that had laid the groundwork for the reformation of French society, *Société des Amis des Noirs* (Friends of the Blacks), had propositioned Louis XVI for the abolition of slavery in all territories. The King had given his approval. This, in part, accounted for Comte de Mirabeau's interpretation of the Declaration of the Rights of Man and of the Citizen as extending to all people, regardless of color.[21] Saint Domingue became the laboratory for the universal application of the declaration. French planters contesting the ideas of the revolution insisted that that edict of liberty was for French citizens and should in no way affect the established patterns of race relations in the colonies.

However, mulattoes interested in establishing their full citizenship lobbied in Paris for rights to be extended to the colonies. As a result, four hundred mulattoes eventually achieved the full status of French citizenship—but not before Vincent Ogé and a band of mulatto militia revolted in Saint Domingue. Planters refused to accept the new rights conferred on the mulatto class. Poor whites were equally self-contradicting in their responses. On the one hand, they were indignant that they could lose their symbolic status conferred by the accident of birth; on the other, they were eager to reap the promises of the revolution and the anticipated benefits of class dissolution. Although Ogé and his companions (twenty in all) were quickly crushed, the debate over color was fully established.

The example of Ogé spurred Africans and African-descended peoples in the colonies to give voice to their repressed grievances. In the summer of 1791, blacks revolted on the northern part of the island, thereby involving themselves in the debate on color. Over two thousand whites were killed, and increased agitation and pressure were brought to bear on the French Assembly. Angry at the colonists for attempting to suppress the mulattoes, the French Assembly was now horrified at the consequences of continued slave oppression. Nevertheless, each colony was granted its own local colonial assembly, thereby appeasing the planters.

In France, Louis XVI was beheaded, and the Jacobins came to power. European powers stood ready to exploit France's internal strife by acquiring its colonies. Saint Domingue became the testing-ground of French politics: the dynamics of everyday life assumed a momentum that promised hitherto inconceivable political and social realignments. Concerned with power and recognition, all those involved—the mulattoes, the poor whites, the blacks, the planters—constantly swapped loyalties. The revolting blacks under the leadership of Toussaint L'Ouverture had earlier taken refuge on the Spanish side of the island. The mulattoes were also building their own army against the French colonials and the blacks. As a result, French colonial authority in the region was shattered. Faced with the threat of war in Europe, the Jacobins conceded by declaring full liberty to the colonies. With this proclamation, L'Ouverture was able to return with his troops to French Saint Domingue. He quickly consolidated his power over the northern sector of the colony, whereas André Rigaud, a mulatto, held power in the southern region.

How L'Ouverture rose from the ranks of slavery to become brigadier general in 1796 is one of the great narratives of heroism.[22] L'Ouverture's brilliance not only in exercising power but also in understanding the dynamics of power gained him respect both within and outside of the island. He understood the importance of economic stability and was able to revive a fast-disintegrating colony by persuading the liberated blacks to go back to work on the plantations. Healthy commerce became his diplomatic linchpin. With a strengthened economy and the prospect of exploiting the conflicting ambitions among the colonial powers, L'Ouverture was able to negotiate a relationship (however fragile) with France, Britain, Spain, and even the United States. As Nicholas Halasz comments in

Rattling Chains: Slave Unrest and Revolt in the Antebellum South,
L'Ouverture was always careful to balance "the claims of the various foreign powers in an arrangement suitable to him."[23] In diplomacy with European and American emissaries, L'Ouverture was advantaged by having
educated white defectors who worked in his service. He himself was not
illiterate, but almost all of his black followers were, and it was necessary
to use all available sources to negotiate a place for the island in the world
of nations.

By 1800, having consolidated his hold on the north, L'Ouverture successfully attacked Rigaud, who controlled the southern section of the island, thereby wresting control of the whole of French Saint Domingue.
Although L'Ouverture's rule would suffer constant threats from European powers—specifically, France's designs for the re-institution of slavery under Napoleon and his brother-in-law, General Leclerc—repeated
defeats of the French army by L'Ouverture's free blacks continued to stay
the menace. Even after L'Ouverture was eventually tricked into captivity
and imprisonment in France, his successor, Jean Jacques Dessalines, perhaps learning from the fate of L'Ouverture, embarked on a campaign to
remove any threat of European reassertion of control over the island.
Dessalines expelled or exterminated all whites. He abolished the political
distinctions between mulattoes and blacks and declared Saint Domingue
a black nation under the name of Haiti.

Remarkable as a century of revolts, the eighteenth century closed with
continued revolution in the island of Saint Domingue, or Haiti as it was
now called. Joshua Coffin's 1860 publication, *An Account of Some of the
Principal Slave Insurrections,* summarizes slave revolts over two centuries
in the Western Hemisphere. From New York City to the islands of the
Caribbean to the mountains of South America, suspicious fires, murders,
conspiracies, open rebellion, and insurrections increased with the rising
traffic in slaves and attested to the most turbulent era in the Americas.[24]
Only in Jamaica did the number (though not the intensity) of rebellions
decrease, simply because, as Eugene Genovese explains in *From Rebellion
to Revolution,* the pacification of the Maroons through treaties with the
British had generally curbed Maroon sympathies for runaway slaves.[25]
Thus, the slave revolts of the eighteenth century would influence the ab-
rogation of slavery in the next century. It is not insignificant that the nineteenth century dawned in the wake of Saint Domingue's changing status,
with power in the hands of former slaves. Genovese has noted that "the

interrelated revolutions in France and Saint-Domingue created a new system of international power and a more coherent revolutionary ideology."[26] Indeed, there is enough evidence to suggest that Saint Domingue reverberated in the minds of colonialist and would-be imperialist nations, such as the United States. The immense impact of the Saint Domingue revolt has, in recent times, been rightly assessed by other historians such as Thomas Ott in *The Haitian Revolution 1789–1804*, Robin Blackburn in *The Overthrow of Colonial Slavery*, Carolyn Fick in *The Making of Haiti*, and Michel-Rolph Trouillot in *Silencing the Past*.

To the extent that L'Ouverture was able to stage, negotiate, and maintain the economy of a liberal doctrine for the people of Saint Domingue, the repressed humanity of blacks was acknowledged (at least tacitly) by white overlords everywhere. The dramatic action of revolt in Saint Domingue invited, even demanded, a specific historical response from its white counterparts and open-ended, intergroup reassessment of established sociopolitical labels of identity. For blacks in search of a redeemed identity, Saint Domingue was a model for negotiating their place in the world. Indeed, as Genovese observes, L'Ouverture's success as a diplomat indicated—to whites as well as blacks—that a new world history had dawned.

Saint Domingue in American Slave Revolts

Gabriel Prosser

Although whites seemed reluctant to enter into dialogue with the reproduction of a new black identity, as evidenced in Saint Domingue, slaves in the Western Hemisphere were eagerly decoding the power relations brokered by L'Ouverture and later, Dessalines's army. Similarly, this dynamic can be read in the Prosser conspiracy of 1800 near Richmond, Virginia.[27] Although the plot of insurrection initiated by Gabriel, a slave of Thomas Prosser, was foiled by two slaves who belonged to another plantation, the visionary imagination of Prosser provides an index of L'Ouverture's discovery that in forging history, black survival as an independent people, for all practical purposes, would occur in both dialogic and dialectic terms with other national and political bodies.[28] The slaveholding community of the South was astonished to discover Prosser's rationale, refusing to accept that a slave could contrive such a politically charged insurgence. Prosser selectively shared his plot with a few slaves, who in turn informed other slaves of the conspiracy. Prosser's brilliance lay in his ability to strategize rather than in any conviction that a large number of slaves was necessary to initiate the plot. Inspired by religious conviction, he believed that he needed only a few committed men to achieve his goal. Although Prosser refused to speak during his trial, many others who were implicated in the plot confessed. It is from their testimonies that the conspiracy can be reconstructed for posterity.

What the prosecuting tribunal heard struck terror in slaveholders everywhere. The insurrection was to begin with the extermination of planters and their families in order to secure an area as an operating base. The revolt was to start with just a hundred men armed with crude, homemade weapons: once the uprising began, Prosser predicted that others would follow. He intended to capture strategic bridges and then march from a relatively obscure base to Richmond, Virginia, with some two thousand slaves armed with their masters' arsenals. In a letter published by the *Boston Gazette,* and cited in Coffin's *Slave Insurrections,* a Richmond citizen wrote:

> By this time, you have no doubt heard of the conspiracy, formed in this country by the negroes, which, but for the interposition of Providence, would have put the metropolis of the State, and even the State itself, into their possession. A dreadful storm with a deluge of rain, which carried away the bridges and rendered the water courses every where impassable, prevented the execution of their plot. *It was extensive and vast in its design. Nothing could have been better contrived. The conspirators were to have seized on the magazine, the treasury, the mills, and the bridges across James river.* They were to have entered the city of Richmond in three places with fire and sword, to commence an indiscriminate slaughter, the French only excepted. They were then to have called on their fellow negroes and the friends of humanity throughout the continent, by proclamation, to rally round their standard. . . . Two important facts have been established by the witnesses on the different trials. First, that the plan of the plot was drawn by two Frenchmen in Richmond, and by them given to the negro General Gabriel, who is not yet caught; and secondly, that in the meditated massacre, *not one Frenchman* was to be touched. It is moreover believed, though not positively known, that a great many of our profligate and abandoned whites (who are distinguished by the burlesque appellation of *democrats*) are implicated with the blacks, and would have joined them if they had commenced their operations.[29]

Although the writer, like many Virginians of the time, was wrong in believing that the French instigated the intended insurrection, he was correct in conjecturing that Jacobin sentiments were strong in the hearts of the slaves. In Prosser's camp, destroying whites simply meant destroying white oppressors, the slaveholding families. It did not mean white Frenchmen, white Methodists, white Quakers, or for that matter, poor whites with whom slaves and free blacks shared certain class similarities. It is rumored that Prosser planned to create his own banner with the slogan "Liberty or Death." Prosser also intended to incite the Catawba Indians of that region in addition to recruiting blacks from distant communities.

Of course, none of these plans came to fruition, because they were betrayed. The leaders, and in some cases supposed leaders, of the intended insurrection were hanged. Herbert Aptheker has commented in *American Negro Slave Revolts* that the "precise number of those executed cannot be given with certainty, but it appears likely that at least thirty-five Negroes were hanged, four condemned slaves escaped from prison, while one committed suicide in prison."[30] The seeds of revolt seemed widespread in the slave population, so a general amnesty was later granted by Governor Monroe in order to cover up an affair that confirmed the insecurities of the slaveholding world. For many years afterward, documents pertaining to this particular attempted insurrection remained sealed.

Why, indeed, would a revolt that never occurred have instilled such widespread fear among planters long after it was aborted? Certainly, the shroud of secrecy imposed on the trials and executions inspired legends about Prosser. Some believed that he was never killed, that he eluded capture by sailing to Saint Domingue. Others said he was tied to four horses that, pulling in four different directions, tore him to pieces. Both blacks and whites in the antebellum South danced to popular songs about Prosser's "defeat."

Prosser's conspiracy was directly responsible for the attempts in 1800, 1802, and 1804 by the General Assembly of Virginia to secure a place of banishment for rebellious slaves and, in particular, free blacks, who by their very presence constituted a threat. The assembly failed in its attempts. Coffin concluded in *Slave Insurrections* that the "conspiracy of General Gabriel and his coadjutors was, therefore, the occasion, if not the cause, of the formation, in 1817, of the Colonization Society, whose great object was, by removing all disturbing causes, to make slavery secure, lucrative, and perpetual."[31]

In the discourse of slavery, antebellum writers tended to perceive black identity as subsumed by the national issues of race and progress. In-group and out-group interpersonal relations circumscribed social and political definitions of identity. In revisiting the Prosser story in the twentieth century, Arna Bontemps, in his historical novel *Black Thunder,* inverts Prosser's much-trumpeted defeat as a victory. On black creativity, Eric Sundquist has written that "Bontemps followed the tradition established by black antebellum writers—Douglass's 'The Heroic Slave' is the pre-eminent example—of tying slave revolt to the moral principles of the Age of Revolution and making African-American access to the language of liberty a primary trope."[32]

Bontemps also applies L'Ouverture's revolutionary thinking to the character of Gabriel in *Black Thunder.* The evidence for this imaginative recasting is not far-fetched. When Prosser's conspiracy was uncovered in 1800, panic-stricken whites had envisioned a multilayered plot to destroy the slaveholding world, which included political enemies with Jeffersonian principles, religious plotters such as the Methodists, French revolutionary enthusiasts, supposed help from Saint Domingue, and internal help from Northern abolitionists. This self-perpetuating psychological coup-d'état among the slaveholders in effect paralyzed the slaveholders' dreams of a plantation haven.

Slaveholders seemed not to have given credit to the fact that Prosser could imagine such a plan, but their fears were confirmed by coconspirators willing to divulge the plot. It appears that Prosser had hoped to harness sympathies from a fast-dividing America. He did expect support from people of his own color, but he was quick to advise his men to destroy equally those blacks who seemed to support their masters. Moreover, he expected support on the basis of class solidarity, anticipating that lower-class whites, for love of liberty and equality in both social and economic terms, would forge an alliance with them, thereby provoking a popular uprising. Besides, the surprising suddenness of the revolt would have political ramifications. Should his plans fail, however (Prosser at least was practical in this respect), he intended to retreat to a mountainous enclave and fight to the death.[33]

Like Saint Domingue's L'Ouverture, Prosser contrived a plot in which the very identity of blackness was intricately implicated in the political choices of the wider white community. The racial dichotomy of in-group–out-group categories was challenged by Prosser, who was seeking to define blackness beyond the boundaries of color or nation. Prosser's envisioned cross-racial alliance of the disadvantaged not only assumed the full humanity of blacks but also indicated society's evolving awareness of new formations of power in both national and global terms.

Denmark Vesey

This same awareness was demonstrated by Denmark Vesey, a free black of Charleston, South Carolina, in 1822. Vesey's plot to destroy whites and secure freedom for slaves immensely surprised the white slaveholding community of Charleston. Why, they wondered, would a black man, whose personal freedom was not at stake, risk his life through acts of insurrection? The testimonies of slaves who were implicated with Vesey and of whites whom Vesey had confronted verbally reveal, at least partially, the major grievances that preoccupied Vesey and precipitated his obsession with the notion of total freedom for all blacks. Vesey's own social entanglement with the "peculiar institution's" policy on slave sexual relations is foremost. Although he was free, the children he fathered by slave women became slaves themselves. It galled him that he could sire children over whom he had no legal rights. This condition and the general helpless estate of the bonded had in fact prompted him to ignore an opportunity to migrate to Africa. He was concerned with relieving the affliction he witnessed daily in the South.[34]

For a man of his abilities, this desire to do something about an unjust system was not wishful thinking. Vesey had bought his own freedom and was gifted in many ways. He had traveled the world over with his master, Captain Vesey, whom he had served for some twenty years. He could read and write, and spoke several languages. Moreover, he was a distinguished carpenter in Charleston. He was also widely feared by the colored population, for he sought every avenue to make clear his rhetorical position on slavery, a position most could only share in secret. As reported by J. Hamilton, the intendant who compiled the accounts of the Vesey case in *An Account of the Late Intended Insurrection,* many slaves were persuaded by Vesey's impassioned appeals from the Bible. Others were convinced by his abolitionist rhetoric, in which he claimed not only that the North was supportive but also that Congress had declared blacks to be free, thereby implying that the slaves' rebellion would only be reaffirming the law. Even the skeptical and fearful were captivated by his stories of Saint Domingue.[35]

To contend with the insidious fear that dominated the lives of the slaves, Vesey provided a justification for his claims by appealing to the principles of the U.S. Constitution and the need to practice the same. He also created a narrative incorporating the mystique of Saint Domingue as a trope of white terror. Blacks saw in him the qualities of a fearless leader, and many enlisted in his growing organization. So bold were the plans conceived by Vesey that Thomas Wentworth Higginson described him in terms of the stature of the revolutionaries in Haiti.[36] Had Vesey's plans not been betrayed by a slave named Devany on May 25, 1822, and corroborated a few weeks later by another slave who had been enjoined by his master to spy on the conspirators, it seems likely that the insurrection would have had far-reaching effects. Backed by key intimates such as Peter Poyas, Mingo Harth, and Jack Purcell (better known as Gullah Jack)—slaves who commanded considerable respect and power over other slaves—the carefully conceived plan was discovered only a week before it was to be implemented.[37]

As with the Prosser conspiracy, the memory of Saint Domingue featured significantly in the Vesey plot, so much so that one of the appointed leaders, Monday Gell, appealed for solidarity by writing to President Boyer of Saint Domingue. As Higginson related, "the letter was about the suffering of the blacks, and [Gell wanted] to know if the people of Saint Domingue would help [the plotters] if they made an effort to free themselves."[38] Vesey also persuaded his followers that, in conquering Charleston, a total extermination of whites was necessary; this method had been employed in Saint Domingue. Saint Domingue was thus the precedent for both Prosser and Vesey. That their intended revolts never occurred and that most of the circumstantial evidence had to be reconstructed without the help of the leaders who engineered the plot made the specter of Saint Domingue even more fearful than it in fact was. White fear of another Saint Domingue caused white slaveholders to increase slave repression and was an unspoken terror continually reinforced by rumors of possible black insurrections.[39]

What were the gains that Vesey hoped for? Conversant with the politics of the day, Vesey wanted to take advantage of white political dissension over slavery and to secure at some level American support for his agenda. He expected international support from the English, who were now strongly committed to antislavery principles. He also looked to Africa and Saint Domingue for aid. Nonetheless, the facts remain vague, because those who were truly close to the particulars of the plot, men like Peter Poyas, died without revealing the details of the plan.

In retrospect, Vesey's political expectations were more symbolic than they were practical. Vesey was more assured of creating an international drama of the plight of Africans in bondage than of actually securing immediate freedom for his afflicted brethren. What he surely anticipated was the vengeance of an enraged slaveholding community that, reinforced by other slaveholding states, would launch a counter-attack against the insurrectionists. Although there is no way to tell what might have happened had the insurrection succeeded, it is significant that Vesey had a practical plan to save the plotters, should their ultimate dream of a free black society fail: Vesey and his coconspirators hoped to commandeer ships and sail for Haiti with as many goods as they could carry.[40] Much like Israel is to its exiled children, Saint Domingue became a spiritual escape for enslaved blacks, an imagined homeland.

Indeed, the fears the Vesey plot generated in Charleston seemed irrational considering that in actuality, Saint Domingue had neither political nor military clout to aid dissidents on American soil. Moreover, America had signed a pact with Saint Domingue in which L'Ouverture agreed to restrain volatile persons from entering the United States. But neither blacks nor whites seemed to have cared about the implausibility of intervention by a black foreign power. What was significant and affecting was the fact that a black power existed at all in the West at a time when racial theories on the natural inferiority of blacks "justified" slavery. Consequently, Saint Domingue became a highly referential symbol with contrasting emotional associations for both blacks and whites. To the former, it stood for pride and promise; to the latter, for humiliation and anxiety. The political *presentness* of Saint Domingue carried, in Murray Edelman's words, "strong emotional and ideological associations" in the United States. Its potency as a political symbol is that it was "remote, set apart, omnipresent as the ultimate threat or means of succor, yet not susceptible to effective influence through any act we as individuals can perform."[41] Thus, Saint Domingue was a highly manipulable symbol in the slaveholding South. To whites, if it remained the stuff of dreams that never quite came to pass (as in the case of both Prosser and Vesey), the slaveholding communities could believe in their own invincibility. To blacks, Saint Domingue offered an alternative narrative of identity that was not circumscribed by the in-group–out-group or master-slave dynamics of American politics.

Haitian defiance of European domination offered slaves a political and social identity not controlled by a national agenda. In that sense, slaves had a context for understanding their condition while at the same time wielding implied power over their oppressors. Plotted revolts therefore became unreadable, elusive, internalized—an unconscious aspect of slave identity. This unpredictable character of the slave psyche threw into sharp relief the vulnerability of whites.

Nat Turner

In Southampton, Virginia, in 1831, without warning and without suspicion from either whites or blacks, Nat Turner struck. It seemed that the phantom of Saint Domingue had been inspirited in his person. Nat Turner confided his plans to only four blacks, who initiated two others. Unlike Prosser and Vesey, Turner claimed that his directive was singularly from God. He did not spend years dreaming up strategies. The opportune moment arose not after lengthy deliberation but from a sign he interpreted as providential. When an eclipse of the sun occurred in February 1831, Turner decided to attack. Quietly and swiftly, he and his six companions moved from plantation to plantation killing every white person they encountered.[42]

The confessions of Nat Turner seem to suggest that the tribunal had expected Turner's plot to be connected with the now familiar narrative of Saint Domingue and, most likely, with some wider national or global conspiracy. Turner claimed no such affiliation, noting only that the same thoughts of freedom might prompt others to do what he had done.[43] It did not seem to matter to Turner and his men that they had no carefully prepared plan or counterplan, that no grand revolutionary scheme motivated their actions. The simple desire to be free was at the heart of their decision to strike at their oppressors.

The court regarded Turner as a religious fanatic who was misguided in his actions, and was blind to the fact that a desire to cultivate the heroic nature that his family had bequeathed to him underlay Turner's actions. Turner repeatedly stated in his confession that from early childhood he was impressed with the knowledge that he was born for some great purpose. Relatives and other slaves had constantly remarked that he was not suited for slavery. It was common knowledge that Turner's father had run away from slavery; Turner himself had once disappeared for thirty days, although to the disappointment of other slaves, he had returned and submitted himself to his master. Given his quick-wittedness, natural curiosity, and intelligence, he was probably acquainted with narratives of revolts in America and abroad. Yet, in his hour of need, biblically inspired wrath on his enemies would be his only real weapon, not dreams of a popular uprising. Turner couched the deliverance of enslaved blacks in terms of a mandate from God and as part of his prophesied calling, which was nurtured by his unshakeable belief in the human dignity of black people.[44] The parallels between Turner's act and the Saint Domingue resistance lie in the invocation of equality, the latter in the rhetoric of the French Revolution and the former in biblical terms. In either case, the rhetoric of European thought paradoxically provided the rationale for the overthrow of the unjust order.

It is ironic that Turner's unsophisticated plan was the most effective ever staged in the United States. One man, with a clumsy strategy, effected the indiscriminate death of fifty-five whites within forty-eight hours. The fact that he was not avenging himself for any immediate personal wrong (he attested that his master was fair) and had no ties to a larger conspiracy was, without rhetorical guise, the clearest statement that slavery was inherently wrong, a fact that continued to elude the slaveholding South. The machinery of Turner's success, short-lived though it was, was the spontaneous support from other slaves. Slaves who had no prior knowledge of the plot quickly joined forces with Turner: a party of seven grew to a contingent of sixty. "Prophet Nat" had planned to continue with his plot until he had secured freedom for his people. Although in the aftermath, innocent blacks were murdered at the hands of white mobs, Higginson observes that the impact of the revolt caused nine states to quake at the realization that "a Nat Turner might be in every family; that the same bloody deed might be acted over at any time and in any place; that the materials for it were spread through the land, and were always ready for a like explosion." Because of Saint Domingue, Nat Turner could not be dismissed altogether as an anomaly. The slaveholding society soon realized that Saint Domingue was no longer a remote threat to the status quo; it was throbbing in the veins of the seemingly quiescent black population.[45]

The Saint Domingue–Amistad Connection

The constant threat of slave revolts that haunted slaveholders in the southern states had its parallels in the precarious Middle Passage from Africa to the Americas. Numerous slave rebellions are recounted in the personal diaries of sea captains and other journalistic accounts.[46] Nineteenth-century slave revolts on land and sea had their spiritual ancestry in the actions of eighteenth-century freedom fighters along the African coast, especially the Guinea coast. One such example is the nine-day battle onboard *Little George,* a Rhode Island vessel that was embarking on a return voyage to the United States with slaves from Sierra Leone. On June 6, 1731, thirty-five male captives rose against the crew, killing three guards, taking control of the ship, and successfully plotting their escape. The captain and remaining crew members resisted, but all attempts to regain control of the ship failed. With the help of the cabin boy, the African revolters steered the ship and its human cargo (sixty captive men, women, and children) along the Sierra Leone River, docking nearby the departure site.

Similarly, the Amistad Africans' tale of horror in the Middle Passage crossing was reversed in their favor when they successfully took control of *La Amistad* in dangerous waters. Many a slave dreamt of being among the few successful mutineers, but most attempted mutinies failed. Some slaves might have succeeded in killing a few crew members, but rebellions were usually quelled and contained. The technological invention of disposable hatches to flush slaves into the Atlantic ocean—in the event that British patrol boats accosted slave ships (in violation of the 1807 treaty for the suppression of the Atlantic slave trade)—served as convenient devices to manage rebellions onboard ship. The hatches created enough terror to subdue slaves in transit, but many undermined such strategies by choosing freedom in death. Suicides and behavior that courted death were typical occurrences on slave ships. Despite the extreme security measures enforced on slave ships, "rebellion rivalled disease as the greatest killer on the passage from Africa to the Americas." Some slaves preferred the fatal wrath of the ship's crew to a life of slavery in the New World.

Such mutinous behavior continued in the New World, especially in places where the ratio of slaves to whites was very high, such as Saint Domingue. Much like the Middle Passage revolts, the Saint Domingue rebellion was founded on the desire for freedom from oppression. Narratives of resistance were kept alive in slaves' shared memory of cultural stories. For this reason, slaveholders usually separated slaves who shared similar language ties, both during the crossing and in the New World. The Saint Domingue rebellion made possible other forms of resistance. It is also not altogether unlikely that some of the Amistad Africans knew about the uprisings in Saint Domingue and the Guinea coast, especially through the stories of black merchant seamen.[47]

Although historically related, the Saint Domingue takeover and the Amistad revolt were expressed differently. Whereas the latter was a mutiny by fifty-three Africans whose clear goal was to return to the land of their birth, the former was a people's revolution, its immediate concern being freedom and the end of slavery and dispossession. The Amistad Africans' major concern was to escape the alien world of the West. Navigating eastward to freedom seemed the only comforting proposition, and flight was a familiar course of action. In contrast, the blacks of Saint Domingue knew well the site of their rebellion—their island—sometimes better than the island's white landlords. Legitimate claims to mastery of their own fate were forged not in flight—that is, a return to Africa—but in rootedness in this new terrain; Haitians were determined to make a home for themselves in the New World. Besides, blacks sought to foster for themselves the intellectual, social, political, and economic exchanges they had observed and grown accustomed to in colonial life.

On the African continent, however, most Africans who were safely out of the reach of white enslavers still had little or no contact with Europeans. Thus, for those unfamiliar with the West, such as the disenchanted Amistad mutineers, a return home was the only viable and satisfying prospect. Whereas the blacks of Saint Domingue were concerned with negotiating their full sovereignty and gaining recognition from other Western nations and were able to maintain their new status of liberty, the Amistad captives were arrested two months after the revolt, in Long Island Sound.

Another difference is that Haitians' appeal for human recognition was initiated and sustained by the sword, thus imposing a narrative of terror on slaveholders. The Amistad Africans' appeal for human recognition started with the sword (specifically, sugar cane knives) but was sustained by the courts and the Africans' persistent self-declaration that they were not slaves. Aware of the implication of New World slavery, the Amistad captives deliberately translated their appeals into the rhetoric of the antislavery movement. They cultivated American public sympathy by invoking the narrative of terror imposed on blacks in the Middle Passage experience.[48]

How the Amistad captives expressed their resistance gave the incident a singular place in history. Unlike a similar mutiny led by Madison Washington of the *Creole* brig, which sought help from the British at Nassau, the Amistad captives sought their freedom, ironically, from America itself—a putatively free nation that sanctioned slavery within its own territory.[49] Providentially landing in New England gave them a chance to fight for their human rights. Had the ship landed on southern shores as the two Spaniards Jose Ruiz and Pedro Montes hoped, the Amistad story might not have survived as even a footnote to history. Given the turn of events in the Amistad trial, however, the celebrated outcome has become a marker in world history, especially in terms of how it addressed the question of slavery.

It is in this specific historical context that the Amistad story shares the glories of the Saint Domingue revolt. There are indeed several structural similarities between the two events. Both resisted the naked realities of slavery. Both were successful, even though their collective impact has only recently begun to receive full recognition. Both, in their respective ways, were unprecedented and unique. The Saint Domingue revolt was significant because, as a parallel to the French Revolution and the changes that were rapidly engulfing Europe, it redefined black political identity on a world scale. Equally, the Amistad revolt shaped events in both America and Africa and highlighted the potential for positive relationships to exist between championing antislavery whites and blacks who were contesting the "peculiar institution."

Saint Domingue in the Literary Imagination

The Saint Domingue and Amistad events have inspired many artists and engendered copious amounts of narrative production. The Amistad incident has been celebrated in the poetry of Robert Hayden, and the Saint Domingue event evokes revolutionary fervor in C. L. R. James's *The Black Jacobins*. Herman Melville, the nineteenth-century American writer, early on linked the two historical events in "Benito Cereno." Although Melville's narrative revises Amasa Delano's account of a slave revolt that occurred in the South Seas near Chile, he draws from both the Saint Domingue uprising and the Amistad case to comment on America's courtship of its slaveholding communities. Both the Amistad drama and Melville's exploitation of it in "Benito Cereno" demonstrate how multiple methods of resisting oppression have helped define identities of blackness.[50]

In *A Narrative of Voyages and Travels in the Northern and Southern Hemispheres,* Amasa Delano tells the story of the Spanish ship *Tryal* that had sailed from Valparaiso on December 20, 1804, bound for Lima. On December 26, the seventy-two slaves onboard the *Tryal* took possession of the ship, killing twenty-five crew members. They also commanded the second captain, Benito Cereno, whose life they had spared, to sail for the slaves' homeland in Senegal. Don Benito sailed with the intent of staying close to the shoreline until their water ran out, hoping that he and his remaining men would somehow escape in the ship's boat.

On February 20, 1805, they anchored near the island of St. Maria where the American Captain Amasa Delano's ship *Perseverance* was watering. Unaware of the true dynamics of power aboard the ship, Delano refreshed the *Tryal* with food and water. The slaves posed as captives and compelled Don Benito and his men to participate in the farce. Although Captain Delano witnessed many unusual circumstances onboard the *Tryal,* such as revolt leader Babo's bold conversations with Don Benito, he was nearly duped. The deception was unmasked when the Spanish captain leaped into Delano's boat as Delano and his men pulled away from the *Tryal.* Witnessing their captain's impulsive move, some of Benito's men jumped overboard. Attempts by the slaves to escape with the *Tryal* were thus forestalled by Delano's men, who suppressed the Africans and took control of the ship.[51]

In retelling Delano's adventure, Melville drew on both the well-known Saint Domingue story and the Amistad case. The latter was unfolding at a time when he himself was experiencing a life of oppression as a sailor on his first career voyage to Liverpool. In her essay, "The Riddle of the Sphinx: Melville's 'Benito Cereno' and the Amistad Case," Carolyn Karcher asserts that the oppressive character of Melville's own career as well as the riveting Amistad case, "the stuff of exotic adventure fiction," deeply impressed the author's consciousness. In re-envisioning Delano's account, Karcher has said that Melville "seems to have borrowed as extensively from news accounts of the *Amistad* as from Delano's *Narrative.*"[52] For example, the description of the *Tryal* and its suspicious character was informed by newspaper accounts of the "piratical" schooner Amistad.[53] In an essay on New World slavery, Eric Sundquist also notes that even though a number of slave revolts were well documented by 1855, when Melville published "Benito Cereno," "the more famous case of the Amistad . . . is even more likely to have been on [his] mind, not least because the enactment of the revolt resembled that aboard the [*Tryal*] and because the slave leader, Cinque, was viewed as an intriguing combination of guile and humanity."[54] Melville's Babo, the charismatic leader of the *Tryal,* seems to have been modeled after Sengbe Pieh.

In "Benito Cereno," Melville changed the *Tryal* in the original Delano account to *San Dominick,* and imbued his *La Amistad*- and *Tryal*-based story with the iconographic image of Saint Domingue. Thus, Melville expressed "the theme of balked revolutions through an elaborate pattern of suppressed mystery and ironic revelation." [55] Invoking Saint Domingue, Melville suggested that the ultimate outcome in the fight against slavery would be favorable to the slaves, a fact he did not want his readers to forget.

Melville's obsession with the horror of Saint Domingue reinforced the "narrative of terror" in "Benito Cereno." Believing they cannot secure their freedom by any other means, the slaves kill Don Alexander Aranda, owner of both the ship and its human cargo, and replace *San Dominick*'s figurehead—the head of Cristobal Colón (Columbus)—with Aranda's skeleton. Below the new figurehead, the slaves write "Follow your Leader," a warning to the remaining Spaniards to cooperate with the slaves' plans. The conflict onboard the *San Dominick* depicts violence as an inevitable reality in the abolition of the master-slave dichotomy. It also predicted that the economy of slavery that Columbus had instituted in Saint Domingue would one day be overturned by the slaves' mastery over their colonial lords. [56]

An oft-revisited scene in Melville's work, which captures this "historical drama of vengeance," to use Sundquist's expression, is the shaving scene in which Don Benito nervously submits himself to Babo's seemingly spontaneous decision to offer him a routine shave: "Altogether, the scene was somewhat peculiar, at least to Captain Delano, nor, as he saw the two thus postured, could he resist the vagary, that in the black he saw a headsman, and in the white a man at the block. But this was one of those antic conceits, appearing and vanishing in a breath, from which, perhaps, the best regulated mind is not always free." [57]

Delano observes the scene but fails to grasp its full significance. Similarly, Melville seems to be saying that America failed to be enlightened by slave revolts and conspiracies that would otherwise provoke revelation. Rather, the twin strategies of denial and repression suppressed the meaningful messages of various forms of slave resistance. Delano epitomizes a national system that claimed a benevolent paternalism to its slave population but remained blind to the implications of slavery. The complicity of the North in the consolidation of slavery is also evident in Melville's sketch of Delano. It was the Northerner Delano and his men who reversed the gains made by the slaves by restoring them back into slavery. Delano aimed at profiting as much from the revolt as the naval officer from New York, Lieutenant Gedney, had hoped to profit from salvage rights to the *Amistad* and its human cargo.

Many critics have accused Melville of reinforcing the racism of his day by not only engaging the revolts but also enthusiastically detailing their suppression.[58] Indeed, Melville's delineation of the terror that preoccupied white minds accurately reflected the West's response to slave uprisings. The mechanics of suppression seemed to have been the slaveholder's answer to fear. Moreover, in Melville's marriage of the Amistad and Saint Domingue episodes, he conveyed the message that slave revolts in American society could be both violent and successful. In this sense, Melville's depictions are expressions of the *Tryal* incident and illustrate the narrative of resistance: diverse circumstances provoke multiple responses from the oppressed and demonstrate the complexity of interpersonal dominance. As Karcher argues further in "The Riddle of the Sphinx," the Amistad incident had the intriguing figures that could complement Delano's experience in the South Seas, but the successful outcome of the Amistad crisis could have blunted Melville's objective in "Benito Cereno"—to delineate the terror that such revolts evoked in the white world.[59] The Saint Domingue resistance contained the image of terror Melville needed to actualize white psychological responses to slave revolts.

Delano's *A Narrative of Voyages* ended with the microscopic detailing of the violent elimination of the African revolters, first by the vengeful Spanish crew and then by the courts in the city of Conceptión, where the surviving slave revolters were sentenced. The penalty was "death, which shall be executed, by taking them out and dragging them from the prison, at the tail of a beast of burden, as far as the gibbet, where they shall be hung until they are dead. . . ; that the heads of the five [leaders] first be cut off after they are dead, and be fixed to a pole, in the square of the port of Talcahuano, and the corpses of all be burnt to ashes."[60] Similarly, "Benito Cereno" highlights the gory details of the Spanish crew's violent response to the mutineers of the *San Dominick*.[61] Slaveholders' obsession with the instruments of torture was an attempt to eradicate the source of their fear by disavowing the potency of resistance.

Although Melville's narrative focused on the spirit of denial endemic to his generation, he himself attempted to make an issue of the slaves' humanity. "Benito Cereno" suggests that the continued suppression of slave revolts (or the denial and marginalization of successful revolts) cannot result in the salvation of whites.[62] The final (fictionalized) conversation between Delano and Cereno shows that the political struggle for black liberation epitomized by Saint Domingue and the Amistad case reverberates in the culture in the form of historically important narrative "memories." In response to Benito's incessant and mournful obsession with the slave mutiny long after the ringleaders have been hanged, Delano says:

> But the past is past; why moralize upon it? Forget it. See yon bright sun has forgotten it all, and the blue sea, and the blue sky; these have turned over new leaves."
>
> "Because they have no memory," [Benito] replied; "because they are not human."
>
> ". . . You are saved," cried Captain Delano, more and more astonished and pained; "you are saved; what has cast such a shadow upon you?"
>
> "The negro." [63]

Don Benito's final statement, "the negro," is a harrowing rebuke of a society that failed to understand either itself or those it held in captivity. The shadow of the Negro (black agency)—or its equally interesting inversion, the Negro's shadow (white agency)—is a motif that describes the inseparability of black and white in the New World: black defines white even as white determines black. The interdependence between black and white, between in-group and out-group, are demonstrated in Don Benito's inextricable relationship to the memory of "the negro," the "other." Melville's narrative stressed the enormous psychological costs of slavery—for all parties. "Benito Cereno" is about the relevance of blackness to whiteness. By inscribing themselves in the narrative memory of the West, slaves have produced history, even as much as they have been produced *by* history. The master's freedom and full humanity, in Melville's view, could not be realized without the recognition of his slave's full humanity.

Resistance and Identity

The Saint Domingue revolt and the Amistad case had separate but lasting impact on American society. Saint Domingue, in particular, was the first full-scale resistance of global proportion. In presaging the Gabriel Prosser, Denmark Vesey, and Nat Turner rebellions, Saint Domingue both contributed to and amplified the political significance of slave unrest on American soil. Such widely known cases were instrumental in creating a cultural memory of slave resistance. The Amistad case further challenged this public memory. In the narrative of New World slavery, it would seem that rebellious activities were not an aberration but a pattern of behavior consistent with the repressive polities that produced them. Across the centuries, Coffin, Aptheker, and many other historians have explored the actions of slaves that, falling short of outright revolt, ultimately rendered the institution of slavery unproductive, unprofitable, and dangerous.[64]

By undermining the legitimacy of the "peculiar institution" both in rhetoric and revolt in the United States, slaves and free blacks disavowed the strategies of denial employed by a dominant society that chose to consolidate the union rather than eradicate the specter of slavery. Under tremendous pressure from the American Colonization Society to send them back to Africa, blacks quickly learned to articulate their claims as legitimate American citizens. Rather than acting philanthropically, the Colonization Society proposed repatriation and resettlement as means to eliminate the problem of "the Negro."[65] Blacks did in fact identify with the national interests of the United States in that the revolutionary processes, which birthed the nation, spoke to the deepest desires of their own hearts. But the national blight of an exclusionary system that contradicted the tenets of freedom inscribed in the Constitution accounted for blacks' ambivalence and the pessimism that caused some blacks to sympathize with the aims of the Colonization Society.[66]

Consequently, prominent political personalities such as David Walker and Frederick Douglass were caught in a paradox: they identified with America's revolutionary fervor but rejected its institutional practices. Their response was a two-pronged weapon of slave rebellion and free-black rhetoric, which wreaked immense psychological havoc on pro-slavery arguments. We know, for example, that the publication of *Walker's Appeal . . . to the Coloured Citizens of the World*, by David Walker, unleashed fear and commotion in the slaveholding South. An indictment against slavery and racism and a blueprint for Negro freedom, the *Appeal* aroused black people to unite as a race, to be aware of their God-given relevance to the world, and to push for political participation in the American system. Peter Hinks has observed that Walker's concern was to build "a sense of national identity and collective mission among blacks founded on their special relationship with God."[67]

Both the injustice of the South and the hypocrisy of the North were also called into question by Frederick Douglass. Douglass's most popular anti-slavery speech, "What to the Slave is the Fourth of July?" addressed to a packed hall in Rochester, New York, in July 1852, highlighted black ambivalence toward the promises of independence. Douglass stated that although blacks could identify with the mindset of a pre–Revolutionary War America, in which the nation's desire for freedom mirrored black concerns, they could not identify with a post–Revolutionary War America that stunted its own growth by keeping blacks in chains. Thus, Douglass declared that the fruits of the Revolutionary war would be fully realized only if America freed its slaves. Noting that at the nation's inception both blacks and whites had the same status, Douglass appealed to the common ground of shared identity. In the same breath, however, Douglass signified the dichotomous potential implied by the Declaration of Independence. As historic precedent, independence held the promise that blacks would one day be free, even as it held the threat that this freedom would be achieved, as in America's case, through the violent means of war. Although Douglass himself refrained from advocating violent slave revolts—as evidenced by his choice of depicting the *Creole* brig revolt in his four-part novella, *The Heroic Slave* (instead of, say, the more provocative Amistad revolt of which he was certainly aware)—he did make it clear that active rebellion was preferable to passive victimhood. Madison Washington, the hero of the *Creole* revolt and the protagonist in *The Heroic Slave,* symbolizes Douglass's message. Only by engaging the assumptions of slavery and racism could blacks transform the structural politics of racial identity to their benefit. The interaction, then, between the dramatic actions of the Amistad and the contexts of other slave revolts caused the nation to confront its racial policies.

Nonetheless, African American contestations of the politics of identity in the nineteenth century functioned differently in Africa, where the drama of black-white confrontation had begun. The dialogue engendered by slave revolts and other forms of rebellion in the Western Hemisphere radically mutated on the African continent, where European policies of colonization were systematically replacing the geopolitics of the slave trade.

Sengbe Pieh and ECOMOG, street mural by Amadu Tarawalie. Photograph by Tim Waites.

Behold Africa, street mural by Isah Kabbia. Photograph by Tim Waites.

Black Ruler, street mural by Isah Kabbia. Photograph by Tim Waites.

Margru. Beinecke Rare Book and
Manuscript Library, Yale University.

Kali (or Kale). Beinecke Rare Book
and Manuscript Library, Yale
University.

Kinna (or Kenna). Beinecke Rare
Book and Manuscript Library, Yale
University.

Grabeau (or Grabo). Beinecke Rare
Book and Manuscript Library, Yale
University.

Portrait of Lewis Tappan. Amistad Research Center, Tulane University.

The Mende Mission. Amistad Research Center, Tulane University.

Amistad Memorial, 1992, cast bronze, by Ed Hamilton, sculptor, Louisville, Kentucky, commissioned by the Amistad Foundation, New Haven, Connecticut, in 1991. Photo by Harold Sharpero, New Haven, Connecticut.

CHAPTER THREE

The Amistad Returnees and the Mende Mission

The contact between Europe and Africa, established through peaceful patterns of trade from West Africa to North Africa to the Mediterranean and European worlds, dated back to at least the eighth century. These patterns dramatically changed around the fifteenth and sixteenth centuries when explorers, seeking a trade route to India, made direct contact with Africans on the west coast of Africa. Needing watering places en route to the East, the Europeans developed ties with the indigenous coastal peoples, ties which seemed limited to peaceful transactions of legitimate trade. European goods, such as textiles, beads, and durable metal wares, were exchanged for prized articles such as ivory, gold, wood, and beeswax. It was not long before the indigenous peoples themselves became the most desirable goods—as slaves—in this enterprise. Slaves were highly valued in the European market as a labor force in the New World territorial expansion and as viable "currency" in the circulation of manufactured goods.

From the sixteenth to the nineteenth century, then, Africa increasingly became an international commercial center in which the slave trade was the most profitable venture. While the western and southwestern coasts of Africa were the sites of procured slaves bound for Europe and the Americas, the central and eastern regions of Africa had their own complex arrangements that supplied slaves to the Arab world and to Europe. The plunder of Africa and Africa's resistances and collusions generated specific and varied historical impulses in the many cultural and geopolitical groupings and regions of the continent.[1]

Those who decried the dark history of Europe's ambitious colonizing processes—members of antislavery movements as well as Africans in Europe and America—proffered different approaches for its amelioration, if not for its outright abolition.[2] In the 1780s for instance, Granville Sharp, an Englishman, championed the idea of founding a new home in Africa for destitute Africans who were known as the "black poor" in England. Winning his government's political and financial backing, he resettled over 400 Africans on a small tract of land he purchased from the leader of the Temnes, King Naimbana, near the mouth of the River Rokel on the West African coast in 1787. This Freedom province, renamed Granville town by the settlers, was later burned down by King Jimmy, King Naimbana's regent, because of a dispute he had with the settlers.[3]

Colonization Initiated

Although enormous profits were being made out of the prevailing slave economy by European merchants and investors, men like William Wilberforce, Thomas Clarkson, Zachary Macaulay, and Granville Sharp fomented dissent. Public sentiment finally pressured the British Parliament to accept not only the unchristian and immoral nature of the slave trade but also the gains that could accrue to Europe from a legitimate commercial enterprise *with* Africans rather than *of* Africans. Africans such as Olaudah Equiano and Ottobah Cugoano also lobbied the British government, claiming that Europe would be better served economically and morally if more humanizing relations with Africa were instituted.[4] Antislavery advocates Wilberforce, Clarkson, Sharp, and others decided to test their theory by founding the Sierra Leone Company, a trading post in the rebuilt Freedom province renamed Freetown, in 1791. Their goal was to discourage slavery through legitimate trade, to resettle former slaves and freedmen from Europe and America, to populate the province with captives recaptured at sea, and last but not least, to Christianize the region through missionary influence and Western education and culture. The Nova Scotian settlers who arrived in Freetown in 1792, more so than the Maroons from the West Indies who later followed, were mostly committed Christians and were considered to be capable emissaries for the antislavery agenda.[5]

Nonetheless, the company's dream for Freetown to become a gateway to anglicizing Africa was hampered by many factors, chiefly, poor foresight as to the financial and health needs of colonial subjects; the social and political squabbles among the different settler communities and between the settlers and the Sierra Leone Company itself; the French attack of 1794 in which Freetown was destroyed; and the suspicions, hostilities, and later, attacks from the Temnes. The company was operating at a loss and was faced with political problems for which it seemed unprepared. Thus, when the Atlantic slave trade was abolished in 1807, it seemed logical to sign the company's assets and responsibilities over to the British government which, like other European powers at the time, was busy carving out empires throughout Africa, Asia, Australia, and the New World. Inevitably, the suppression of the slave trade led to the expansionist policies of the British. Thus, in 1808, Freetown became a British colony.

The Missionaries Step In

Europe's colonizing principle certainly revived missionary fervor among Christians in Europe. Islam is believed to have impacted some communities in Sierra Leone as early as the twelfth century. By the early part of the sixteenth century, Roman Catholic priests were attempting to Christianize parts of the coastal regions. Nevertheless, Sierra Leonean indigenes generally maintained their own traditional religions and belief systems; converts to either Islam or Christianity were few.[6] This trend began to change with the political and cultural reconfiguration initiated with the Sierra Leone Company and its settler communities. Displaced from their former origins, most West African recaptives and settlers from the West were receptive to missionary teachings.[7] By the end of the eighteenth century, the Church Missionary Society (CMS) comprising Anglicans, Wesleyan Methodists, and Nova Scotian Methodists had established workable missionary agendas with varying results.

Following the conclusion of the Amistad trial, the American Missionary Association (AMA) dispatched five missionaries—William and Elizabeth Raymond, Henry and Tamar Wilson, and James Steele—to accompany the Africans to their homeland in 1842. These AMA missionaries were effective in reaching Africans because they associated closely with both converts and non-converts and effected change in the mission field mostly by example rather than by ecumenical rhetoric.[8] Given their relative success and the political and social complexities encountered by the American missionaries in their dealings with the Amistad Africans and others, we can gauge the impact of the missionary enterprise in Sierra Leone and its implication for the colonization of the region.

Colonialism is the domination of a society by a superior militarized nation and the process of instituting policies that would effect its dominance in both explicit and implicit ways. It has been argued that "missionaries were part of the political process of creating and extending the right of European sovereignty over 'newly discovered' lands."[9] The passing of the colonizing baton from the Sierra Leone Company to the British government in 1808 upholds this theory. In turn, the consolidation of the British crown in Sierra Leone was further enabled by the missionaries who followed its flag. Indeed, the Amistad committee solicited the British administration's help in assuring the safety of the mission team as they attempted to resettle the Africans and start a mission of their own. Consequently, the missionary indisputably served as "an agent of a political empire, a representative of a civilization, and an envoy of God."[10]

Although the missionaries' unifying aim was to Christianize the "natives," the British and American approaches to missionary work reflected the different cultural and ideological values of their home countries.[11] For example, the British missionaries, like other colonists, tended to live apart from Africans and were somewhat removed from their personal concerns, whereas the Americans lived and worked closely with the Africans and introduced the Protestant work ethic. The mediating processes of Western cultural and social perspectives informed their work, leading to a mindset complicit with colonization. This milieu dictated the paternalistic and condescending attitudes adopted by the missionaries and produced narratives of mastery that defined their ethnocentric positioning. Missionary letters to the home front exemplify how this colonizing principle was perpetuated.

Letters from Sierra Leone

The letters from Sierra Leone are significant not only because they shed light on the Amistad trials and those involved but also because they partially reconstruct the events that transpired in the African phase of the Amistad story.[12] Given the widespread publicity of the Amistad case, the international attention it received, the political cost to the Van Buren administration, the unusual legal maneuverings, and the unprecedented outcome, it is understandable that twentieth-century scholarship has focused mainly on the legal matters in the Amistad trials and the implications for issues such as property law, natural law, and higher law.[13] Some scholars have even dramatized the legal proceedings through novelizing, but their scope is limited to the American phase of the Amistad story.[14] Exceptions are scholars of religion, who are often interested in examining the missionary outgrowth of abolitionism.[15] It is ironic but not altogether surprising that the events of the African phase have either been totally ignored by historians, wrongly misrepresented, or delivered in a narrative style that precludes any serious analysis of the subject matter.

Perhaps renewed academic interest in the Amistad story will produce scholarship on this forgotten phase of the Africans' journey. One way to approach a reconstruction would be to investigate which aspects of the story were retained, mutated, and reformulated in the local history of nineteenth-century Sierra Leone.[16] Through oral tradition—dialogue, folktales, songs, proverbs—the cultural memory of the Amistad may be perpetuated and lead to further reconstructions of events from that century. A more accessible strategy adopted here is to examine the letters that have been preserved in the AMA archive at the Amistad Research Center.

Although it is unfortunate that very few letters written by the Sierra Leoneans have survived, those that exist create a picture of the unfolding events affecting the writers' lives. From the vantage point of the AMA collection, however, scholarly research is limited mostly to the testimonies of missionaries in the field. Missionary letters themselves present an unbalanced picture because the correspondence to which the missionaries were often replying is not available in the AMA archive. The context of the letters' contents must therefore be carefully discerned. Moreover, the letters are subjective in viewpoint, belying both racial and cultural preconceptions. The letters occasionally offer decipherable "facts" and at times, outright hearsay and gossip. Conflicting information also indicates that unverified, unconfirmed rumors were believed by the correspondents. After one hundred sixty years, it is admittedly difficult, and sometimes impossible, to categorize information transmitted to the AMA home base in the United States. Interpretations by modern-day researchers or readers must, then, be carefully filtered not only through an epistemological understanding of place and time in history but also through the critical apparatuses that determined the discourses of the past.

Ostensibly, the discourses of the missionaries took a variety of forms and expressed different levels of allegiances and contentions with the sponsoring organizations. In William Raymond's case (he was the lead missionary with the Amistad Africans), his complaints about AMA activities demonstrated a certain ambivalence toward the imperial culture under which he himself was operating. Raymond complained, for example, that the organization's publication was misrepresenting his words to the American public. In one letter, he acridly wrote that he was taking "a great deal of pains this time that you may have no reason to complain of my chirography so that I may have no reason to complain that the sense of my letters is altered by the printer. I know that my letters need correcting for I am not a scholar but many times *this sense is altered & I am made to say what I never meant to say.*"[17] Perhaps, where Raymond expressed opinions that tested his own cultural beliefs or even emulated some traditional practices in Sierra Leone, the AMA editors in the United States rewrote his sentences to conform to what they imagined he would have *liked* to have said. That is, through such "censorship," they effectively reinscribed a colonial master text that marginalized the African worlds Raymond described. This tendency to misread setting and context, not to mention intent, should alert researchers to the metadiscourses that often pass for fact. Epistolary accounts from the missionaries were influenced by their expectations, cultural preconceptions, emotional temperament, and personal or missive agenda.

In general, the letters report on a number of different topics, including the affairs of the mission; the progress the missionaries were making; the everyday struggles with the original Amistad Africans; the pervasiveness of the slave trade; the social, cultural, and political consequences of the trade; missionary involvement in the lives of non-Amistad Africans; and budgetary matters. These letters paint a certain picture of the AMA experiences in Sierra Leone between 1842 and 1882.[18] As such, they are worth revisiting to highlight some of the major accounts in the establishment and early work of the mission.

On January 13, shortly before the *Gentleman* berthed at Freetown, both Kinna and Sengbe—two of the original Amistad Africans—wrote to Lewis Tappan, thanking him and all the "good people in America" who had helped them secure their freedom. They expressed their joy at once more seeing their native land. Sengbe had even said that in two years' time, he would revisit the United States. The journey to Sierra Leone had been, for the most part, uneventful. However, Sengbe's letter did fore-shadow trouble.

> Mr. Tappan,
> Dear Sir,
>   Captain good—no touch Mendi people. All Mendi people love Mr. Tappan. Mr. Tappan pray for Cinque and all Mendi people all time, and Cinque and all Mendi people pray for Mr. Tappan all time.
>   You give Cinque two white men and one colored man to go with Cinque. We stay Sierra Leone. Cinque can't help because it no my country. We go my country, I help very much. . . .
>   We catch Sierra Leone very quick now—I think tomorrow morning—I very glad. Two years your Cinque see ship—Mr. Raymond glad, Mr. Steele glad—then I go back and see Merica. I go my country, I make house and take care of white man. . . . I thank all Merica people, for they send Mendi people home. I shall never forget Merica people. Your friend,
>   CINQUE.[19]

This letter conveys not only the joy of returning home and gratitude for the help rendered by sympathetic Americans, but it also indicates Sengbe's perception of his role in the unfolding Amistad story. As far as he was concerned, he was in charge. The missionaries had been *given* to him. He was willing to allow two years for both Raymond and Steele, leaders of the intended mission, to settle down happily, but he himself already anticipated returning to America before finally assuming his role as caretaker. The vision of himself as leader would, of course, spell trouble, as evident in several arguments between Sengbe and Raymond and Steele.

Raymond wrote to Tappan that during the journey on the *Gentleman*, Sengbe had exhibited distrust for the missionaries.[20] The revolt leader had been sullen and uncooperative and had asked some questions that bluntly demonstrated his suspicion of the missionaries' design. The argument began when Sengbe discovered a cask below deck containing bottles of rum. While in the New Haven county jail, the Africans had been taught by the missionaries that it was unchristian to drink alcohol, not only because it was proscribed but also because the jail overseer, Colonel Pendleton, had sold rum to the Africans, who were ignorant of its effects. On finding rum in the ship, Sengbe accused the moral crusaders of duplicity and suspected ulterior motives. However, Raymond assuaged Sengbe's fears when he discovered that the captain of the *Gentleman* kept a supply of rum for his own purposes. Nevertheless, Raymond was incensed at how this one act by a nonchalant captain could jeopardize the missionaries' desire to gain credibility with the Africans, whom they had only come to know shortly before the trip to Africa.

Yet another crisis occurred on landing. Under the impression that he was in charge of the trip, Sengbe had decided that the entourage should go directly to his village where, as agreed earlier, they would eventually settle. However, the missionaries expected to stay temporarily in the more agreeable capital city of Freetown, to acquaint themselves with both the new country and the British colonial officials with whom they would need to interact in years to come. Having clearly been the leader of the Amistad captives in times of great need, Sengbe was not ready simply to relinquish his authority to that of the missionaries. He argued vehemently. Steele attempted to convince Sengbe that they still intended to follow the original plan, although certain preparations first had to be made for the move to Mani, Sengbe's hometown. When it was rumored that they would not eventually proceed to Mendeland, Sengbe once more argued with Steele and became distrustful of the entire endeavor.

The ideological and conceptual differences between Sengbe and the missionaries in light of unexpected changes in plan increasingly disrupted communication. Steele wrote Tappan that he was concerned Sengbe's unmanageable attitude could influence the other Africans. After Steele scolded Sengbe (as Steele reported in a letter to Tappan), Sengbe reluctantly agreed to remain a part of the mission team.[21]

Indeed, the Supreme Court victory of the Amistad case in America would undergo a severe test in Africa. Already, things were not going well for the missionaries. Mapping out their mission into the hinterland was proving more difficult than they had envisaged. Some of the Amistad survivors, as they met relatives or received news of their whereabouts and as they became more comfortable in their own cultural space, simply abandoned the group. Others stayed, but they were restless and bored, anxious to begin searching for their families. To save the mission, Raymond decided to move the group to York while Steele was in Mende country scouting for a suitable location.[22] Had the missionaries better understood the Africans' desires and ambitions and the traumas associated with their still displaced identities, they might have given greater consideration to the delicate situation as partners rather than assuming the quasi-imperial position of masters. Raymond and Steele's early letters show their frustration and impatience that so many Amistad

Africans were leaving. In a letter of December 21, 1843, Steele remarked with disappointment that only the children and about ten adults were still with them.[23]

To add to the troubles, Sengbe received news that his village had been burnt to the ground because of the "war road palaver" (slave catching). He was devastated. All his sufferings and endurance abroad were negatively compensated by the "gift" of a vanquished and vanished village. The fate of his wife and three children was unknown: they had either been killed or sold into slavery, neither of which was a comforting prospect. Sengbe's sense of loss and displacement was manifest in his own confused career afterward. He could not decide whether or not to stay with the missionaries. He slipped away but returned for a while, finally helping the missionaries secure a location in Mende territory. Sengbe's personal loss of land and family symbolized a cultural loss. Having fought for his freedom in the United States, Sengbe returned not to freedom but to the reality of territorial wars instigated by the still thriving slave trade. Endless wars between and within ethnic groups resulted in the devastation of entire villages.[24]

The missionaries felt betrayed. Bad news marred the triumph they had envisaged. British missionaries in Freetown thought the AMA team reckless for wanting to locate their ministry in the war-ravaged hinterland. Ready as they were to pursue their goal with single-mindedness, the dangers, diseases, and disappointments confronting them proved insurmountable.

There were other tragedies. Steele did not seem to have the stamina for the climate, and soon fell ill. The Raymonds' baby died. For unknown reasons, the West Indian couple, the Wilsons, soon left the team. It was alleged that Henry Wilson later abandoned his wife, Tamar.[25]

Further letters to key officers in the AMA committee confirm the continued travails of the Amistad team. Steele returned home due to ill health. Without the Wilsons, a missionary team of five was suddenly reduced to two, Raymond and his wife, Eliza, as she was often referred to in his letters. The couple later returned to the United States to recover their health and to raise funds for the mission, and Eliza Raymond eventually returned permanently. Reputedly, she had been a good "mother" to the Amistad children, but her personal tragedies and her consequent emotional problems, which her husband identified as a "mental aberration," made her incapable of withstanding the trials of missionary life.[26]

In spite of his personal ordeals, Raymond succeeded in purchasing land in Kaw Mende from Chief Harry Tucker, the cunning Sherbro strategist who, like other formidable chiefs, had secured his kingdom by going on the "war road." In a letter to Tappan, Raymond indicated that he had heard that Kaw Mende was "a permanent slave market" with "Spanish influence." Once the mission was established, he had the formidable task of enduring the work alone for two years before help was sent from abroad.[27] Raymond was a faithful AMA representative, and was the only white man in that region for that length of time. He reported that months would go by without any contact with other whites, because few whites ventured so far afield and the demands of the mission school meant infrequent trips into the more diverse community of Freetown. Raymond's sanguine personality helped in these times of adversity. He seemed, however, to have clashed too often with some of the Africans. That he was morally upright and committed to the struggle was unquestionable.[28]

Nevertheless, Raymond's impatience with the Africans was manifest in his expectation that they should live a far more stringent Christian lifestyle than their cultural background and tragic experiences in the Americas had prepared them for. Eventually, his unreasonableness and perpetual scolding discouraged the Africans. Sengbe, for instance, left the mission because he and Raymond differed on matters of lifestyle. Sengbe had brought with him a woman he had met on one of his intermittent desertions of the mission. Raymond did not approve of her, so Sengbe left the mission once more.

Raymond's troubled letters give us many insights into the precarious destiny of the Amistad Africans. It is true that while only about eight of the Amistad returnees felt settled at the mission, a few others lived close by in surrounding towns and villages. Others, like Sengbe, would visit the mission after long breaks. However, as Raymond stated in his fundraising tour in America in 1843, the desertion by the Africans was positive, in a sense. As they moved around in search of relatives or fortune, the Amistad Africans continually told their story and spoke incessantly about the mission. In this way, they spread the fame of, and encouraged respect for, its work. This increased the mission's credibility among the powerful chiefs and other local rulers. In fact, Raymond claimed in February 1846 that his name was "a safeguard to any person anywhere between here and the Mendi country. Nobody can trouble anybody or anything that belongs to 'the white man.' This I know savors very much of egotism but it is only the simple truth."[29] This was indeed the truth; the colonizing discourse created a level of credibility (through military might and other methods of subjugation) that could not be ignored by the Africans. Many of the Amistad returnees rightly felt that the mission was a symbol of their experiences abroad and part of their new identity in Sierra Leone. Their pilgrimage to the mission kept news and gossip flowing from Raymond's pen.

Thus we learn in one letter that Sengbe had "emigrated to Jamaica" and, in the next sentence, that Tamar Wilson, from what Raymond could learn, was "living the life of an open prostitute."[30] However, because this was pragmatic correspondence, Sengbe Pieh, Tamar Wilson, and others tend to be referenced only in terms of the mission objectives of spiritual conversion. Comments about the Africans reflect the "good nigger/bad nigger" image popular in American discourses of the nineteenth century. This rhetoric also infuses Raymond's writings about "the flock." The Africans were "good" if they were receptive to Christianity and "bad" if they opposed it. Thus, Sengbe was a "bad nigger" because he did not cooperate with the missionary agenda.

In April 1842, Steele wrote Tappan about "the influences of the villainous Singui who has caused us much of our troubles." Such rumors soon demonized Sengbe. As his trips from the mission lengthened, Sengbe was labeled a bandit and a slave dealer. While these blatant rumors continued to taint Sengbe's character, Tamar Wilson, in contrast, was shrouded in mystery. Her "fall" was highlighted, but what occasioned the breakdown of her marriage was not divulged. We learn later that Henry Wilson reportedly returned to New York alone and continued to be a clergyman. What we never learn about is what transpired between the black missionaries and the white missionaries to cause the former to abandon the group within a year of their arrival at Freetown.

In another letter from the Kaw Mende mission, Raymond writes of the endless wars ravaging the countryside because of the slave trade. Two chiefs, Kissicummah and Sisiwuru, had joined battle in Mperri, the home of Fuliwa, one of the Amistad Africans. It is uncertain whether Fuliwa was residing in the town at the time the letter was written or whether he was visiting his father there. In either case, Fuliwa, along with James Covey and Sa, another Amistad African, happened to have been in Mperri village when the fighting broke out. Fuliwa's father and Sa were killed. Raymond wrote that:

George Brown (Fuliwa) Henry Cowles (So-ko-ma) and James Pratt (Sa) were in the town when it was attacked. George and Henry escaped. James was taken; Henry and James slept in one bed. When James found the town was taken he delivered himself up and begged for his life, telling the man to whom he delivered himself that he belonged to me. The man happened to know me and he promised to save him. Afterward, Johnson (Kinna) and Covey met with him and they begged for his life. The man said he could not kill him. The man left him in a house and went some way. Another man not knowing the agreement that had been made saw him and killed him.[31]

This letter points to the evolving role of the mission as the conscience of the community and as the moralistic yardstick in a disintegrating society. The stabilizing potential of the mission provided "normative ideologies of amelioration recognized as the Civilising Mission or the White Man's Burden." Because the connection between the anarchic state of the colonized country and the colonizing agent was suppressed, what was made visible—the goodwill mission of the Christian world—justified and consolidated imperial power.[32]

This process suggested a complicitous relationship between the colonial administration's aggression and the missionaries' benevolence. The continual slave wars conducted in order to satiate demands in the West put in jeopardy the lives of the Amistad returnees and all other Africans in the hinterland. The Amistad returnees were in constant peril of being recaptured into slavery or even slaughtered. James Covey later lost his life in one of these wars. "The vicissitudes of negotiating their every day existence" demonstrated the dire reality of a nation in peril.[33]

The increased significance of the mission circulated widely, and many people in warring disputes who were unconnected with the mission sought redemption for themselves or their children from Raymond. The structural relations between displacement on the one hand and stabilization (according to a new order) on the other, succeeded in making Africans feel inferior about their own cultures. Abraham's analysis of the policy of "divide and rule" instituted in the provinces of Sierra Leone by the colonial administration worked to the administration's advantage. "There is no doubt that it was part of the colonial strategy to fragment in order to establish firmly the colonial hegemony. Once it was established, a reverse process began—that of amalgamation."[34] Suddenly, traditional approaches were inappropriate to deal with new conditions and social fragmentation. Suddenly, the colonizer's methods seemed superior, natural, and logical for resolving the people's crises.

In one letter, for instance, the mission was informed that Kali had been taken in a war in "a town within gunshot of Mungray." Although this particular letter does not state whether Raymond was able to save Kali, he must have done so because the mission was in the habit of redeeming, or re-buying, captives who were involved with the mission in some way. For instance, Teme's brother was redeemed from slavery by Raymond. In fact, the mission became a symbol of redemption in the war-torn hinterland. As many as two hundred people at one time sought refuge there.[35] The very innocence and goodwill of the mission in accepting so many "redemptees" highlights the intricacies of the socialization process through which Africans themselves became complicit with established systems of domination. African encounters with Europe had evolved into an inextricable colonizing process. The slave trade was such a pervasive force that it corrupted every major institution.

The AMA committee in the United States found itself in a difficult position on receiving Raymond's letters chronicling redemptions. The idea that an abolitionist missionary could participate in the slave trade, even for benevolent purposes, was anathema to committee members. What they failed to realize was that colonization and Christianization were symbiotic. The alternatives to redemption (i.e., murder or enslavement in the Americas) left the committee with no other choice but to accept Raymond's redemption policy. It might be tempting to interpret the mission's acts of redemption as actually contributing to the slave wars, but it is only fair to judge the mission in the context of its credibility to the warring groups. Because the conservative Raymond as a rule refused to trade in slaves, tobacco, rum, or firearms, which were the principle means of exchange in the region, his motives were judged, by indigenes and missionaries alike, as pure.[36]

Against the mission's ethos, Raymond became politically involved in persuading the chiefs to call off the wars and invest their resources in a trade other than slave dealing. He even had to compromise his high ideals of "untainted Christian service" by sending certain gifts, such as tobacco, as a peace offering to the chiefs. The chiefs were slow to respond, and with Raymond dying of yellow fever in 1847, he did not see the fruits of his labor.[37]

By August 1848, under the directorship of Raymond's replacement, thirty-one year old George Thompson, the mission began to realize the results the AMA had hoped for.[38] Thompson decided on a systematic approach. First, he solicited monetary support from the parents of children who lived at the mission. Second, he wrote letters to local rulers, such as King Kissicummah, appealing for both institutional and financial support.[39] Several months later, he wrote a letter to Chief Caulker asking for military assistance to fend off bands of marauders.[40] The devolution of authority by foreign missions to the indigenes was an excellent strategy that compelled the local leaders to assume more responsibility for the welfare of the mission. A "successful" colonizing mission was one in which the Africans themselves internalized the colonial process.

The ongoing warfare among the people, however, continued to affect the mission's progress. Thompson concluded that the slave trade was the "principal cause of all these wars and that can only be stopped by the spread of light and truth."[41] To this end, Thompson spent two and a half months journeying from town to town, making peace in the country. By the beginning of the following year—January 1850—Thompson had successfully mediated between warring parties, and peace was established in Kaw Mende. Consequently, with the cessation of the wars, life steadily became normal. Food was abundant. Education was now highly treasured, and both the chiefs and the local people sent their children to the mission school.

As the work of the mission developed over the years, other branches were opened. Black and white, male and female missionaries were sent by the AMA from the United States. Many of them died from malaria within a few weeks of their arrival. The Amistad African Margru and other later protégés of the Kaw Mende mission, such as Barnabas Root, also served as missionaries.[42] Indirectly, then, the 1839 revolt onboard the *Amistad* schooner greatly influenced the cessation of the slave trade in a region that was notorious for its slave markets. Indeed, by 1882, when it was absorbed by the United Brethren in Christ (UBC), the AMA had already transformed the country irrevocably.

Stability in a New Sierra Leone

Through their participation in the colonial process, the Amistad Africans both facilitated and contested the nature of the colonial discourse, which affected both colonizers and colonized. In a mission that was largely unplanned and unpredictable, Africans had room to contribute and shape the direction of the colonial process. Sierra Leoneans were severely traumatized by the slave trade, but the AMA mission (*within* the colonial process that was now an indelible emblem of modernity) provided positive influences that contributed both economic and educational stability to the people of the country. Sierra Leone has benefited tremendously from the processes set in motion by the Amistad incident. Despite a murky past, Sierra Leone still evinces the "positive consequences" of the AMA mission.[43] Clara DeBoer has noted that the missionaries "left a greater impact on Africa than the graves of their dead would indicate. They had given the Sierra Leone area its first sawmill and two printing presses, had reduced the Mendi and Sherbro languages to writing and had produced translations of the Gospels as well as grammar for use in schools."[44]

Indeed, many of the Amistad Africans remained unconverted, but others, like Margru (renamed Sarah Kinson, later known as Mrs. Edward Henry Green) followed the new faith. The abolitionist Lewis Tappan was greatly encouraged and once commented that if Margru were the only fruit of all the travail of his abolitionist endeavors, she was indeed worth it.[45] Margru had returned to the United States to study at Oberlin College in Ohio. She later returned to the mission to head the school's female department. Committed to the objectives of the mission, she was made head of the mission school and later put in charge of the mission branch at Manya Station. Her husband, the British-educated African Edward Henry Green, was also on the staff.[46]

American Missionary Association activity in Sierra Leone led to the founding of many churches and two reputable academic institutions that are still in operation today: the Albert Academy for boys in the nation's capital, Freetown, and the Harford School for Girls at Moyamba. The immense benefits of such institutional endeavors are evident in the rise of "a nationalist elite which pressed for independence. Significantly, the first Prime Minister of Sierra Leone, Dr. (later Sir) Milton Margai, and the first Executive President of Sierra Leone, Siaka Stevens, were both products of American mission primary schools in the southern part of the country, and, later, graduates of Albert Academy."[47]

Many non-Amistad Africans also benefited directly from the first mission school. Thomas Tucker (a grandson of Chief Tucker who had sold land to the missionaries) and Barnabas Root completed further studies in the United States and worked for the AMA: Tucker as a teacher in a freedmen school in Virginia, and Root as a pastor for freedmen in Alabama. Root returned to Sierra Leone in 1874 and with the help of the mission, simultaneously ran a church and a school in his hometown, Debia, until he died, apparently of tuberculosis. A dictionary of the Mende language on which he had labored for years was preserved and later brought to America by another minister. Tucker stayed on in America and in 1887 co-founded with Thomas Van Gibbs the State Normal School at Tallahasee, Florida, known today as Florida A & M University. Tucker became the school's first president. Thus, under the auspices of the AMA, Africans worked among African Americans in the southern United States, serving in professional capacities as teachers, doctors, and theologians.

We can conclude that although missionary work in Africa was essentially legitimized and validated by the colonizing principle, missionaries, like the Africans they hoped to convert, were often unpredictable factors in the colonial process. Indeed, a number of missionaries were ambivalent about the colonial process and their contributions were sometimes at odds with colonial administration policies. The intervention of missionary discourses, while an important mode representing the apparatuses of power, also articulated and often signified complex relations with colonial subjects. It is therefore not surprising that in Sierra Leone, as in many other African nations, the (missionary-) educated Africans were among the most militant groups to agitate for self-rule and independence from the colonial government.

PART TWO

Reinventing the Present

Seize on the sense, don't seize on the word.

SIERRA LEONEAN PROVERB

CHAPTER FOUR

Sculpting History: African American Burdens of Memory

Since the 1980s, an increasing number of scholars and performance artists have been using a variety of media to make the story of the Amistad a living memory. Through pamphlets, public lectures, plastic arts, the fine arts, fiction, drama, poetry, film, and even a floating museum (a model of *La Amistad* at Mystic Seaport in Connecticut), the Amistad is fast becoming a greater presence in public memory.[1]

In his foreword to *Black Mutiny*, William Owens captures the reasons why the Amistad story might have meaning in today's world:

> No institution in America has its origins in an event of such dramatic power as the American Missionary Association and the *Amistad* story. This is truly one of the great contemporary myths of the American folk. The myth of the *Amistad* would be much easier to live with if it were not historical, if it had its origins in primordial imagination. . . . The power of this drama lies in the symbolic representation of its leading characters and in the heroic dimensions of its staging.[2]

Indeed, the synchrony between the Amistad narrative and the artistic expression of that narrative has always been apparent. This, in part, explains the use of what I have called the quasi-historical genre, rather than traditional academic history, to memorialize the incident. Influenced by the interdisciplinary theory and practice of cultural studies and performativity, many scholars prefer a dramatized translation of the Amistad events to a disengaged, seemingly objective delivery of their research.[3] Owens, for instance, prefers a dramatic retelling to the usual scholarly documentation of history.[4] The conceptual framing of the Amistad story as a performance of culture has also been considered by historian Howard Jones, who contends that the Amistad incident "contained the ingredients of a national melodrama."[5] Jones concludes that "[a] novelist telling this story would be accused of taking an excursion into fantasy."[6]

To many nineteenth-century New Englanders, the Africans' appearance in their territory was a melodrama in living color. Locals and visitors to New Haven filed around the New Haven green to gape and gawk as the Amistad captives exercised daily outside the jail, even going so far as to pay admission. The performative dimension of the situation was readily apparent.

Many plays dramatizing the Amistad and its surrounding events began at this time. For example, in the fall of 1839, an Amistad production titled *The Black Schooner, or the Pirate Slaver Amistad* played to packed houses in the Bowery and a number of other theaters in New York.[7] Like other Amistad performances of the nineteenth century, the play has not survived. It was not until the centennial celebration of the Amistad incident in 1939 that Owen Dodson wrote *Amistad*, the earliest surviving play.[8] Considering the dramatic nature of the Amistad revolt, the celebrity status of the trials, and the jailhouse "performances" of the Africans, it is a wonder that many more plays have not survived.

In recent years, however, scholars and artists, such as the African American playwright John Thorpe, have contributed to efforts to commemorate the incident in the United States. Just as Dodson did for audiences in the depression years, Thorpe has reinterpreted the Amistad revolt by developing a dramatic retelling of the story for contemporary audiences.

African American Drama

Perhaps the greatest dilemma facing African Americans today is not so much the struggle with double consciousness through which they have come to know themselves, but more so the moral dilemma of recognizing their collective memory. Living on the periphery of the dominant society as a marker for white identification, blacks have learned to negotiate both the advantages and disadvantages of their marginal existence through what W. E. B. DuBois has called "second sight" and "twoness" in *Souls of Black Folk*.[9] On the one hand, double consciousness as an art of survival offers a concerted response to America's long history of oppression.

On the other hand, the consequent collage of memory in double consciousness offers a ruptured narration of rememberings.

How to stage what black artists knew of the experiences of being black in white America often called for rhetorical strategies that could access simultaneously the resolve of blacks and the sympathy or guilt of whites.[10] The mimetic representation of what Samuel Hay has termed the "inner life/outer life" of blacks has often been modulated by anxieties over white misinterpretation and the need to present positive black images and to protest the social conditions of blackness.[11] In their daily existence, African Americans have refined, as it were, the moment-by-moment art of crisis management. Yet, in the metaphoric staging of the self, African Americans have often either recoiled from or been paralyzed by the weight of remembering the very realities they have survived. Usually, the trace, the recall, the in(ter)vention of the painful past, has produced a more searing wound than the occasioned crisis. This, in itself, is not necessarily a bad thing.[12]

We can argue that the conflicted and fragmented recollections of slavery, for instance, signify the love/hate relationship of African Americans with self-recognition through memory. Toni Morrison has consistently urged blacks to embrace the history of slavery, not as an act of paralysis but as a dynamic tool of self-recognition.[13] The past, though traumatic, is still the measure between the hegemonic realities of self and other.

Memory, however, is by nature revisionist. In *Memory: Surprising Insights into How We Remember and Why We Forget*, Elizabeth Loftus notes that memory is selective and self-serving: "motivated forgetting" is the attempt to forget what is unpleasant and remember what is enjoyable.[14] We forget harmful information and retrieve material that is comforting. Understandably, then, many African Americans balk at their own historical past and are highly selective about their African past. For example, the glorious days of the pharaohs, the far past, are preferable to the colonial past; bucolic scenes of peaceful African communities are more tempting to contemplate than war-torn impoverished African nations presented on television.

In the production of African American cultural history in particular, this ambivalence is profoundly reflected. Afrocentric theorization is notable for its selective construction of racial history. In general, it has encouraged blacks "if not to forget the slave experience which appears as an aberration from the story of greatness told in African history, then to

replace it at the center of our thinking with a mystical and ruthlessly positive notion of Africa that is indifferent to intraracial variation."[15] Nonetheless, according to its theory, afrocentricity positions the dilemmas of
self-recognition and the inequities of self-development in reference to
African American history of oppression, disempowerment, and dispossession.[16] The emotional outbursts and seeming overreaction that have
frequently marked racial incidents or accounts in the United States further confirm the deep psychological scars of memories seemingly forgotten but never lost.[17]

Many black artists have attempted to represent this struggle against the
debilitating effects of slavery and racism by seeking to define their role as
not only dramatists but specifically, as *black* dramatists. Focusing the
world they live in through the lens of the racism they have experienced,
they attempt to present to both black and white audiences the crushing
reality of a pained existence. Part of their attempt to articulate this racial
struggle can be measured, according to W. E. B. Du Bois, by the commitment of black artists to their community:

> The plays of a real Negro theatre must be:
> 1. *About us.* That is, they must have plots which reveal Negro life as it is.
> 2. *By us.* That is, they must be written by Negro authors who understand
> from birth and continual association just what it means to be Negro today.
> 3. *For us.* That is, the theatre must cater primarily to Negro audiences and
> be supported and sustained by their entertainment and approval. 4. *Near
> us.* The theatre must be in a Negro neighborhood near the mass of ordinary
> Negro people.[18]

Although in 1926, when Du Bois formulated these principles, serious
black drama or theater was yet to emerge for the mainstream, black
folkplays performed in churches, schools, and colleges did in fact meet
Du Bois's goals.[19] Enacted by mostly amateur groups for occasions specific to their localized communities, black artists explored serious social,
political, and moral questions.

Interestingly, black drama seems to have been double-voiced: while en-
tertaining and educating blacks, its messages have been clearly directed
at whites, the absent audience. Black artists and audiences were restricted
to revealing their rage and distress among themselves because they were
situated far from the dominant society that oppressed them.[20] For its part,
white society was used to a different representation of the Negro on

stage—white actors in blackface, nonthreatening caricatures circumscribed by white privilege.[21] The dilemma of the black artist, James Weldon Johnson noted in the 1920s, was that his or her audience was "always both white America and black America," a double audience that held contradictory and antagonistic points of view.[22]

The real souls of black folk would not become familiar on the mainstream stage until the late 1950s, when Lorraine Hansberry's *A Raisin in the Sun* broke through to white audiences. To be sure, the conceptual and artistic qualities of Hansberry's play were rooted in other plays of the black tradition, which had preceded *Raisin* and, in essence, nurtured it.[23] The struggle to present the real Negro in his or her everyday struggle for meaning in an alien world has been a longstanding tradition on the black stage. Moreover, the black theater has often used American history of oppression and resistance as resource material in helping black audiences define who they are and where they are in the struggle.[24] Seeking to be not just the chroniclers of the past but, more important, the visionaries of the future, many artists have been engaged in the production of black identity through the exploration of existing revolutionary material.[25]

Of the roots of black revolutionary theater, Errol Hill has reviewed a number of historical plays that have made "a significant contribution to black art and black consciousness."[26] Revolutionary theater offers prototypes that help define the meaning of black identity. Indeed, Hill has shown that many slave revolts in the Western Hemisphere have been rich fodder for black playwrights and have occasioned celebration on the black stage.

Hill explores William Henry Brown's *King Shotoway*, which dramatizes the insurrection of the black Caribs on the island of St. Vincent in 1795; Randolph Edmonds's two liberation plays, *Nat Turner* (1934) and *Denmark Vesey* (1939); and Owen Dodson's one-act play, *Amistad* (1939). Hill also discusses William Branch's 1954 production of *In Splendid Error*, a play in which the hero, Frederick Douglass, examines the implications of the use of violence in the fight against slavery. Douglass's expressed ambivalence toward the subject of violence is questioned by the revolutionary zest of the white abolitionist, John Brown, who endorses the immediate, albeit violent, eradication of slavery. Also analyzed are plays engendered by the Haitian Revolution, including William Edgar Easton's *Dessalines* (1893), C. L. R. James's *The Black Jacobins* (1936), Aimé Césaire's *The Tragedy of King Christophe* (1963), Derek Walcott's *Haitian Earth* (1984), and Langston Hughes's *Troubled Island* (1949).

These plays serve as milestones of collective memory for the black community because they reenact significant events in the quest for black liberation and global recognition and are in themselves critiques of the present and visionary models of racial justice. Thus, in meeting the needs of its community, black drama has become, to borrow Rhett Jones's phrase, "the vanguard of the black struggle." [27]

The Amistad incident may be considered a prototype for the black struggle. The Amistad encounter as interpreted by two African American playwrights, Owen Dodson and John Thorpe, illustrates both the meanings attached to the past and the relevance of that past to the present. Both playwrights engage the Amistad past from the cultural standpoint of their own respective historical realities. They feel an overwhelming responsibility not just to recreate a historical past but to critique and modify audience responses in the process. In other words, the theatrical text, space, or performance, offers the artist an opportunity to repeat the past through revision.[28] Joseph Roach defines the phenomenon of repetition as "an improvisatory behavioral space" in which "memory reveals itself as imagination." [29] The lived memory of the cultural, racial circumstances in the present is instrumental in the artist's re-creation or imagined configuration of black history. Almost sixty years apart in their conceptualization of the Amistad revolt, Dodson and Thorpe give us a sense of the temper of their respective historical eras, and they offer us a perspective on the evolving notion of the politics of identity.

Owen Dodson (1914–1983)

The Amistad revolt was revisited in 1939 not only as a commemorative symbol of black achievement, but also as a "re-memory" of history articulated through a performance of Owen Dodson's play, *Amistad*.[30] Then a student at Yale, Dodson was invited by George W. Crawford, a prominent black lawyer in New Haven, Connecticut, to write a play marking the 100th anniversary of the Amistad revolt. The play was to premiere at Talladega College in Alabama, April 1939, and was part of a larger centennial celebration during which the Savery Library at Talledega was dedicated and the famous Amistad murals by Hale Aspacio Woodruff were unveiled.

Throughout the fall of 1938, Dodson researched the Amistad incident. He had a keen eye for detail, to which his notes in the James Weldon Johnson Collection at Yale attest. James Hatch, his biographer, writes in

Sorrow is the Only Faithful One that "Owen worked furiously on the play commissioned by Talladega, scribbling ideas on backs of dining-hall menus while he ate dinner, writing late at night while others slept. By Thanksgiving, he had created *Amistad*, a pageant with sixty-eight characters." [31] From his university residence at 74 Lake Place, Owen revised the play during the period December 1938 through January 1939 before sending it to Lillian Voorhees, Talladega's (white) director, "with a caveat not to make any changes that would affect the drift of the play." [32] Voorhees reduced the cast to fifty members, but Dodson was nevertheless pleased with the production. Not only has *Amistad* survived in manuscript form, but so too have Dodson's supporting notes and comments about the play, which enhance our understanding of the circumstances surrounding his writing. [33]

Dodson's play opens "near the shore of a little village not far from Havana." According to stage directions, when the curtain rises, the audience should get the impression of innumerable slaves sprawled on stage, wondering where they are and what the future holds. The narrator immediately begins to describe the mood of the scene—one of death, despair, and fear. Note the high oratory of the opening scene the narrator relates:

> From those shores they have come
> Where anguish spilled over the sand,
> Where the sea was a hum of cries
> When the life hand took leave of the death hand. [34]

These words set the tone of the play and offer a sense of Dodson's reading of the Amistad incident. In contrast to the gloomy outlook of his opening lines, the narrator proceeds to tell us of the more pleasant setting from which the Africans have just been taken. He gives a romantic image of the Mende country as a place full of corn, cotton, and fig trees, a place "with panthers running / and lions running; their long manes on the wind." [35]

Throughout the next four deck scenes, the plot approximates historical accounts: the revolt occurs, followed by Montez and Ruiz's deception and the eventual capture of the Africans at Montauk Point. Later scenes feature the Africans' jailhouse experience and the Supreme Court trial.

Presented as a prince, the son of one of the prominent chiefs of his country, Sengbe Pieh (rendered Cinque in this play) emerges as the undisputed leader among the captives. His dignity, compassion, and courage are dramatized through his passionate oratory, an art the factual Sengbe

Pieh was widely respected for during his testimonies at court trials.[36] In the play, Cinque continually stirs his restless and unhappy companions with words of encouragement and in song, he evokes memories of Africa:

Keep the jungle stars then.
Keep them shining in your eyes.
Keep the long white shore,
And keep the songs we sang,
And our drum music beating in your heart.[37]

The power of Dodson's writing is his ability to employ lyric elements to great advantage. Dodson's choric free verse uses the imagery of death, fear, and blood to convey the gloomy prospects the Africans must confront in the West. The repetition of key phrases such as "jungle star" and "shining eyes," with only a slight variation here and there, enhances Dodson's thematic message that slavery is the embrace of death. The act of staring into the face of death, and searching out the stars as if to read their destiny, is impressed upon the audience through the Africans' seeming obsession with those who have died on the passage and been thrown overboard to the sharks. The chorus's lines are often interspersed with repeated calls for the removal of the dead from among the living:

Why don't they unchain the dead one,
He is staring at one star only.
I can't reach to close his eyes . . .
He died staring at one star only
Jungle star.[38]

Death assumes a redemptive role as memory: the white crew cannot erase the dead captives' ties to Africa (the "jungle star").[39] Their countenances impart a message of hope to the surviving Africans. Thus, the living captives hail death as an ally. Thus, although the Africans ward off death and recoil from it, this form of victimization metamorphoses into an instrument of self-assertion. By robbing the slave master of the desired object of appropriation—the black body—the slaves inscribe their own agency.[40]

Death also becomes the birthplace of life. It is in the hold of the ship, which constitutes the womb of death, that the slaves weave a scene of hope in which they conspire to take down their persecutors, especially Celestino, who threatens them with cannibalism. The narrator comments on this one bright moment:

Keep the jungle stars shining in your eyes, . . .
Cinque, with the saw he found
Freed his chains, . . .
And in the blackness of the underdeck
he found freedom gleaming.[41]

Like the Christian motif of the star of Bethlehem, the jungle star symbolizes the Africans' unwavering focus on Africa as a place of hope and
salvation.

Dodson reinforces this religious motif of death and rebirth by casting
Cinque as a Christ figure who saves himself and the other captives from
the hell of slavery. In the rebellion scene that follows, Dodson presents
Cinque as one who takes no particular joy in the death of his enemies.
While other freed captives desire revenge on their captors, Cinque is only
concerned with justice and truth. It is Cinque who stays their hands from
a marred victory:

We have killed to be free and we are free.
We did not kill for hate,
We did not kill for revenge,
We cannot kill now for blood.[42]

Astute and pensive, Cinque bears the posture of the suffering Christ in his
words at the close of the third scene: "It is finished. "

But the drama is just unfolding. Cinque soon joins the other Africans
in expressing his anger against Montes and Ruiz, who have deceived them
by sailing to the United States instead of to Africa:

Cinque: We spared his blood
To lead us home
We found him steering westward. Kill.
All: Kill! Kill! Kill!
Cinque: By the blood of the slain,
By the scars we bear,
By the misery.
Kill.
All: Kill! Kill! Kill![43]

This episode in scene four demonstrates Dodson's sensitivity to the
emotional complexities evident in crisis situations. Cinque expresses his
struggle between being Christ-like to his enemies and being vengeful like

his enemies in the decision to kill the Spanish captors. The tension between killing for freedom and killing for vengeance is clearly delineated in Cinque's confrontation of the classic paradox between revolts (which are often seen as unplanned acts of desperation) and revolutions (which often register as orchestrated manifestos to save the oppressed).[44] The heroic ideal of freedoms won is often defended by less glorious strategies, especially when heroes are forced to play by the enemy's rules.

As Dodson wrote years later in a review on black playwrights, it is "not easy to celebrate naked truth, passion and honesty. There are startling visions to be seen, shocking insights. The fearful knowledge that no man in this land has not been affected by the imbalance of justice."[45] Dodson presents the humanity of his main character by carefully cataloging his psychological struggles. Cinque's dilemma—to spare or kill the Spanish deceivers—is eliminated when the Africans are arrested by Lieutenant Gedney and his men. In this way, Dodson affirms the Africans' fateful actions of self-defense in the revolt of 1839, without wallowing in sadistic, vengeful destruction like that portrayed in the movie, *Amistad*.

In interpreting Sengbe Pieh as a Christ-like figure, Dodson shows the strength of his conceptual imagination while also offering an artistically innovative interpretive reading of the historical account.[46] Although Dodson's hero is oratorically adept, the playwright submerges this quality in favor of the suffering Christ image, so that Cinque comes to embody the pillaged continent of Africa. Dodson's objective is to refocus audience attention not on the seemingly arbitrary victory in the American judicial system, but on the unwarranted and unjustified sufferings of African and African-descended peoples on both continents.

A key element of Dodson's narrative of pain occurs in the Supreme Court trial scene. Unlike earlier trial scenes that are only briefly described by the narrator of the play, the Supreme Court scene is framed by events happening in the Amistad captives' prison cell. In jail, Cinque is seen reading aloud from the Bible, his sense of the Lord being on his side, while the defense arguments of both Adams and Baldwin fade in and out of his meditation.[47] This is a compelling moment: Dodson isolates and downplays the legal victory by subordinating it to a higher power. Such dramatic moments in *Amistad* rescue the play from any monotony of lyric repetition and add the symbolic and resonating force of Christianity familiar to African Americans.

In fact, the Amistad victory did not mean freedom for those in bondage throughout the Americas. It also did not change the facts of slavery and colonialism still plaguing both the Americas and the African continent long after the Amistad affair. Indeed, in the play, the Supreme Court victory is overshadowed by the narrator's ambivalent response to the return trip awaiting the Africans. "It is over," the narrator says,

> But nothing has healed these days
> The scars are in the spirit
> Not the bone.
> This evil is spread over Africa now like nets
> To catch the black hunter still, . . .
> The hand of the world have lit a fire over Africa
> And the smoke is rising . . .
> rising. . . .[48]

The narrator not only comments on the evil of slavery, which foretold the precarious career of the Africans in a homeland ravaged by the slave trade, but also addresses the scars slavery had left on Africans in the Americas.

As far as Dodson was concerned, there was really nothing to celebrate in the Amistad victory one hundred years after its unfolding. The Amistad revolt symbolized the continuing struggles Africans and their descendants were facing in the imperialistic stranglehold of European and American powers. For African Americans like Dodson, who lived through the aggressive colonization of Africa by the West, white oppression had cast a net over all of Africa, and the illusions of a romantic homeland could not be courted. That the play was composed after the Great Depression and before the Second World War is reflected in a pessimistic ending that captures the tensions of homelessness and social dis-ease negotiated daily by African Americans.

The satiric qualities of Dodson's play, *Divine Comedy*, produced a year earlier, echo loudly in his 1939 production of *Amistad*. *Divine Comedy* depicts the frustrations of African Americans and their despairing experiences during the worst days of the Great Depression.[49] World history was bleak in 1939: the depression hit African American communities particularly hard, a second world war threatened, and imperialism was already an oppressive reality in Africa.[50]

Staring into the face of a grim future, Dodson expressed his despair in a scribbled note not included in *Amistad*: "Missionaries tell Cinquez they are going back to teach his people. Cinquez sees that his land will never be the same. He sees that all his efforts for freedom have been in vain. . . . Cinquez sees that these are the beginnings of the great imperialistic wave in Africa. So although Cinquez wins in the end it is a dark victory: They will have them in the end." [51] Dodson's most memorable poetic line, "sorrow is the only faithful one," seems to bear witness to his convictions about the outcome of the Amistad encounter beyond the court trials phase. Even though Dodson was very young when he wrote *Amistad*, the marks of sorrow and racial anguish were already apparent in his dramatic work. In particular, the untimely death of his mother added to this marked acquaintance with the history of sorrow. [52]

In writing about the Amistad victory, Dodson could have been writing about himself and about his generation, which although ambitious and eager to participate in the American dream, was impaired from the start by white racial prejudice and discrimination. Despite Dodson's natural talent and his promising career as an artist, his race and his color severely limited his opportunities. Racial prejudice was a frustrating reality, and the Jim Crow South where most intellectuals were segregated (at that time, blacks could teach only at black colleges) was an unflinching confirmation to the young artist for whom sorrow was a second shadow. [53] Dodson's interpretation and understanding of the Amistad revolt, then, was filtered through both the realties of racial intolerance in America and the oppressive colonization on the African continent during the first half of the twentieth century.

It is also significant that Dodson's reading of the Amistad story derives from a uniquely African American perspective radically different from most Amistad scholars who are white. For Dodson, the central aspects in *Amistad* are the figures of Cinque and the other Africans, not the trials or their legal teams. Rather than giving primacy to the American landscape, Dodson foregrounds Africa's engagement with imperialist history. The legacy of slavery and its present-day implications are the meditations of the ending. Thus, Dodson questions an American judicial system that could momentarily deliver a few Africans (the Amistad case) yet leave millions of African descendants in chains. The burden of present memory, inscribed especially in America's Great Depression and the colonial enterprise in Africa, led Dodson to revise previous white depictions of an Amistad victory by anchoring the Amistad story in the realities of his day.

John C. Thorpe (1947–)

Unlike Dodson, who lived through some of the most depressed years of the twentieth century, African American artist John C. Thorpe was born after the Second World War and came of age in the later years of the Civil Rights movement. Thorpe witnessed the growth of black theater from its revolutionary protest stance of the black nationalist 1960s to the self-conscious aesthetic realism of the 1980s and 1990s.[54] Consequently, Thorpe's interpretation of the Amistad incident followed a different route informed by his generation. Considering the complex forms of expression racism has assumed in the last quarter century, Thorpe knew that the political contextualization of identity would need to be addressed through a more political, perhaps less angry, reading of the Amistad story.

Thorpe's vibrant 1996 play, *Chap Am So: A Historical Drama*, re-enacts the historical accounts of the Amistad incident and demonstrates the intimate connection between modernity and slavery. The Middle Passage experience of the Amistad Africans is explored in the context of several key factors: nationality, identity, location, and historical memory. Although the play is faithful to the historical specifics of the Amistad incident itself, Thorpe is sensitive to the multiple international relationships (involving the governments of Spain, England, and the United States) that dictated the destiny of the Amistad captives and were responsible for the global transformation of the moral and political landscape.[55]

Thorpe is also concerned with the intimate ties between past and present, examining the flows and exchanges between different time frames and highlighting in particular the significance of the interim.[56] Time and space are relational "in their articulation with racialized being."[57] The play's thematic sophistication and sensitivity can be attributed to Thorpe's sojourn as a Fulbright scholar at the University of Sierra Leone (Fourah Bay College) in 1990, as well as to his numerous years of experience in the theater. Throughout his long theatrical career, Thorpe has assiduously stressed the social problems of the inner city and other race and gender issues.

Chap Am So begins where Dodson's *Amistad* ends.[58] In *Amistad*, the "hand of the world has lit a fire over Africa / And the smoke is rising;" in

Chap Am So, the play opens with the destroyed village of Mani (Sengbe's hometown), and Sengbe's "spirit" is sitting in the ashes. Thorpe goes beyond Dodson's interpretation to demonstrate that hope can rise out of the ashes of death, a theme which Dodson himself had earlier taken up in his play but later dropped.

Whether one reads or watches a performance of *Chap Am So*, it does not take long to understand who or what Sengbe's "Spirit" represents (the character is female). From the first speech made by "Spirit," Thorpe puts the village of Mani in the context of global time and space. "Spirit" introduces Sengbe not only as a hero, but as one who is intimately involved in the circularity of time:[59]

> Reverse the steps. Walk backwards . . . no run, back to where the village of Mani is awakening. What is so special about this village? It has given birth to, nurtured and protected . . . a person. Before him has come the great liberators Katuma of the Congolese tribes, Moses of the Israelites and after him will come Harriet Tubman and a man named King. A person has the gift to lead others. Not only by ideology but to physically lead. Look to the sky. Why do all the geese follow one? The gods have given the gift to one and one only in a span of time. The one can lead the way. The one can make the circle *(she begins to draw a circle in the dirt)* . . . close. The one can take the chains that drag one across a universe and he can Chap Am So.[60]

With this introduction of the historical specifics of the Amistad story from the mid-point of the narrative (that is, the return to Africa where Sengbe discovers a vanished past as symbolized by his burnt-out village and his new relations with the Western world), Thorpe places the audience in the center of that narrative circle. This circle of time demonstrates the interrelatedness of the different historical epochs. The past, present, and future constantly collide in an attempt to produce meanings out of history. Again, the use of the circle also illustrates the African conception of the unbroken seasonal cycles of life, the unborn, the living, and the dead.

This strategy—carefully maintained throughout *Chap Am So*—is consolidated in the play's structure, which expresses the symbol of circularity in its narration from freedom to slavery, to freedom. Repetition of language and reiteration of imagery reinforce the concept of circularity in the play. Rather than presenting a static past, Thorpe's use of the circular introduces a flow, a movement, that engages everyday reality. "Spirit" imparts this imagery in the opening scene when she describes one of two paths leading out from Mani:

> It cannot be seen. It starts with two bent blades of grass, grows to become a footpath, broadens to become a road. The road becomes a highway. . . . The highway explodes onto a beach which is washed by a great causeway. . . . The ocean becomes yet another beach. A beach that becomes a road, then a footpath and again just two blades of grass. They cross and close behind us. Here is another village. A village in a strange land where the not-natives eat human souls, enslave mankind.[61]

Thus one village (in Africa) leads to another (in America). In this dynamic picture memory, to remember is to repeat—not the exact past but a reinvention of the past. Thus, through memory, or the return, circularity becomes an active engagement with the past and an imaginative connection with the future.

Thorpe takes his readers on a narrative and performative journey that encapsulates and retraces relationships transcending temporal and spatial dimensions. The play from this point on is sequential, but it is constantly disrupted by the overwhelming presence of "Spirit," who defies the chronological order of things by constantly revealing events before they happen and also by prompting Sengbe and the audience to recall the past. Through constant communication with the audience, "Spirit" evokes a collective "social memory." [62]

Like Dodson, Thorpe uses the basic plot of the historical Amistad, but Thorpe's introduction of "Spirit" demonstrates his bold attempt to use the Amistad to engage the larger history of Africans. "Spirit" serves both as Sengbe's spirit or conscience and as the ancestral spirit representing the wishes and desires of the forbears. It is also significant that "Spirit" is a woman, because the historical account of the Amistad revolt included only adult males (forty-nine men in all) and no adult females. The gender ratio onboard the Amistad certainly was not representative of a typical Middle Passage experience. For example, the infamous Tecora that brought the Amistad slaves across the Atlantic included both males and females. In essence, the Amistad incident was tangential to the Middle Passage narrative itself. Thus, the gender distribution on the Amistad schooner represents a specific set of preferred slaves that were being moved from one island location to another.

"Spirit," then—an adult female character—is a refreshing presence and better represents the typical situation in the Middle Passage crossing and the contribution of women in other slave revolts. In other scenes in *Chap Am So*, other African women, including Margru (who was just a child in the historical accounts but is a grown woman in the play), are intimately involved in the rebellion on the *Amistad*. Within the play, "Spirit" is supposedly invisible to the other characters but visible to the audience and to Sengbe, who converses with her throughout the play. Thorpe uses the sometimes contradictory concerns between Sengbe and "Spirit" to portray the psychological struggles leading up to the revolt. Presented as a split-subject—Sengbe-in-the-flesh and Sengbe-in-the-spirit—the hero's internal struggles underscore his humanity, an integral message of the play.

By brilliantly eliminating the problem of a voiceless hero—through the creation of "Spirit"—Thorpe manages to evoke an image of the reality onboard slave ships. Obviously, under the savage control of slavers on the *Tecora* and the *Amistad*, Sengbe could not have been physically assertive or talkative in his subjugated state. It is only through the artistic expression of an embodied presence that the audience becomes intimate with the hero's thoughts. Thus, we are acquainted with the method by which "Spirit" pushes Sengbe to make categorical decisions in the play. Vibrant and assertive, she profoundly demonstrates the dominance of mind over flesh.

In this portrayal, Thorpe touches on a very sensitive issue that caused much debate during and after many slave revolts in the Western Hemisphere. Whites had always believed that only whites were capable of conjuring conspiracy, since slaves were not expected to be intelligent enough to conceptualize intricate strategies to liberate themselves. Thorpe's use of "Spirit," then, echoes Melville's challenge to his white readership. In "Benito Cereno," Melville foregrounds the *mind* rather than the body of Babo through the elaborate plot that Babo and other revolters stage onboard the *San Dominick* to deceive the naive American, Amasa Delano.[63] Sengbe's "Spirit," Thorpe insists, is the brain behind the revolt. "Spirit" is the one who instructs Sengbe to kill before he is killed.[64] Both by persuasion (self-encouragement) and the realization that liberation would come only by the act of resistance, Sengbe emerges as the hero of the Amistad revolt. "Spirit" is so integral to the plot that she not only

"steers" Sengbe in the play but also prods the audience into suitably re-
acting to the plot.

Representing the individual (Sengbe), the community (the Africans onboard the *Amistad*), and the ancestral legacy, "Spirit" becomes the em-
bodiment of African memory. She not only critiques the present against
the historical realities of the past; she also foreshadows future events
through hints or outright statements of fact. "Spirit" thus encourages
audience identification with the cultural memories of the Amistad story.
Embracing time and space, Thorpe effectively uses "Spirit" to "remember" the past in the context of the present. The goal is not to surprise the
audience with what they do not know but to stress what they should already know, as if to say simply, "this is history, this is life." Although executed on a more simplistic level, Dodson's play also used this strategy of
historical specificity. However, Dodson's play offers a more dichotomized
explanation of the interrelations between blacks and whites, masters and
slaves, in-group and out-group.

In contrast, Thorpe's play focuses on the in-between, the shifting and
subtle balance of power between African slave traders, slaves, and Euro-
American slave dealers. Perhaps the strength of Thorpe's *Chap Am So* is
the balance he is able to maintain among the varying articulations engendered by the historical events of the Amistad. He is able to probe a situation sufficiently to reveal the complexity of the issues at hand. For instance, in Act One, the slave dealers Blango (a corollary for Blanco) and
Alvarez negotiate their claims to power in the trade in human flesh. While
Sengbe begs for his life, the audience witnesses the shifting tensions in the
relations between black and white slave dealers and between masters and
slaves:

> *Blango:* I never lie. These are the best slaves I have ever sold you. Young men
> captured in the interior. Women, wise in the ways of tending fields and of
> tending a man. Babies to feed your future crop of slaves. I should charge
> more. . . .
> *Alvarez:* You cry too much for a rich man. You have become wealthy in this
> business and wise in the ways of catching-up. Catching-up a man, woman
> or child. Catching-up a friend or an enemy. Catching-up a political rival.
> Maybe these are not slaves taken in war. Maybe some are innocent, Blango.
> *Sengbe:* . . . Could you sell your brother into this? You know stories of this
> place. No one has ever returned. Where are you sending our people? Have
> you been there? Is it true what they say, that these are men who they say

eat the very souls of other men? Why Blango? . . . I have been taken un-
fairly . . . for no reason.

Blango: No reason? Hah! I have the best reason of all Sengbe. I am short on
the promised number of slaves for today. . . . Consider yourself lucky that
you don't know where you are going. It may save your life eventually. No,
I don't know where the merchandise goes. . . . It is a known fact that we
do not expect or accept returns.

Alvarez: I don't want that one. I don't need some trouble-maker among these
people. . . .

Blango: Like the other white men who have come here, you are weak. You
don't have the stomach to do your own work. Thin skinned, white skinned
boys playing at a man's game. This is not slavery. This is war and if you
quit, where would you go? The rich men that profit from you would send
you to that hell you fear.[65]

Unlike the historical account in which he is European, Blango here is
represented as a rich, ruthless African slave dealer who brings the slaves
from the interior to traders such as Alvarez, who is represented as a
Spanish slave dealer.[66] Alvarez wants to sell slaves, but his disadvantaged
position as a middle man implies that he can be cheated by a shrewd
dealer like Blango. He is also subordinate to those whose interests he
serves on the African coast: rich, white entrepreneurs who control the
trade from abroad.

Aware of the power he wields over Alvarez, Blango mocks Alvarez's
middle, weaker position in the complex chain of the slave economy:
"I could kill you as invaders. I could take these slaves and sell them
to another weak white warrior."[67] Furthermore, by labeling Sengbe
and Alvarez as the "reluctant slave" and the "reluctant master," respectively, Blango underscores the negotiable terrain on which race and
class relations operated during the slave trade years. Alvarez is obviously afraid of Sengbe's innate rebelliousness. Blango's intervention in
this explosive relationship between potential slave and master posits the
slave master's identity on the would-be slave's recognition of the master's
power over him.[68] Power, masculinity, and race are interrelated in the
construction of identity.[69] Thus, Blango says to Alvarez while handing
him a whip: "Here Alvarez, train your own beast. I know these people. If
he does not see you as the unchallenged master before getting on the ship,
your life will be in very great danger. Show me that the weak white warriors are not women. Show that you are who you say you are . . . a master."[70] Thorpe portrays the construction of identity as intricately inter-

twined in the complex relations between masters and slaves, and between men and women.

The complexity of identity is further explored in the context of the Middle Passage experience, which introduces new negotiations and representations in the lives of slaves. Thorpe's exposition of the shifting tensions that exist even within groups that have the same goals precludes any naive assessment that shared racial or class distinctions automatically create unity.[71] Skin color, location, origin, and language are not necessarily determinants of identification or similarity of purpose. This issue is revisited frequently in the play. For example, Antonio, from whom the slaves expect some sympathy, cruelly taunts them about being cannibalized. In the historical account, Celestino, not Antonio, taunted the Africans.[72] Antonio claims no kinship with them when they appeal to shared racial and cultural traits. He has learned to forget his own color by refusing to be a witness to the past, by selectively "forgetting" the horrors of the Middle Passage to which he has been and remains an accomplice. Responding to Sengbe's appellation of "little brother," Antonio states: "You are sadly mistaken my friend. No man is my master . . . and my brother? My brother is my brother, but I know not where to find my brother. Try another road. That road is closed." Antonio closes all avenues of racial alliance.[73]

In this exchange between Antonio and Sengbe, Thorpe comments on the fragmentation of kinship ties and the unraveling of the social fabric of African communities. The success of the slave trade hinged on the deliberate erosion of interethnic and intraethnic cohesion. Laws that underlay the moral and social fabric of peoples and nations in Africa were summarily dismissed in the discourse of slavery. Slave catchers, traders, and chiefs employed numerous devices to avail themselves of the lucrative trade.[74] The Amistad captives themselves enumerated various reasons why they were sold to slave dealers at Dombokoro.[75] The breach of trust in these transactions was exacerbated in the Americas where white planters deliberately instituted class conflicts through elaborate codes according to skin color (with definitions such as mulatto, octoroon, nigger) and other social divisions (such as field hands versus house slaves). Another policy of the slaveholding world was to separate slaves of the same ethnicity to minimize the possibility of slave revolts on the plantations.[76]

In an attempt to construct their identity within the intricacies of the slave world and its demands, New World slaves had to forge new forms of interaction. The Cuban slave in Thorpe's play, for example, only dreams of being free, not of returning to Africa. Another character, James Govie (a correlate for the Amistad interpreter Covey), also remarks in his conversation with "Spirit" that America is the only home he knows. As slavery weakened ties to the cultural homeland in Africa, then, it also inspired a different set of communal values in the Americas. "Spirit," however, insists in her conversation with Govie—the only character other than Sengbe to whom she reveals herself—that Africa remains, forever, the origin and link of the dispersed black race.

Insisting on a theme of return, Thorpe's message at this point in the play is directed at his African American audiences who have already made a home for themselves in America: "Walking about does not automatically make a man free. . . . The people you see walking about are wearing invisible chains. The worst kind of shackle. Because they cannot be seen they cannot be sawed upon or broken." [77] To forget one's African homeland, one's history, is to lose one's freedom. Thorpe reminds his audiences that the Mende captives' identities were forged in their strong desire for the homeland, their rejection of the identity imposed on them by their captors, and their insistence on the geopolitical identification of themselves as Africans.

The play nonetheless emphasizes the theme of survival, which at the time was tied to the emerging movement for emancipation in the United States and elsewhere in the New World. Just as the Amistad captives needed to keep their Spanish captors alive to enable them to retrace their steps to Africa, so too did the abolitionists feel impelled to help blacks in their fight for freedom. Thorpe highlights the history of black-white alliances, such as that represented in abolitionism, but also portrays the complex struggles to define the nature and direction of the fiery convictions against slavery within such sympathetic organizations. The contemporary realization that broad-based coalitions are necessary in the struggle for social justice echoes throughout *Chap Am So*. As essential as such coalitions were during both the nineteenth-century antislavery struggles and the more recent Civil Rights undertakings, a platform of commitment will be needed in any future quest for racial justice. Thus, Thorpe uses collective memories of the historical past to map out the possibilities of the present and the potentials for the future.

The ending of *Chap Am So* is hopeful and foregrounds the return to Africa. Unlike the opening scene of the play which is set in the ashes of

Mani, the final act depicts a scene that is pregnant with possibilities. At the mission in Sierra Leone, Margru is seen teaching the Amistad story to a group of children who represent the future of Africa. Sitting in a circle around Sengbe's grave, Margru and the children spin the narrative thread of the Amistad story in a song honoring the Amistad hero. In this dramatic return of memory, the children are advised to cultivate the noble, unflinching personality of Sengbe Pieh by believing in themselves. The play ends with the children shouting "Chap Am So!" which means "Resist!"[78]

Thorpe reminds us that the Amistad Africans, despite their precarious journeys on the Atlantic and in the Americas, returned full circle to Africa—but the return was not to a romantic Africa without conflicts. The call to "chap am so," relevant to the nineteenth-century Sierra Leone of the Amistad Africans, resounds in the ongoing struggles in present-day Sierra Leone. Thorpe also encourages Americans to participate actively in the re-"vision" of the historical Middle Passage past.

Sculpting Historical Identity

Public recognition of the need for the United States to develop its own cultural memory of the Amistad story led the Amistad committee of Connecticut in the 1980s to research ways to memorialize the revolt and its subsequent developments.[79] Historians and artists have done much to keep the story alive, and the nuances of the Amistad saga have subconsciously entered the culture through names such as "Cinque" in the black community[80] and the word "Amistad" in the world of publishing.[81] Nevertheless, the Amistad story needs to be recognized as a national rather than a specific local event. Together with the mayor's office in the city of New Haven, Connecticut, the Amistad committee was able to market its ideas for celebrating the Amistad at a national level and in 1990 received permission to build a monument to honor the Amistad heroes.

It was through this endeavor that Ed Hamilton was chosen out of 71 national competitors to erect a sculpture commemorating the Amistad event. Although Hamilton had successfully completed two major commissions on black legendary figures previously (namely, representational projects on educator Booker T. Washington and boxer Joe Louis), this eighty-thousand-dollar memorial commission was the greatest creative challenge Hamilton had yet embarked on in his public career.[82] Prior to the submission of the initial concept in the competition, Hamilton educated himself about the story, with which he was unacquainted beforehand. Hamilton was deeply moved by the dramatic unfolding of the Africans' attempts to free themselves from an impending destiny of bondage. He was not only challenged by the dramatic narrative of the Amistad revolt but also readily identified with the captives' story, which he recognized as his own legacy.

Like other artists at the first submission stage, Hamilton turned in a single representational figure of the Amistad hero, Sengbe Pieh. The Amistad committee then selected five finalists, but sent each sculptor back to the drawing board. The selected models were by Clarence Shivers of Colorado Springs; Tina Allen of Los Angeles; Jerome Meadows of Washington, D.C.; James Lewis of Baltimore; and Ed Hamilton of Louisville, Kentucky. After reviewing the submissions (each artist had presented a single figure concept), the committee was able to better define for itself and articulate to the artists its intentions. Although the committee originally envisioned an approximation of Nathaniel Jocelyn's widely known portrait of Sengbe, it soon deemed that a solitary figure would be inadequate; a broader, more dynamic concept was warranted, one that would capture at a glance the enormity of the Amistad story.

In a face-to-face interview and discussion with the adjudicators, Hamilton was able to glean the committee's vision of the project. He sensed the need to place the figure of Sengbe Pieh not only in the context of his New World struggles but also in the reality of his African past and future. The fact that the Africans desired to return home and succeeded in doing so distinctly changed the dynamic of the discourse of helplessness in America to a discourse of self-realization in Africa. A narrative sculpture that could capture both an American and an African contextualization would be the only satisfying direction for such a challenging task. While at the interview, Hamilton was also able to visit the intended site in New Haven.

Back in Kentucky, Hamilton began a long, contemplative process. His idea developed from two sources, one of which was the famous painting of "Washington Crossing the Delaware." [83] The story did not exactly fit, but the form of the prow of the boat in the painting impressed the artist. Hamilton's sketches of a prow (a three-sided figure) led to his drawing a figure *within* a prow, rather than on top of it. This prompted him to rethink the project in bas-relief. Sometime later, at a Sunday morning service at a church in Louisville, Hamilton was struck by the iconographic symbols on a cloth adorning the church pulpit and inspired to rework the piece as a narrative in triptych. Hamilton noted that "in the middle of this embroidered piece were three rings—interlocking rings. But the key to it was that just in the inner circles of the ring was a triangle. On each side of the triangle the ring of the circle came out just enough to give you a feeling that something was on the [other] side of that triangle." Based on this interconnectedness, Hamilton created a three-sided model in which each panel is artistically and contextually related to the other two panels. Hamilton commented further:

> If you notice on the whole sculpture, each side tends to be connected to the other side. In the right hand corner at the top, there is a young boy with a wool cap, Kali. His arm is outstretched in Africa and if you notice he is pointing, almost pointing to the bird just above Sengbe's head. Then on the courtroom side his body is in America. It's like he is in both lands. He's say-ing, I want to go back to Africa but I'm in America now, I've got to deal with this thing. The lower right hand corner of the bottom of the piece are bodies represented in a slave ship. They literally turn into the wooden balustrades of the courtroom side. Then from the courtroom balustrades all of that turns into the wharf where [Sengbe] is standing saying his goodbyes.[84]

Like John Thorpe, Hamilton engages memory as a theme of circularity: the past, present, and future all flow into each other and are dependent on each other for their full meaning.

Hamilton's three-sided conceptual figure captures the three key events of the Amistad story: the first scene represents the capture of the Africans from their homeland. Hamilton rejects the atrocious acts of kidnapping and offers instead a peaceful moment in time in the African world. He preferred to place Sengbe "in his own space and time" prior to the unex-pected intrusion from the outside world. In this first conceptual segment, Sengbe Pieh is walking toward his farm and has casually picked up a stick which lightly rests on his left shoulder. In the background, we envision a world peopled with men, women, and children who are engaged in every-day activities. The subjects' cultural stability and beauty are also symbol-ized by the Bundu mask. This Mende mask symbolizes the initiated mem-bers in a secret society for women.

Sengbe's peaceful life, however, is destined to be disrupted. The tilt of Pieh's head coupled with the far away look in his eyes suggest an air of expectancy. Moreover, the westward path of the flying bird overhead, the same direction in which Pieh is positioned, foretells his impending westward journey and his inevitable fate of displacement in the West.

The second panel of the monument portrays the familiar courtroom trials of the Amistad story. A transformed Sengbe Pieh, in European clothes, stands confidently in defense of his life and the life of his friends. He faces the Spanish slavers and their pro-slavery prosecuting team on the other side of the courtroom. Whereas the faces of notable abolitionist supporters and other Amistad captives are clearly discernable in the top right hand corner of the sculpture, the opposing team, in the top left hand corner, is represented as symbols of evil. This caricature of the prosecuting team is Hamilton's way of taking a moral position on the issue of slavery. Their obscure, somewhat contorted expressions symbolize the bad memory of slavery, the nightmare experience of bondage, that the captives were resisting.

The third side of the monument depicts a rather aged Sengbe Pieh—book under arm, bag packed, right foot resting on a stone, left arm lifted in a didactic pose—altogether suggesting a resolute air of confidence in the future. He stands at dockside. The cargo and ship in the background represent the return of the captives to Africa. The bird has changed its path eastward. Pieh does not face the same direction as the bird, as he does in the first panel; rather, he faces the viewing audience, seemingly ready to tell his story to the world.

This third segment represents the dual destiny of Africans in America. The "I-am-here" nature of Sengbe's pose suggests Africans' new residency status in the Americas, whereas the background etching implies the return of others to the home continent. On a metaphorical level, the pose also speaks to the Du Boisian double-consciousness that confounds the African who has been marked by American racism, if not by American slavery. Sengbe's exposure to the modern, colonial world order not only transformed him, but also made his return to Africa a changed experience.[85]

All three sides of the monument depict Sengbe Pieh as the dominant figure, while details surrounding each key event in the Amistad story are chiseled into the background in both literal and figurative forms. Hamilton's compact narrative interpretation in fact won him the commission. His past record as an artist whose work portrayed "great strength" paled in the face of his first real attempt at a public narrative. The decision of the jury (comprising men and women from varying walks of life) was unanimous. With the Amistad commission in hand, Hamilton now faced transforming a fourteen-inch clay model prototype into a fourteen-foot bronze monument destined for an open-air alcove on the steps of City Hall in New Haven—the very site where the Amistad Africans had been jailed in 1839.

Back in his Shelby Street studio in Louisville, Kentucky, Hamilton was putting finishing touches to the Amistad monument when he realized how bare the flat top of the monument was. He had originally conceived the model as a three-sided structure, but the thought that people would be looking down at the monument from city hall windows challenged his imagination. Now emotionally tied up with the monument, he felt uncomfortable with this emerging fourth side.[86] Without notifying the Amistad committee, he decided to carve the overarching trademark story of the Middle Passage at the top—a historically sound judgement, for the Middle Passage crossing, while sometimes undecipherable, even unspeakable, has never been without meaning. The result was a textured representation of the Atlantic with the submerged, drowning body of a man, his face and hands barely above water.

In this fourth panel, Hamilton reminds us of the slave trade and all those who did not survive, the slaves who were lost but not forgotten. The tense interplay between life and death depicted in this final segment spills over in the form of rain drops on the three-sided structure. Hamilton seems to suggest that the story of triumph implied by the triptych structure is made possible only by the memory of deathly struggles, a memory those in the present must perpetually recall. Also remembered are the millions who died in the Middle Passage, either from the gruesome pressures of the journey itself or as a suicidal act of liberation from the terrifying prospect of slavery.

The fourth segment brings to mind mass suicides that occurred in the Middle Passage. It also recalls the fate of an individual, Foone, one of the Amistad Africans who was reputed to have deliberately committed suicide by drowning while on remand at a Connecticut farm.[87] One can hardly look at the fourth segment of the monument without recalling Foone's death, an event that helped hasten the repatriation of the Africans to their homeland. His death is representative of other blacks across the American landscape who have sought freedom in death.

The parallels between the African American and the Amistad African stories are articulated in the triangular Amistad memorial, which evokes the triangular slave trade that sealed the fate of so many. As depicted in the third panel in particular, the Amistad incident is not just the story of Sengbe Pieh and other Africans who returned to Africa, but is equally the story of the African Americans who never left the Americas. Perhaps what is singularly intriguing about the Amistad monument is that Sengbe is representational because he seems to speak with, rather than apart from, the other figures in the bronze casting. The background images remain compelling because they tell the story of the Middle Passage and symbolize (in the courtroom segment, the second panel) the African American rite to citizenship, and because they configure African anxieties for nationhood and universal acceptance.

Each segment of the monument is revealing, but in the complex mixture of concrete and abstract forms, there is the impression of something not being told, of something left to be discovered. Hamilton himself disclosed that part of his intention was to make the visitor's experience of viewing the monument fulfilling but incomplete. This "incompleteness" would signify one's metaphoric identification with the repeated attempts by the Africans to secure their freedom and signal the need to return to one's heritage.

Hamilton admits that his narrative merely evokes the key events of the Atlantic crossing: it does not tell the whole story of the Middle Passage. His deliberate casting of the story in a sculptural triptych and his compelling, overdetermined narrative on the memorial's fourth side illustrate his attempts to unburden his own personal memory as a sculptural epigram. As an artist with great creative potential, Hamilton tends to pour the vibrancy of his own life into his interpretation of past events. His ability to coax the tenderness of life out of inanimate objects gives his historically inspired pieces a dynamic connectedness with the world in which he and we live.

Like most African Americans, the circumstances in his life constantly force him to confront the past. His memories of the segregated South in which he grew up feature significantly in his interpretation of present experiences. Hamilton vividly remembers a time when Louisville blacks not only lived in segregated housing but also used segregated parks.[88] Although the Civil Rights years changed all of that, it is to his own personal past that Hamilton returned as he searched for suitable subject matter for the Amistad monument and for an object with unique significance. He found a good-sized, slightly bent stick at Chickasaw Park in Louisville where he had often played in the days prior to integration. Today, cast in bronze and resting on Sengbe Pieh's shoulder, this stick has found a lasting place in the Amistad monument in New Haven. Hamilton thus blends the Civil Rights era with the African past and speaks plainly to the singular destiny of both continental and diasporic blacks. For posterity, the stick also suggests a revolutionary spirit that celebrates life, both in spite of the past and because of it.

Much like playwrights Owen Dodson and John Thorpe, Hamilton has adopted a personal approach to the story of the Amistad. For each artist, the revolutionary fervor of the revolt is foregrounded, and Africa occupies a primary place in the engagement with history. The intervention of memory for the African American is thus demonstrated in the *presentness* of interpretation and in that interpretation's capacity to direct the future.

The three-thousand-pound, fourteen-foot cast bronze memorial stands as a symbol of harmony between races and as a symbol of unity within the black race itself. This memorial speaks not to a desired past, but to a hopeful future born out of a critical past. It represents not reality, but the possibilities that can be negotiated when memories are meaningfully employed in the articulation and expression of fractured identities.

CHAPTER FIVE

National Identity: The Dramatic Return of Memory in Sierra Leone

The literature on collective memory suggests that a society's selection and ascription of significance to a historical event is not an arbitrary process.[1] In public discourse, memory is constructed and deployed to achieve a number of strategic ends. How a particular society understands its past is significant to how that society constructs its present values. The past is "a social construction shaped by the concerns and needs of the present."[2] In other words, because the past helps us interpret our present-day reality, we are careful to select material that will in fact serve the purpose of interpreting the present. Past events are commemorated "only when the contemporary society is motivated to define them as such."[3]

Many collective memory scholars believe that the nature and interpretation of present-day reality significantly determine the direction that reconstruction of the past takes. To be sure, both the past and the future exist in present time because our activation of "the events that constitute the referents of the past and future" are based on our interpretation of the present.[4] The past is not "final and irrevocable" as so often believed; rather, it is "as hypothetical as the future." So, whether the past is mythical or implied, its validity lies in the position it occupies in society's shared consciousness or collective memory; a past action must have occurred for the present to be what it is.[5]

By extension, the Amistad events are believable because they happened *in fact* and led to the establishment of the mission in Kaw Mende, Sierra Leone. The Mende mission was the result of abolitionists' desire both to continue the work of Christianizing the Amistad Africans and to initiate mission activities throughout Africa. The evidence of the Mende mission and its contributions to the nation are still very much evident today.

Nevertheless, the Amistad events of 1839–1842 hardly registered on the consciousness of the nation of Sierra Leone or on that of later generations of Americans. Although the result of the revolt and trials in the Americas played itself out in Sierra Leone, it left no impression on the collective memory of the nation. Why did the nation forget this story? More important, why does the nation only now remember? The Amistad event was an incident that Sierra Leoneans, before the 1980s, never identified with as part of their national history, but the validity of this past has recently taken its place in the shared consciousness of the people. As Clifton Johnson has noted, it is mainly artists and writers in the United States, who have kept the "drama of the Amistad incident" alive in the American imagination.[6] For Sierra Leoneans, unfortunately, ignorance of the grand events of the Amistad story has largely robbed them of a victorious national identity. In recent years, however, the Amistad story has been birthed in the imagination of Sierra Leonean artists.

It would seem that up until 1992, the Amistad was only an inherited past, that is, an implied objective past. The Amistad's factual existence in the past did not necessarily lend itself to an inherited memory. Although the Amistad Africans evidently talked a great deal about their experiences in the West, there is no evidence that their story received national attention. It would seem that Sierra Leoneans actually *forgot* the Amistad story. What, then, does it take to remember the collective past? Constructionists, or theorists of the past, see tradition and commemorative rites as transmitted through a "guiding pattern" to "subsequent generations." This transmission is important because, as Barry Schwartz has stated, "Stable memories . . . creat[e] links between the living and the dead and promot[e] consensus over time."[7] Apparently, the Amistad account entered into history but not memory.

Although the mnemonic structure of the oral tradition—the guiding pattern common to the Sierra Leonean people—was in place when the Amistad Africans returned home, other structures necessary for the story's transmission seem to have been displaced. Most of what we recall today about the Amistad is culled from written history about the events in the United States. Those that followed in Sierra Leone were largely transmitted through the letters of missionaries to their home base in the United States. Given that even today a large percentage of the Sierra

Leonean population is illiterate, the existence of written chronicles could never have transformed history into memory in such an oral tradition–based culture.

We should also remember that the Amistad captives returned not to freedom but to a land under colonial rule. Slave wars raged in the hinterlands, creating a very unstable and dissonant environment in which to transmit memories over time. Moreover, British colonial education characteristically discouraged all national histories by subsuming them and imperially substituting its own history. Colonial Britain instilled in Sierra Leoneans an attitude of self-cynicism.

This attitude of self-cynicism can be seen in the legendary resistance of Bai Bureh, a Temne chief, to the attempts of the British to impose a hut tax on Sierra Leonean natives. The colonial administration in 1897 attempted to curtail the deteriorating relations between the different ethnic groups and clans by imposing a house or hut tax throughout the hinterland. Since the natives were to pay either in cash or in kind—mainly in the form of produce from the land—the district commissioner hoped to stop the interethnic raids incited by the continued demand for indigenous slave labor necessary for the cultivation of farmlands owned by chiefs. This assumed "good intention" on the part of the colonial government lacked sound judgement. A. B. C. Sibthorpe, a shrewd Sierra Leonean historian of the era, has noted: "That a people not accustomed to pay[ing] tax to their natural Kings, and without knowledge of it in their traditions, that such a people, their Chiefs and their Kings, would easily submit to taxation ought not to have been supposed. Common-sense should have dictated that they all would act 'as a bull unaccustomed to the yoke'." [8]

The colonial power's naive arrogance agitated the citizens in the protectorate on whom the levy had been imposed; this led to armed resistance in some districts. Historian Joe Alie has stated that Bai Bureh, a resilient general and military strategist, initiated "successful guerrilla warfare" against the colonial government;[9] his actions incited other communities to aggressively resist the hut tax. Lives were lost on both sides of the struggle, but government forces won. Although Bai Bureh gave himself up nine months later, he had evaded capture for months and his name, to British ears, commanded a certain fear and respect. Although he became a state prisoner and was banished to the Gold Coast until 1905, it is on record that the queen pleaded that Bai Bureh be treated humanely. He did return to Sierra Leone and was reinstated Chief of Kasseh.

Sierra Leoneans now view Bai Bureh's ingenious resistance ambiva-
lently. To their minds, Bai Bureh's legendary ability to make himself in-
vincible in defiance of British might has a victorious ring, but, being a
practical people, Sierra Leoneans concede his mortality in his ultimate
surrender to the British. In recalling the Bai Bureh story, Sierra Leoneans
negotiate the ambiguity of victory and defeat, of invincibility and mortality. "Distancing" themselves from both the British conquerors and the conquered natives, Sierra Leoneans—in a spirit of cynicism almost unique to
them—are unruffled spectators in the game of life. They ironically comment upon and condense major events, such as this song based on the Bai
Bureh story that has been passed on from generation to generation:

Bai Bureh was a warrior
He fought against the British,
The British made him surrender,

I ala Kɔrtɔr Maimu
"E Kɔrtɔr Maimu, E Kɔrtɔr Gbekitɔng,"
I ala Kɔrtɔr Maimu.

The first two lines of the song are chanted as historical fact, untainted
by social commentary. The third line sharply deviates from this objective
slant. Bai Bureh does not surrender to the British, as the story officially
goes, but the British "make him" give himself up. Rendering Bai Bureh
passive rather than active, any residue of heroism that might have accompanied his decision to surrender himself is erased from the picture.
(No reference is made to the fact that he was restored to his former position as chief.) Consequently, in the fourth, fifth, and sixth lines of the
song (the Temne words in translation are: "He hollered, 'Master, I beg,
oh, Master, I beg, oh, Master, It's enough.' He hollered, 'Master, I beg'")
the singers distance themselves from the great warrior's then predictable
fall by ridiculing what was perceived to be a personal failure.[10] Sierra
Leoneans are generally intolerant of failure, so they absorb Bai Bureh's
failure—and by extension, the nation's—in practiced indifference to the
idea of success.

Moreover, the settler communities, the Krio people, who were the elite
in the nation, tended to identify with the colonialists more so than with
the indigenes. This "psychopathology," as Frantz Fanon would put it,
aptly describes the fault lines along which the very idea of nation has been
forged.[11] Thus for Sierra Leoneans, their collective memory as a nation

easily translates into collective amnesia, especially when what they remember highlights the present failures of the nation.

This ambivalent and unstable character of the national memory, as exemplified in the story of Bai Bureh, was certainly more marked when Sengbe Pieh and the Amistad Africans reached the shores of Sierra Leone. Various disappointments meant that the victory they had celebrated in America all but dissipated once they reached their native land. The missionaries and the Amistad returnees had to change their plans to build a mission house in or near Mani, Sengbe Pieh's much talked-about village, because it had been destroyed. Many of the Amistad Africans began to question the authority of the missionaries. Raging slave wars further jeopardized their already precarious position. And perhaps most poignantly, the "past" the Amistad returnees had tenaciously fought for through the American court system in order to return to Sierra Leone no longer existed. Sengbe's ambivalent relationship with the mission—returning intermittently while attempting to seek his fortune elsewhere—was analogous to the changed and unpredictable landscape to which he returned that contributed to his lifelong restlessness. Desouza George describes Sengbe as a man who "could not quite gather the bits and pieces together again."[12]

Under these conditions of return to their native land, the Amistad group had little cause to rejoice about and eventually pass down a glorious story of victory in the United States. With the ever-present danger of being recaptured into slavery, the issue of their survival remained unresolved. This reality, coupled with the fact that there was a struggle for power between Sengbe and Raymond over who should lead the mission in Sierra Leone, slowly but surely changed the nature of their "positive" experiences in America. The hegemonic centrality of the colonizing presence of the British, and the missionaries in West Africa, demonstrated the peripheral situation of the Africans. Thus, the master narratives of the colonial administration circumscribed any representation of the Amistad narrative as a victorious experience for the Africans. In fact, as Raymond rightly concluded while touring the United States in 1846, the testimonies of the Africans, especially the discontented and the double-minded, helped to extend his authority and the influence of the mission in Kaw Mende.[13]

It is not at all surprising, then, that Sengbe and the other liberated captives seemingly chose to forget their own story. Their limited agency in the continuing Amistad story probably prompted the neglect and, later, cessation of the story's continuity through the oral tradition. Liberated Africans, in general, seem to have handed down and established in the minds of Sierra Leoneans not their sporadic victories of eluding capture, not even their achievement of freedom after capture, but their irreducible conviction that *captivity is a way of life.* The experience of Sengbe Pieh in his native land, as well as the experiences of many Sierra Leoneans thereafter, did not constitute a suitable milieu in which to commemorate their past.

Why, then, is the Middle Passage experience receiving such attention in Sierra Leone today? What commemorative processes have led to the institutionalization of the Amistad revolt? During a visit to Sierra Leone in April 1994, I examined the means through which diasporic memory of the Amistad event has been articulated in the Sierra Leonean society. I discovered that through the cultural performance of the Amistad revolt, Sierra Leone has restored the significance of the event in the production of its national identity. Drama has been the most prevalent form of cultural performance in awakening this national memory.

African Drama

Drama or theater is prevalent in African cultural performance.[14] Cultural performance, as employed here, embraces the participatory practice of African drama.[15] As in all human societies, theatrical and dramatic elements are intertwined in almost every aspect of African social life. These structural elements underpin religious rituals and other civic organizations of African peoples. A basic component of the oral tradition, theater, in all its varied forms, serves as a significant medium in transmitting information to the continent's vast rural and urban populations. Unlike written literature, drama derives from expression in the oral tradition, the basic level of social interaction that is integral to African culture.

The orality of theater is such a powerful force in many African countries today that even the mostly Westernized leadership in these countries recognizes its potency as the only practical way to communicate with the indigenous populations. The power of theater is also rightly viewed by African leaders as both a useful and a dangerous weapon in the hands of the masses. Politicians know that theater is a double-edged sword: it can work as an effective campaign tool but can, simultaneously, be utilized by opposing parties, dissidents, or radicals to expose social injustice and other corrupt practices in their government.

In *The Truthful Lie,* Biodun Jeyifo cites several examples of the many political ends to which theater can be put by rival political parties in Nigeria. The social impact of the Yoruba Travelling Theater is evident in its popular appeal and wide representation in Nigeria.[16] Many international agencies are also appreciating theater's pedagogical reach in the developing world. International agricultural and health organizations are bypassing ineffective and corrupt government efforts and are using local theater groups as vehicles for reaching the masses with their programs.

Theaters with such social purposes have generally been classified under the rubric "theater for development" or "popular theater."[17] Theater for development is proving effective in many communities in Africa. In a study conducted in the West African nation of Burkina Faso, Joy Morrison observed that performance is a central communicative art form in Africa. "African performance differs from that in the West because it is part of the whole fabric of African life and culture, existing as part of the larger communication environment which includes dance, drama, storytelling, music, games, and visual arts."[18] Penina Muhando Mlama has also noted that the "essence of popular theater resides in the use of dramatic media to 'communicate for development' by involving the members of the community at every stage of the process."[19] Among other examples, Mlama cites the Mkambalani Workshop in Tanzania as a project which encouraged women to cultivate their communication skills through participation in theater. The success of the project was partly judged through the larger issue of socio-economic problems, which the communication debates addressed.[20]

In Sierra Leone, the communication skills of the theater have also been effective in transmitting life-saving counsel to the people. Both international and national agencies, such as UNICEF and the Sierra Leone Departments of Health and Education, have employed the services of local theater groups, such as the Freetong Players, to communicate the structural aims of these agencies to both urban and rural populations that cannot read or write English, the official language of the country. Through "an innovative educational initiative," these agencies have collaborated with the Freetong Players in targeting issues such as "poor school enrolment, low level community awareness about issues such as safe motherhood and oral rehydration."[21] Artists implement music, dance, proverbs, and plays to communicate the desired developmental skills. For instance, in the process of teaching young mothers how to care for their infants, artists may enact the proper use of a feeding bottle or demonstrate the need for inoculation against debilitating diseases. Considering the alarmingly high infant mortality rate in Sierra Leone, one can appreciate the vital significance of purposeful theater.

To what extent this community service has affected the nature of contemporary theater in Sierra Leone cannot be adequately assessed, but it should be noted that formal theater organizations in the last fifteen years have undergone a radical change in perspective. Whereas amateur groups were the prevalent force in the past, professional groups are now occupying center stage; whereas most plays in the past dealt mainly with love stories or domestic themes, such as conflicts between mothers-in-law and daughters-in-law, many plays today endeavor to explore serious historical and political issues that question the nation's present decadence and warn against a devastating future. The incipient power of the people to participate in their own political future—a future that has been left, for the most part, in the hands of corrupt politicians—is being tapped into by young, politically conscious theater artists. At the grassroots level, these artists are committed to empowering the people through the art of effective communication.

It is in this mode that two Sierra Leonean playwrights, Charlie Haffner and Raymond Desouza George, invest in the people through the use of historical drama. In *Amistad Kata Kata* and *The Broken Handcuff or Give Me Free,* respectively, Haffner and Desouza George use the Amistad story to raise people's awareness of their cultural place in the politics of nation-building.[22] Both Haffner and Desouza George, active participants in the theater for development, know the value of anchoring their plays in the cultural traditions of the people in order to assist the formation of collective identity and promote individual agency.

Amistad Kata Kata

Charlie Haffner employs traditional processes of social learning in his play *Amistad Kata Kata* and in so doing, contributes to the cultural awakening of a nation undergoing a crisis of identity. Although Haffner himself learned about the Amistad story in an academic setting, it was the oral tradition employed by the professor that arrested Haffner's attention.

In 1986, as a student at the University of Sierra Leone's African Studies Department, Haffner attended a lecture by American anthropologist Joseph Opala on Sengbe Pieh's role as the leader of the revolt onboard the *Amistad* slave ship. Profoundly affected by what he had heard, Haffner was inspired to write the play *Amistad Kata Kata*.

The project proved to be a rude awakening. The writer pondered over the extent to which he, like others around him, had been alienated from some of the most significant moments in his country's history. He had wept when he heard the story. Haffner was so affected by the Amistad story that his concept of the theater took on a whole new meaning. Disregarding an education that had taught him more about the Industrial Revolution than about the history of his own country, he and his professional theater group, The Freetong Players, began building what he called "a theater of relevance," a theater that would raise the consciousness of the people by making them more aware of their own history.[23]

For some twenty-six years now, Haffner has been a prominent figure in theater circles in Sierra Leone. His activities in the last ten years as the full-time director of Sierra Leone's leading traveling community theater group have catapulted him to unprecedented fame both nationally and internationally. Born March 26, 1953, Haffner displayed from a very early age a natural love for the theater, a passion that has blossomed into a professional career as a playwright, director, teacher, and actor. He has trained others, including entertainers in the traditional arts, teachers, dramatists, religious leaders, and youth in all twelve districts of Sierra Leone, to better communicate development ideas to their own communities. Disseminating cultural and historical information through the medium of popular theater, Haffner and the Freetong Players have motivated others and actively participated in raising the social and political awareness of the Sierra Leonean people.

Haffner's play, *Amistad Kata Kata,* is a product of this political strategy of theater-with-a-purpose. The play premiered at the British Council, Freetown, in May 1988. According to Haffner, the audience was shocked the first time it heard the Amistad story. Why did the Sierra Leonean public not know of the heroic ventures of the Amistad captives prior to the production of this play?

Haffner addresses this question and introduces the historical figure of Sengbe Pieh, which for many audience members was a revelation. In the first scene, a history student, pen and paper in hand, questions an old woman, "Grama," in Sierra Leone's major lingua franca, Krio, as they walk along a footpath to an ancestral ceremony in honor of Sengbe Pieh, one hundred fifty years after the Amistad revolt:

> *Grama:* Soon we shall be at Kaw Mendi, the home of Sengbe Pieh. . . . It is along this same path that Sengbe was captured 150 years ago. We are quite early, in time for the ceremony.
>
> *Student:* Yes the ceremony is tonight. I am happy I made it after all.
>
> *Grama:* Are you? (laughter) Please help me with some tobacco (student helps to fill and ignite pipe and Grama makes a few satisfying puffs). You see, my son, our people have a tradition which is based on the belief that a person survives after death, and it is the surviving personality spirit that enters the land of the dead.
>
> *Student:* I agree with you Grama. From my readings I have discovered that nearly all African peoples have some kind of ancestral culture. I think I remember reading about eh . . . I think the Mendes call it *tindyamei* or so. . . .
>
> *Grama:* You are quite right my son. In order for the spirit of the dead ancestor to "enter" his "new country" that spirit has to first cross a river. It is here that the *tindyamei* or crossing rites come in.
>
> *Student:* Ehn. . . I see. Grama, let me take these points down (as he writes down the information laughter by Grama).
>
> *Grama:* Ah you people! You are always writing. Our bookmen of today (laughter).[24]

The opening scene presents the tensions that exist between two kinds of knowledge. The old woman represents native African knowledge, which preserves the history of indigenous peoples in the oral tradition. Western knowledge is exemplified by the university student, who relies on the usual Western representations in books rather than on the cultural reality around him as the validating source of his own cultural experience. This scene sets the tone for the rest of the play and provides a focus for the audience.

Indeed, the political pedagogy of cultural history in Africa demands that we acknowledge the grounds of culture on which we stand. Adebayo Williams has argued that "cultural production in Africa must necessarily engage the great cultural tradition of African societies in their concrete and individual specificities." Arguing about the need to communicate differently in Africa, Williams endorses a "Derridean revolt" against the means and methods of Western discourse: "The privileging of reading over other perceptual and cognitive modes is itself the reflection of an historical alienation of the sense and of a profound disarticulation of the organs of perception in the process of capitalization. . . . [H]earing and seeing are as important—if not more important—than reading."[25] The primacy of orality, and thus of oral communication, in Africa cannot be overemphasized.

A crisis of modernity is further depicted in this same scene. As Grama continues to explain ancestral customs, the student continues to question the validity of her claims:

> *Grama:* Our ancestors can be angry with us and as a result become very vengeful towards us because they were wronged during their lifetime or after . . .
> *Student:* Hmmm. (writing, takes a deep breath) I see . . .
> *Grama:* What do you see? You see nothing son. You bookmen and leaders fail to see that it is our ancestors that offer us guidance and counselling throughout our never-ending stream of life. But when a child is well fed does he not look upon a grave as an ordinary heap of earth?
> *Student:* Surely, Grama, ever since I was far younger than this I have heard of names like Shaka the Zulu, Sundiata Keita, Mansa Musa, Osei Tutu, yes the Samoris and the Lion of Judah who pitched their strength against the whites and boldly attempted to keep them away from African . . .
> *Grama:* Well, we too had our Bai Burehs, our Manga Sewas, our Ndawas and Kai Londos, our Alimamy Solokos, not to mention Sengbe Pieh. . . . It is a tragedy. But the truth will be out tonight. A snail may run but it cannot avoid its shell. The truth never falters.[26]

Although the play focuses on the all-important cultural asset of reverence for ancestors as a key component in the memory patterns of Africans, Haffner foregrounds the need to question the method by which such memory patterns are assimilated. Grama's confident, relaxed laughter, as she criticizes the student whose absolute faith seems to be in the written word, indicates that the collective memory of the nation has faltered because it has resorted to alien methods of transmitting knowledge uncritically. Grama not only indicts the nation for forgetting the heroic story of the Amistad Africans, but also suggests that the transmission of memory is effective only when the most viable cultural channels are used.

Haffner confronts a major problem in the African condition today: the tendency to elevate the written word to the place of *fact* and the oral to the place of *fiction*. This form of hierarchizing comes with the power and privilege of Western education. Ironically, while some have accessed the privileges of Western education, the vast majority of Sierra Leoneans today are still functionally illiterate. Thus, in the struggle for cultural and political identity, the oral tradition remains the primary medium for effecting change. That is why in most African countries today, the theater for development has become the significant way of communicating with mostly rural populations. Besides, colonial education left little room for indigenous histories to be accommodated and transmitted. The tradition through which Sierra Leoneans transmit rituals and other cultural practices and memories to subsequent generations therefore remains the oral tradition. When the memory of Sengbe Pieh is ritualized in the play, it is done not through traditional educational means but through the performative act of the oral tradition.

When Sengbe's ghost is resurrected, he is angry with the living for forgetting their obligations to the dead. The ghost's refusal of the libation offered by one of the ancestral priests registers the impact of the people's failure to remember their past. Sengbe's ghost is finally appeased by the rhythm of drums, and he finally decides to share with the living the memorable events of his life. His recollection of the events, from his capture on the farm to the trip across the seas, to the court trials in the United States, are performed through a series of flashbacks. These flashbacks enable the audience to see beyond the ghost to the Sengbe Pieh that once was—a hero who fought not just for his life but for the freedom of his people. Asked why he had revolted against his captors, Sengbe replied that he was not born to be a slave: "It is better for me to die fighting than live many moons in misery. And if I am hanged, I will die happy if that will save my people from bondage." In the last scene of the play, John Quincy Adams, in his final submissions to the court, presents Pieh as a hero whose "name would have been handed down to posterity as one who had practised the most sublime of all virtues—disinterested patriotism and unshrinking courage"—if he had "lived in the days of Greece or Rome."[27]

By employing various narrative strategies, Haffner contributes to the evolving national character. Specifically, he adopts a tripartite narrative structure to heighten the meaning of the Amistad story. The three concentric layers start with Grama's conversations with the history student, which serves to frame the larger story. This is followed by the traditional-rites segment in which Sengbe's heroic role is reenacted. In the third and inner concentric layer, Sengbe himself tells the story of the Amistad revolt.

By utilizing the repeating patterns of the oral tradition through the concentric layering of the plot structure, Haffner has attempted to ensure both the "re-memory" of the past as well as the validation of that past.

It is noteworthy that Haffner, a playwright who depends on the pen, understands the significance of adjusting the literary to the realistic demands of communication, the ultimate goal of any writer. Indeed, if written words were enough, then the many books on the subject sitting on bookshelves in the library at the University of Sierra Leone would have made an impact over the years. Written records have had no real impact on the psyche of the nation. On the contrary, it was Joseph Opala's use of the oral tradition in his delivery of academic lectures that led both Haffner and Desouza George to channel the Amistad story through a performative route.

Sierra Leoneans found Haffner's play refreshing for the spirit of optimism it conveyed, but it was of little use to them. In fact, it took Haffner's repeated production of the Amistad play and the use of several modes of presentation—formal theater presentation, street drama, improvisations performed in a variety of settings, and ballads about the Amistad heroes sung on the radio—to convince the populace that the story was not fiction but historical reality. Nonetheless, the play in no small measure introduced the people to a new sense of national and historical awareness. With gratitude, the people embraced the Freetong Players as a theater of relevance, a theater for the people. The play in fact catapulted Freetong Players to both national and international prominence. In 1992, through a grant from the National Black Arts Festival, Haffner and the Freetong Players toured New Haven, Connecticut, where the dialectics of freedom for the Amistad captives had been hotly debated a century earlier, and other cities along the eastern seaboard.

Although denial of the Amistad story was dispelled through constant (re)education, methods by which the story would be made more relevant as both known historical past and "available past," as a commemorative event *belonging* to the people of Sierra Leone, were lacking. The Amistad plays by Haffner and Desouza George were certainly educational to Sierra Leonean audiences. A 1985 stamp depicting the Amistad as a cultural icon also pointed people to their own forgotten history. Despite these commemorations, the Amistad story did not impress itself on the people's psyche as being valid to their own experiences. G. H. Mead's theory of the symbolically reconstructed past emphasizes selective memory based on aspects of the historical past we recall for present-day use. When did this happen for Sierra Leoneans?

In the 1980s, Joseph Momoh, the army chief-of-staff of Siaka Stevens's All People's Congress (APC)—the incumbent party—succeeded Stevens as head of state through an undemocratic process of "heir to the throne." Sierra Leoneans recognized Momoh as Stevens' most trusted bodyguard and were indifferent and cynical about the conferred leadership. As was often the case in the country's long, repressive history, Sierra Leoneans expressed their dissatisfaction with Momoh not with outward protest but rhetorically: they simply rechristened him Josephine.[28] During Momoh's regime, cultural advocates like the American Joseph Opala requested that the APC government commission a publication on the neglected heroes of Sierra Leone;[29] the resulting book, *Sierra Leonean Heroes,* was published in 1988. When Momoh sensed the increasing cultural pride among the people, he himself slowly embraced the language of patriotism. But politicians were generally not known to promote patriotism of this kind. Divide-and-rule had always been the gateway to power. Therefore, the symbolic unity that derived from a sense of historical and cultural awareness was always potentially dangerous to such politicians. Like Stevens before him, Momoh's guarded appropriation of cultural symbols in effect suppressed national pride and identity.

From 1968, the APC ruled Sierra Leone as its personal property and offered very little in terms of national esteem and integrity. Corrupt officials grew fat on bribes, while the people languished in poverty that worsened with each passing year. John Cartwright notes in *Political Leadership in Sierra Leone* that the chronic skepticism of the populace toward institutional politics started with the first two prime ministers of Sierra Leone, Sir Milton Margai and his brother Albert Margai, who were leaders of the Sierra Leone People's Party SLPP then in power (1960–1967). The influences of "the Margais' style of politics had accustomed most people to thinking that politicians were out primarily for their own good, that professions of altruism were to be treated skeptically. Politics was a source of material payoffs, not of sacrifices."[30]

Sierra Leone has been plagued with unprofitable leadership since its independence in 1961. Poor leadership has enhanced anxieties about nationhood and has beset the nation's attempt to define itself as a place of "unity, freedom, justice."[31] It is no wonder that even with the publication of *Sierra Leonean Heroes,* meant to promote the richness and diversity of

Sierra Leonean cultures, the demoralizing lifestyle of the nation's leaders continued to feed the barren trope of cultural nationalism.

On April 29, 1992, the National Provisional Revolutionary Council (NPRC) overthrew the Momoh government in a military coup. The act was received with unprecedented acclaim expressed by artists and young people in search of heroic symbols to match the enthusiasm with which they hailed the NPRC. Opala's work on street art, *Ecstatic Renovations!* analyzes this cultural outburst. Opala notes the series of almost incidental events that have led to the establishment of Sengbe Pieh as a national hero: "The April 29 coup occurred during a symposium at City Hall, named for the Amistad Revolt, and when young people took to the streets to celebrate [the coup], they found a ready-made symbol of their liberation in the form of a twenty-foot model of the ship Amistad on the City Hall steps." [32]

Crowds rushed through the streets of Freetown, joining the confusion and jubilation that followed the announcement of the coup. In their euphoria, they shouted praises both to the military and to Sengbe Pieh, thus making the 1839 Amistad hero the symbol of the 1992 revolution. Indeed, the NPRC government was quick to realize that the cultural zeal awakened by the Amistad iconography was in fact doing the work of the revolution. The birth of the NPRC was, as it were, the birth of a new cultural identity. The political revolution and the cultural awakening were so intertwined that each continued to fuel the other.

Although the NPRC government did not officially sanction the unfolding cultural revolution, it acknowledged its impact on the political scene. Furthermore, because of the Amistad connection, the NPRC regime received recognition in America, which further conferred legitimacy at home. The cultural climate strengthened military leader Captain Valentine Strasser's political base, and in turn, the political revolution made Sengbe Pieh, leader of the Amistad revolt, "the unofficial symbol of the [NPRC] revolution." [33]

Being a people with no previous celebrated legacy of patriotism, Sierra Leoneans have encountered a fresh experience of national pride and historical awareness. Haffner's dramatic representation of the Amistad revolt led to the people's epiphany about their past. The Amistad, as a political icon, has contributed to an alternative definition of national identity. Both the cultural and political awakenings in Sierra Leone have further encouraged identification with other patriotic heroes who lived and died fighting a variety of oppressive institutions within the colonial and post-colonial eras.

The Broken Handcuff

Raymond Desouza George's play, *The Broken Handcuff or Give Me Free,* which was written and produced after the Amistad story had become an entrenched symbol in Sierra Leone, firmly places Sengbe Pieh in the cultural context of both past and present.[34] In particular, Desouza George highlights the relationship between the Amistad revolt leader and other patriotic heroes of the nation. Moreover, he focuses on the need to celebrate neglected Sierra Leonean heroes, such as Sengbe Pieh and the other Amistad Africans.

From the cast of the play, it is evident that this playwright takes more liberties in his writing than the other Amistad playwrights previously discussed. Several of the cast characters do not intersect either in time or in space with the Amistad event. Some (like the former British governor of Sierra Leone, Governor Clarkson) and select national and provincial rulers (such as Sir Milton Margai, Bai Bureh, and Mammy Yoko) are historical figures with which Sierra Leoneans are very familiar. Other characters, such as the narrator Lavalie, the narrator's friend Kakpindi, and Margru's friend Miatta, are invented by the playwright. Also, a contemporary cultural fixture on the music scene, the late Ebenezer Calendar, is included in the play. By making the historical figures rub shoulders with Sengbe—or rather, by making Sengbe rub shoulders with historical figures who are better known on the national scene—Desouza George attempts to elevate the stature of the Amistad hero to national significance. The playwright also uses this commemorative opportunity to indict the nation for vaguely acknowledging, rather than revering and celebrating, all of its heroes.

Raymond Desouza George is a well-known playwright, actor, and professor of theater studies at the University of Sierra Leone in Freetown. Born August 14, 1947, Desouza George has had a long history in the theater—from his recitals in elementary school to his performances with the Tabule Theater group (which received acclaim for representing Sierra Leone at the second world Black Festival of Arts and Culture, FESTAC '77, in Lagos, Nigeria), to his present international status as a playwright and theater professional. In an interview on April 29, 1994, the second anniversary of the NPRC revolution in Sierra Leone, Desouza George mentioned that Sierra Leonean playwrights, including himself, have always desired to preserve their culture, but this zeal has been ill-matched by ignorance of their own past. As a faculty member at the Institute of African Studies at the University of Sierra Leone, he was one of many faculty members and students who witnessed Opala's lecture on past heroes of Sierra Leone, which inspired him to write the play.

Desouza George sees culture as "a powerful political tool" necessary to raise the consciousness of the Sierra Leonean people. Artists, he insists, must motivate themselves, knowing fully well (as in the example of Sengbe Pieh) that if they are not "appreciated by the current generations, they might be picked up by posterity." [35] It is with this hope that in *The Broken Handcuff*, Desouza George attempts to liberate the minds of his audience.

Representing what is truly at stake today, the enslavement of African minds rather than African bodies, he uses a giant handcuff as the backdrop throughout the play. The playwright is galled at the tendency on the part of Sierra Leoneans to ignore those who have offered a lifeline of hope in the nation's past. As Lavalie, the narrator, says to the audience: "My people, I fear for our children. We fought for freedom, then used that freedom to sell our brothers, our fathers, our mothers, our wives, sons and daughters—all we had. Even the things that make us what we are. We killed ourselves in those sales and are still killing our heroes with dishonor." [36]

Desouza George is preoccupied with showing how the history of slavery, the present political era of independence from colonialism, and the future comportment with regard to the past are one and the same. What identity have Sierra Leoneans carved out for themselves? What identity will they yet carve out?

In answer to these questions, an onstage choral group, representing the people, responds by surveying the historical past that is responsible for the present sad state of affairs. Expressing the materialistic decadence of the present society, the chorus bursts into a Krio song:

But all of a sudden
Some strangers appeared
And corrupted some of us
And corrupted some of us
Things filled their eyes

Food filled their eyes
It turned their heads
Clothes filled their eyes
Rum turned their heads
Money turned their heads
It twisted their hearts

Oh my mother!
Oh my father!

The artist's poetic rage is further expressed through the anguished words of Lavalie, who addresses the shame of such a historical past recounted in the people's song.

History is once more embodied in scene three, "Independence Beyond the Grave," when the dead leaders and heroes of Sierra Leone emerge from their graves and converse about the present state of the nation. They comment that the living have forgotten the dead and, in the process, have become culturally dead. This is well demonstrated when Sir Milton, the first prime minister of the nation, in honoring Sengbe with the Order of Sierra Leone Freedom Award, asks for the nation's cultural performers to seal the act of honor with a dance celebration:

> *Sir Milton:* Let me see the National Dance Troupe in action.
> *Lavalie:* Let the drums of the Lion Mountains come out! [pause] Let the drummers, singers, and dancers show their national blend of rhythm and cultural fire! (No response)
> *Sir Milton:* Lavalie, where is the National Dance Troupe?
> *Lavalie:* They live in Aberdeen Village, Sir.
> *Sir Milton:* I know that. You mean the Cultural Village at Aberdeen.
> *Lavalie:* Well, yes Sir! But the roads are . . . well not so much the roads sir, but there are no telephones to summon them here; their costumes are tattered and torn; their properties and instruments largely in need of repairs or replacement. They lack a means of transportation and even their meals are not as regular as before.
> *Sir Milton:* You mean the National Dance Troupe? What do they have then?
> *Lavalie:* Some of them have ulcers, but most of them don't have the physique that will either compliment their costumes or be enhanced by their costumes. So I suggest that we leave our guest of honour to tell the story of his life.

With this sense of the present condition of cultural struggle and decay, Sengbe Pieh takes the audience on a tour of the historical past: the capture of slaves in Sierra Leone, the Middle Passage crossing on the *Tecora,* the auctioning of the slaves in Cuba, the revolt on the *Amistad* schooner, the American trials, and finally, the return to Africa.

What stands out in Desouza George's portrayal of the Amistad account is his exploration of the historical events in Africa that led to the Middle Passage experience in the first place. Grounded in a more immediate cultural context, the play's scenes depict the everyday life of the people— their anxieties about the "disappearing acts" of friends and relatives, and the deception by, and betrayal of, those who have "sold out." The playwright's free use of indigenous languages also adds to the immediacy of the cultural setting.

Also of note is the politics of language deployed in the *Broken Handcuff.* Sengbe, like John Quincy Adams and the American characters in the play, speaks perfect English. Grabo and Burnah, two of the Amistad Africans, speak imperfect English (certain verbs are missing from their lexicon) to indicate, perhaps, their social class among their people:

> *Grabo:* What I do?
> *Brunah:* I am wanting to drinking more water.
> *Grabo:* You to wait tomorrow.

Ironically, Sailor and Whiteman, two characters representing the Spanish crew (Ruiz and Montes are never identified by name in this play), speak in heavily accented English:

> *Whiteman:* "Vi look like very far from land and zis is sri days on zi sea. Vat vi do now?"
> *Sailor:* Vot vi do? Nor! (Angry) Vot I do? You not sail, I sail. I fight ze vind, ze boat fight ze vind . . . Vat I do? I do norsin. I vate.

To diminish the historical importance of the Spanish slave traders, and to denigrate their deplorable career, Desouza George uses language in a self-consciously political manner. The playwright confers not only the quite noticeable accented language on the Spanish crew, but, like the sculptor Ed Hamilton, he drastically reduces the overall prominence given to the Spanish slavers, Ruiz and Montes, in historical representations.

Even the trial scenes, as arranged by Desouza George, lend larger significance to the involvement of the Africans in effecting their freedom than historical accounts of the Amistad otherwise attest. Unlike Haffner's play that seems overcommitted to the trial scenes, an overcommitment that tends to rob the play of much dramatic zest (Steven Spielberg's *Amistad* movie is equally guilty of this type of representation), Desouza George emphasizes the active participation of the Amistad Africans in evoking and maintaining the sympathy of their American supporters. Desouza George is more interested in revising history than in siding with standard interpretations. Thus, in the district court defense trial, Sengbe's defense speech is highlighted rather than those of the defense lawyers. Without waiting for the arguments of the lawyers, Judge Judson rules in favor of the Africans at the close of Sengbe's moving speech. In this way, Desouza George insists on the relevance of the role played by the Africans. The courtroom scene is then transformed into a village arena where a harvest dance is performed to celebrate the victory.

In the meantime, Adams struggles with the decision to accept or reject the Supreme Court case on behalf of the Africans. In Adams's vacillation and doubt, a voice (supposedly that of little Kali) reads Kali's letter of appeal that Adams holds in his hand. The reading of the letter is followed by shouts of "give we free" from the Africans. Desouza George once more impresses his audience with the active participation of the Africans in effecting their freedom. Investing in the rhetorical potency of the Africans' participation, the author once more affirms that the Africans were never docile or powerless creatures in the fight against injustice.[37]

Nowhere is this point more clearly made than later in the courtroom scene when the Supreme Court justices take their seats and Adams proceeds to defend the Africans. The narrator, Lavalie, continually moves on and off stage during Adams's rebuttal, thus disrupting the audience's focus on the trial and marginalizing Adams's centrality to the plot. In fact, instead of Justice Story announcing the verdict in the Supreme Court trial, Lavalie announces the Supreme Court decision in favor of the captives — within the context of American slavery. Consequently, the narrator reminds us of the fact that this specific victory did not affect the condition of the slaves in the South who were "still being subjected to the atrocities of slavery."[38]

In the final scene in the play, "Return, Disillusionment, Death and Burial," Desouza George again indicts the audience for failing to recognize Sengbe Pieh as a valiant son of the soil, as a prophet, and as the "link between two great continents." The playwright further demonstrates that the colonial reception to which the Amistad Africans returned in Sierra Leone was far less than the dignity accorded them prior to their capture and release. Nonetheless, Lavalie's closing speech in the play offers a glimmer of hope. He points out that even if Sengbe's body fell low (he died an old and broken man), his spirit presently soars in triumph.

The playwright's attribution of uncompromised strength to the Amistad Africans confirms his desire to revive the memory of the neglected heroes of the past. Within the context of present-day attempts to memorialize the Amistad revolt in Sierra Leone, then, Desouza George's *The Broken Handcuff* engages the artistic representation of the event in relation to the political determination of Sierra Leoneans to candidly confront the memories of the past. That is, the play examines the past both for its availability and usability in the everyday lives of Sierra Leonean people.

Artistic Parallels in Representation

Artists who invest in historical materials are, to a large extent, committed to accessing the historical past to benefit their communities. As the conscience of their generation, they essentially reflect the historical, social, and political order of their specific societies through an interpretation of history's legacy. For the "text" of history to be accessible to the immediate audience, the relevance and usability of the past must be brought to bear on the present.

Owen Dodson, John Thorpe, Charlie Haffner, Raymond Desouza George, and Ed Hamilton have, to varying degrees of success, attempted to ground the history of the Amistad in the context of the everyday struggles of their own specific historical reality. In his own way, each has made specific claims on black identity by engaging the meaning, or the usability, of the Amistad story in the various political quests for racial equity and national significance.

Concerning the theme of return, which is evident in the four plays and the sculpture, Thorpe, Haffner, Desouza George, and Hamilton adopt the motif of the "soaring spirit" in their respective work. In the Sierra Leonean plays, Haffner and Desouza George use ghosts; Thorpe uses an embodied spirit in *Chap Am So;* Hamilton uses a submerged spirit, strategically located at the top of the Amistad monument; and Dodson uses the "jungle star" from which the Amistad captives draw inspiration. The return of the "spirited" past, however, is not an attempt by these artists to focus on the haunting phantom of wrongs done and evils committed. Rather, this call to memory represents the surge of hope birthed in the struggles of ancestors, their legacies of resistance, and their testimonies of self-recognition both in Africa and the United States.

Hollywood Images, African Memories: Spielberg's *Amistad* and Sierra Leone Culture and Politics

The American mainstream motion picture industry has impacted society politically, economically, and socially. As a powerful social institution, Hollywood's cultural elite influences society through its creation of cultural symbols and its authoritative control of the dissemination of those symbols. From its beginnings in the 1900s through the 1960s, the movie colony, as Leo Rosten labeled Hollywood in his 1941 publication, was not only ruthlessly capitalistic but also ideologically conservative.[1] Hollywood film producers shared the social values of the dominant society. Their representations of Africans, Native Americans, African Americans, and other non-European groups generally reflected their uncritical acceptance of dominant ideological views of the "other." In America, African Americans were either completely absent from movies or were given marginal roles such as mammies, chauffeurs, porters, or shoeshine boys. "Indians" were practice targets for trigger-happy whites, and in "Africa" movies, barely clothed or exotic-looking Africans were displayed as background props.

As part of a Third World attempt to revise the oppressive ideological dominance of Euro-American film culture, African cinema has been concerned with using film to revise the history of "mis-recognition" inscribed by a colonial legacy of misrepresentation.[2] This alternative medium has chiefly focused on "de-colonizing" African minds, raising consciousness, instilling racial and cultural pride, and articulating the potential for a revolutionary transformation of African societies.[3] Unfortunately, in spite of the industry's increasing popularity among Africans, these films are nevertheless marginalized due to limited financial backing and inadequate distribution. Hollywood still dominates and controls the marketing of cultural images globally.

At the micro level, however, the cultural wars in local communities are being fought on a variety of platforms—social, religious, political, ideological—that are not readily accessible to Hollywood giants. The kind of memories created and marketed by Hollywood are therefore continually contested by the real experiences of Africans, alternative cultural media, and dynamic social and political conditions in specific locations on the African continent. Thus, the racist stereotypes prevalent in Hollywood's versions of history are increasingly being resisted at multiple levels of articulation both in the Third World and in the West.[4]

In the last three decades, the colonial representations of blacks in Hollywood films appear to have been mitigated by the increasing number of significant roles that minorities play. This progressive trend began in the 1970s when New Left radicalism penetrated Hollywood. The transmutation of such images has since then improved. One study strongly indicates that overtly racist representations have become taboo, and that whites are much more likely than blacks to be portrayed negatively.[5] Hollywood's carefully packaged positive imaging of blacks, however, needs to be examined closely, because the context in which blacks now appear—even in lead roles—is still marked by a "racial character." That is, while racial tensions and conflicts in real-life situations have increased in the last decade, Hollywood's revised representations of blacks in, for instance, socially palatable "buddy" movies (starring black-white lead roles) potentially subvert the issue of race. Consequently, attempts to be "politically correct" have, in some cases, further consolidated racial stereotypes.

The hegemony of Hollywood ideology, which led many Third World artists in the 1960s and 1970s to establish film companies such as Third Cinema, is very much in place in the 1990s. It is particularly interesting, then, to analyze the ideological positioning of Steven Spielberg's *Amistad* in light of the political and cultural significance of the Amistad narrative in Sierra Leone. Although within the Sierra Leone context, the Amistad story was never commemorated on film, other artistic media such as theater, street murals, and folk songs have been employed over the last twelve

years with positive results. In contrast, Spielberg's 1997 movie has received negative reviews from American film critics, black and white audiences in the United States, and Africans as well. This series of outbursts is
justified not because Spielberg merely approximated historical truth on
screen but mainly because of the decadent ideological perspective from
which he chose to narrate his version of the Amistad story.[6]

Colonialist Reenactments

Certainly, the movie *Amistad* covers some major truths in the historical
account. That Spielberg selectively excluded some issues, however, not
only diminished the narrative power of the Amistad story but also was in-
dicative of regressive ideological positioning. The role of Antonio (the
cabin boy), who sided with the slave masters at sea and who brought
complexity and tensions to the Amistad story, was not represented in the
movie. The replacement of real historical black abolitionists of the era with
the composite fictional character of Joadson (played by Morgan Freeman) distorts the historically significant role African Americans played in
advancing the cause of black emancipation. Roger Sherman Baldwin, an
abolitionist, one of the finest and best defense lawyers in the United States
in the nineteenth century, is rewritten as a no-name property lawyer
(Matthew McConaughey) who claims no political allegiance to either
side of the passionate debate on slavery. Devoid of any real abolitionist intent, Baldwin's pseudo-character is anchored singularly by a presumed
social linkage: his charismatic bonding with the Africans. Also, as key
witnesses for the trial, the four Amistad children who evoked much sympathy in the hearts of New Englanders were excluded from the script. All
these events take a back seat to the sketches Spielberg chose.

Although Spielberg's imaginative use of historical material spurred
heated debates about the intrusion of art into the recorded past, the focus
should be shifted to Spielberg's political and artistic choices: choices that
belie his reliance on the colonial discourse of subjectivization and subjugation for his ideological construction of Africans in the movie.[7] The ideological power Hollywood wields both in the film industry and in public
perception of reality today necessitates the close scrutiny that "serious
race movies," such as *Dances with Wolves, Mississippi Burning,* and
Amistad, receive from film critics, historians, and the general public. The
translation of history through the "culturally overdetermined eye" of the

camera, to use Rey Chow's expression in her work on the theory of ethnic spectatorship, engenders an increasing mistrust of the object of consumption.[8] The evident power relations in *Amistad,* compounded by the varied levels of racial consciousness of the movie's audiences, resulted in hostile criticisms and disappointments and occasionally, in exhilarating moments of identification with the Amistad revolters. Indeed, the multiple levels of consciousness and engagement with Amistad scholarship represented by the movie's multiracial audiences largely outline the politics of memory and the politics of identity at play.

For example, the founder of the Amistad Research Center at Tulane University, Clifton Johnson, though a major historical consultant for the movie, reportedly was exasperated by the historical inaccuracies contained in *Amistad:* "What [film makers] call dramatic license, I call historical error." Johnson further commented that although Spielberg had succeeded in promoting a subject he, Johnson, had labored at for 40 years with little national success, he would now "spend the rest of [his] life correcting the errors" in Spielberg's movie.[9] One fallacy among consumers of media entertainment is the assumption that because the principal goals of commodified pleasure and box office success are primary, serious ideological interventions are not equally occurring. A scholar such as Herbert Gans, who has argued that commerce is more important than ideology, underrates the role of ideology in media communication by ignoring the fact that ideology and capital are twin products. Under the reality check of marketability, ideology is often perceived as inconsequential.[10]

Concerns with ideology—who has the power to be heard in society—and marketability were primary in African American artist Debbie Allen's search for a producer willing to take on the Amistad story. Her choice of the internationally known Spielberg highlights the lack of power among black film makers.[11] Although it is evident that all marginal identities are not equal, Allen nevertheless argued that Spielberg's sensitivity in portraying the humiliation of Jews in *Schindler's List* qualified him to handle the equally sensitive issue of race relations in the Amistad story. Many in the African American community and several film critics have challenged Allen on this point. Spike Lee, for instance, was incensed that a white director could be credited with the ability to portray accurately the American experience of slavery.

Can whites credibly convey the history and legacy of slavery under which blacks still "burn" in this country? The less reductive answer to this question is that in theory, they can. To argue otherwise is to claim the reverse position, that black artists cannot convincingly direct or produce movies portraying white experiences. Ideally, each artist, regardless of race, should be judged both on the merit of an artistic piece and the contextual soundness (ideological content) of that piece. Furthermore, the universal condition of pain and suffering should transcend social and racial barriers. In reality, however, the historical specifics often fail to cross these barriers of identification. The common ground of human communication, at any level in any society, is often exploited to a lesser or greater extent through the existing hegemonic lenses of power.

Interestingly, the politics of identity (in favor of a common ground) in the movie is deployed by the character of John Quincy Adams (portrayed by Anthony Hopkins) when he audaciously demands that unsympathetic pro-slavery justices imagine themselves in the Africans' shoes. Moreover, Adams's rhetorical call on the founding fathers as witnesses to the deliberation in the Supreme Court parallels the undaunted belief of Cinque (Sengbe Pieh, played by Djimon Hounsou) that his ancestors also have a stake in the outcome of the trial. This common ground of understanding between Adams and Cinque propels Adams's passionate defense of the Africans. Spielberg's intense desire to communicate effectively the bridges of identification that were forged in the historical Amistad case (perhaps the best known historical narrative of black and white racial cooperation in America), to be politically correct, and to sell a very "American" story seemingly entangled him in a web of inaccuracies, stereotypes, and insensitive sketches.

To be fair, Spielberg has attempted to cross the barriers of otherness at several levels. On matters and issues that other successful Hollywood (read: white, male) film makers would not even care to touch, Spielberg is willing to risk his reputation. Given the mixed reviews of his earlier artistic endeavor, *The Color Purple*, based on Alice Walker's 1982 novel, his acceptance of the more daunting historical project of the Amistad is rather daring.

But good intentions should not prevent us from critiquing Spielberg's movie, especially since his version is at present the most popular public memory of the Amistad revolt in the United States. Well-meaning intentions do not necessarily translate into non-oppressive representations, nor do they shift ideological ground. If anything, without careful reflection, such efforts indicate a nonchalant, seemingly apolitical and insensitive articulation of otherness. It is hard to escape the impression that Spielberg's *Amistad* offers a history he believes Africans and African Americans need or for which they should be grateful.[12]

Controversy over the basis of the Amistad story, which began even before the movie debuted, presaged the resistance that Spielberg's version would face. The battle over which literary version should be considered definitive started with Barbara Chase-Riboud's ten-million-dollar plagiarism lawsuit against Spielberg's movie company, DreamWorks. Chase-Riboud had several years earlier failed in a bid to sell the movie rights to her novel *Echo of Lions*. When Spielberg accepted Debbie Allen's proposition to direct the movie *Amistad*, he chose to base it on David Franzoni's more commercial adaptation rather than Chase-Riboud's more literary account.

The subsequent dispute over source material became a public spectacle. Chase-Riboud's lawsuit clouded the Amistad story and threatened, for a while, to delay the planned December 1997 release of the movie.[13] The suit and the debate centered on the question of which portions of the *Amistad* movie could have been "stolen" from Chase-Riboud's (still obscure) historical novel, *Echo of Lions,* and which elements of the Amistad story must necessarily be considered public-domain.

Many who took sides in this controversy did so on an emotional basis. Without reading *Echo of Lions* or weighing the merits of the case, many (blacks especially) sided with Chase-Riboud (whom they considered the underdog) against the greater political might of Hollywood. In addition, the African American producer Debbie Allen was viewed with suspicion for partnering with *Amistad*'s white director. If conversations on the Internet are any indication, many advocated a boycott of *Amistad* in support of Chase-Riboud. However, others sympathized with Debbie Allen, who claimed she had knocked on doors for years in her attempts to sell the Amistad idea to the film industry. In either case, racial antagonisms were aroused even before the movie was released.[14]

Besides this sideshow, *Amistad*'s seemingly "heavy" commercialization through several media outlets, including Oprah Winfrey's review of the movie and interviews with its major players, also prompted responses from the viewing public. While many were won over by Oprah's publicly emotional endorsement of the film, others disdained the commercial overtones of Allen and Spielberg's marketing strategies. Amidst the hoopla, the media and the intellectual community were buzzing once more with debate about the place of fiction in history and the role of history in popular culture. An avalanche of documentaries, talk shows, side shows, and the *Amistad* movie itself threatened to overwhelm the relevance of the historical Amistad story and its place in American history.

For most informed black and white viewers, the *Amistad* movie was more disturbing than profound. The historical records paint Sengbe Pieh as an excellent rhetorician. His comportment and his rousing speeches made New Englanders line up for hours in the cold just to secure seats in the courtroom. In contrast, Spielberg's courtroom scenes are tediously drawn out. Apart from Cinque's stream-of-consciousness remembrances of the Middle Passage crossing on the infamous slave ship, *Tecora* (one of the more dynamically narrated scenes in the entire movie)—and apart from Cinque's emotionally charged statement "Give us free"—like the other captives, Cinque is simply *present*. Indeed, the African American novelist Alexs D. Pate, whose visibility soared with the publication of his tie-in book, maintains that he would have liked to have seen certain things done differently in the movie:

> I think the film was good but literarily I felt that we should have spent more time with Cinque in Africa. I think the whole process of his being kidnapped is too profound to be spirited away. The trip from the point of kidnapping to the slave factory was a very interesting period. All of that I would have spent more time with! I would have started there as opposed to the time of rebellion which the film does and would have spent less time on the courtroom stuff. More time on the interior struggle that the Africans go through in captivity because nobody really talks about it.[15]

Historian Jesse Lemisch also took a parallel view in his suggestion that the movie should have focused more on "black agency and group action rather than on "white paternalism."[16]

In spite of actor Djimon Hounsou's dynamic stage persona (his "authentic" looks according to some critics), his character's lack of any articulate verbal action for almost two thirds of the movie far outweighs his stage presence. Cinque and the other Africans have to be content with displaying much idiocy and dumbness in the trial scenes, while prosecution and defense lawyers Holabird and Baldwin spar in a bumbling and often distracted fashion. Perhaps, Spielberg's good intention was to show the helplessness of the Africans who were trapped in a foreign and unfriendly land. Overall, however, the director fails to depict adequately the Africans as active participants in their attempts to redeem themselves from bondage. For instance, *Amistad* never informs the audience that the attention the Amistad Africans received from Yale professors and students who were hired to teach them English helped them in articulating their rights. A good number of the Africans, including Sengbe, could read and write English fairly well before they returned to Africa. Some even wrote letters to John Quincy Adams (none of the Africans met Adams prior to the trial), encouraging him and thanking him for being willing to take the case.

Instead of focusing on the many different contexts in which the Africans articulated their subjectivity, the movie plot seems to pivot on the centrality of Adams. Early on in the movie, Adams is pursued by abolitionist lawyers who need his support. This quest to enlist Adams overshadows the significance of the Amistad Africans' crucial role in the legal battles. Many viewers took offense at this second-class representation of the captives in a movie that was expected to celebrate the ultimate triumphs of the Africans. Had the movie utilized historical information that depicted more dignifying images of the Africans, most audiences, black audiences especially, would have responded differently.

In contrast, and in typical Hollywood-colonialist fashion, the movie errs on the side of the exotic. The film opens with Cinque attempting to free himself by loosening a nail that chains him to the hold of the ship. Artistically, the image is powerful, but ideologically it is a typically Westernized racial construction of Africans. In the opening montage, the facial features of the Amistad hero are presented as, and appear to be, animal-like. The audience barely recovers from this transposed imagery before another powerful scene is presented: the violent mutiny and aggressive, even sadistic killing of the captain by Cinque, which is prolonged in the film and emphasizes standard (white) tropes regarding otherness. Spielberg does not prepare the audience for this mutinous act, and the film never returns to the historical act that specifically incited the Amistad captives to revolt in the first place. Granted, kidnapping and slavery are reasons enough for any group of people to revolt; however, the horrendous rumors of possible white cannibalism that pushed the Amistad Africans to desperately defend themselves is omitted.

In the movie *Amistad,* however, the largely American audiences gaze at the mutinous Africans for about twenty-five minutes without truly comprehending their actions, especially since the Africans speak Mende, the indigenous tongue widely spoken in the southern part of Sierra Leone. Their Spanish captors also speak Spanish, not English. Ironically, the words of the Spanish slavers are translated whereas those of the captives are not, until Americans appear on the scene, at which time subtitles for the Africans are provided. Without evoking the politics of translation here, it is necessary to stress that the association of blacks and violence is so familiar to the American consciousness that rational explanations are often uncalled for. This seemingly spontaneous and visible recognition of black masculinity is a stereotype that is staged repeatedly and therefore resonates as "natural identity." [17]

It has been argued that Spielberg's intention in the revolt scene was to displace Americans as they listened to a language they have never really heard before, thereby enabling viewers to experience the disoriented state of the Africans. This aesthetic privilege is a luxury with which most black audiences cannot afford to identify. For minorities who live in predominantly white cultures, being displaced and disoriented is the normalizing process through which they are compelled to engage the dominant society. If Spielberg's goal was to disorientate, then he succeeded in consolidating ideological representations of blackness as absence and as violent nihilism. Language disorientation, as a strategy to reach white audiences, inscribes a "primitivistic reverence" for the Africans; [18] this "reverence" emanates from a "noble savage" ideology.

To black audiences, this must be an incredible explanation: they are being called upon not only to negotiate their everyday existence as racially marked by violence but also to revise the history of slavery as the incomprehensible violence of black on white. The tie between blackness and violence in the movie reinforces rather than disentangles the mainstream American image of the black male body as violent. The full-bodied presence of actor Djimon Hounsou, coupled with the seemingly endless rage with which he infuses his character, confirms rather than negates the typical American impression of black male violence—uncontrollable anger that is unsupported by a rational response to circumstances. Understandably, there were very few reasons for Hounsou to have been graceful and calm, but the historical Sengbe Pieh was noted for his dignified and enlightened defense of himself and his companions. On the contrary,

Cinque's animal-like breathing in the movie and his tendency to speak in a shouting, angry voice failed to draw the deepened empathy Spielberg seems to have expected from audiences.

Another point of contention in *Amistad* was the pervasive use of exotic African imagery (this was also a flaw in *The Color Purple*), particularly in the victory scene that follows the first legal battle in *Amistad*. While Cinque is absorbed in an argument with his lawyer, Baldwin, about the scheduling of a Supreme Court trial, the other Amistad captives are seen in jail, dancing around a fire. Outside the jail, nervous soldiers, with guns ready, watch the captives curiously. Meanwhile, Cinque's heated argument with Baldwin culminates in his self-exposure: he takes off his clothes to dance away his frustrations by the fire. This scene may be regarded as artistically impressive but its contents remain startlingly bizarre. A fire dance, in the confines of a jail? It is a puzzling scene that makes sense only in light of Western expectations that an African dance around a fire is a necessary ingredient in the definition of Africanness.

Paradoxically, while *Amistad* strives to promote a primitivistic African presence, it simultaneously erases the significance of African Americans' spirited commitment to abolitionism. The black abolitionist Joadson is more of an onlooker than an active participant in the plot. Unlike fervent black antislavery agitators, such as Frederick Douglass and David Walker, who were notably involved in the fight against slavery, Joadson is portrayed as an innocuous, pleasant fellow with little conviction. Even Joadson's personal story, like those of the Amistad captives, is appropriated and rewritten by John Quincy Adams. In a revealing conversation, Adams attempts to solicit from Joadson the captives' story:

> *Adams:* What is their story?
> *Joadson:* Well, they are from West Africa.
> *Adams:* No, what is *their* story?
> *Joadson:* Ah!
> *Adams:* Mr Joadson, you are from where originally?
> *Joadson:* Georgia, Sir . . .
> *Adams:* Does that pretty much sum up what you are? A Georgian? Is that your story? No, you are an ex-slave who devoted his life to the abolition of slavery in overcoming great obstacles and hunches along the way, I should imagine. That's *your* story.[19]

It is rather strange that, given the history of the African American struggle, a character like Joadson would have needed a history lesson from Adams on the difference between external and internal "identities." Most likely, an African American of Joadson's calling not only would have had his own story but also would have understood that story within the larger canvas of the black struggle.

The most redeeming quality in Joadson's role, however, is that he comes to terms with his historical memory through his encounter with his African ancestors in the hold of the ship. In the darkened, blood-splattered hold of the ship, a thousand ancestral voices thrust their way into his consciousness, literally knocking him off his feet. In one of the finest moments in the film, Joadson searches the ship's hold for evidence he can use to help defend the Africans with whom he still cannot communicate. The overwhelming abundance of "memory" he encounters ends this search. Even though this scene is entirely fictional, it convincingly portrays the traumatic effects of slavery in the African American experience; it underscores the dispossession that is still a formidable issue in the present.

Although this pictorial narrative of terror is effectively assumed by Joadson, the privileging of speech in *Amistad* as the province of the white intelligentsia is problematic to the rich rhetorical heritage of African Americans. Perhaps Spielberg was trying to present the broader significance of the gag rule which in the nineteenth century prohibited politicians sympathetic with the cause of slavery from addressing this sensitive subject matter. It was also unlawful for blacks (both free and slave) to testify against whites in southern courts. African American memory was thus called into question by the dominant society not only for its reliability in relation to "truth" but also for its validity in an environment that had already denied the humanity of the witness. In essence, only white men could gainsay other white men. Perhaps Spielberg wanted this point emphasized in *Amistad;* otherwise, the disturbing erasure of the African American voice and the displacement of knowledge and the role of memory ascribed to antebellum American slaves, especially in the free states, defy explanation. Thus, both African American and African agencies in the movie are constricted by the power of white speech. Cinque's heroism, for instance, is filtered through the eloquent Adams who uses Cinque's reasoning to persuade the Supreme Court justices in the Africans' favor. After the court victory, Adams's acknowledgment of Cinque's eloquence, "I used your words to persuade them," is small consolation for his having dispossessed the Amistad hero.

The movie ends with the Africans pensively sailing back to Africa, followed by a coda explaining that a civil war was raging in Africa and that Cinque's wife and children were reportedly missing. Like most books on the Amistad story by Americans, the Amistad Africans' return trip to Sierra Leone and its implied possibilities take on a mystical, shadowy quality. *Amistad* does not attempt to interpret the events that happened after the captives went home to Sierra Leone. Nonetheless, for a story this traumatic, it is gratifying to see slave fortresses decimated by British naval forces (we can succumb to Hollywood catharsis here) and Africans dramatically freed—*Ben Hur*-style—from a life of oppression, an entirely fictional ending.

Colonial Resistances

At this point in time, it is unproductive to argue that Spielberg should not have made this particular movie. For better or worse, Spielberg's *Amistad* aids in exposing a story that needs to be told, in spite of our reservations about the movie's flawed ideological reconstruction. Even the movie's failed box-office records cannot negate Hollywood's ability to impact world audiences with its imposing power of distribution. The impact of *Amistad* has been compelling: public inquisitiveness has been awakened, and those who have denied the pain of history once more confront its ever present reality.

The problem with Hollywood's monopoly over the sale of ideology is that its conflation of imagination and reality is often indistinguishable and misleading. For that matter, the *Amistad* movie's supporting study guide, provided by DreamWorks as a teaching aid for use in schools, repackages the movie as an apparatus of documentary truth, as history. As Eric Foner has suggested, it is hoped that people will head for libraries and begin to read the numerous materials on the history of slavery in America. While the movie might have provided a momentary communal experience of the past based on Spielberg's interpretation, we have to remember that the real history of the Amistad is accessible and available.[20]

In consonance with the sensitivity of the subject matter with which the movie deals overall, we can surmise that no amount of intellectual knowledge on the subject can take away the pain of the past or ease the agony of confronting memories of the past. Chester Fontenot's essay, "Black Misery, White Guilt and *Amistad*," focuses on the powerful effects of this public discourse on movie audiences of mixed races. Commenting on two couples—one white, the other black—who he had observed after the viewing of *Amistad,* Foner notes that both couples "were obviously shaken by the movie:"

> The African American couple moved deliberately, but without specific purpose and direction. It was as if they were adrift on a sea of emotions deprived of the means to navigate their shared pain toward the shores of reconciliation and wholeness. As they walked by a padded bench on the outskirts of the theater, the young woman sat down, placed her head in her hands, and began to weep. I saw her companion come to her side, place a hand on her shoulder, and in an effort to share her pain, ask "Are you alright?" She replied, "I just need to get myself together." The white couple seemed to cling to each other in a desperate attempt to manage the tragedy that had unfolded before them; . . . as if they sought a bond . . . which would allow them to tuck away the collective guilt. . . . I heard the young man ask his companion, "Are you okay?" She replied, "I think I'll be fine." [21]

Whether it is manifested in white discomfort or black pain, *Amistad* forces the American public to collectively reflect on the systematic disfranchisement of the black race in America. Just as John Quincy Adams's invocation of the founding fathers highlights the similarity of purpose and meaning he shares with Cinque and with Cinque's past, so too does Spielberg's movie as a whole challenge Americans of all races to ponder the implications of the past in the present. Our actions in the present undermine, question, affirm, and establish the past, even as the past guides and nurtures the present. For African Americans in particular, the ordeal of revisiting the past underscores the everyday burden of articulating their identity in a world that constantly misrepresents them.

Sierra Leone Memories

Spielberg's historical memory of the Amistad story is radically different from the memory of Sierra Leoneans who have embraced the same. In Sierra Leone, the immediacy of meaning in the Amistad event has elicited a different set of responses that are productive in rendering the past not just an available memory but also a usable memory. Most Sierra Leoneans have had no access to the Spielberg movie, which incidentally was released while a civil war was raging in Sierra Leone. Over the past twelve years, Sierra Leoneans have engaged the Amistad story in various cultural and political orientations. The Amistad story has led them to reinvent images of themselves, both at the individual and national level. Unlike Spielberg's movie, which silenced Africans and African Americans alike, Sierra Leoneans have found their voices through the cultural awakening initiated by the Amistad narrative and reactivated during the military coup of 1992.

The people welcomed the NPRC government of Captain Valentine Strasser, which had ascended to power through the coup. Sierra Leoneans believed that this regime would redeem them from the excesses of previous governments. In fact, Strasser had declared war on corruption. The NPRC was quick to realize the advantages of identifying with the people's sense of rediscovered national consciousness. The popularity of the government at the initial stages was very much tied to the people's sense of freedom to express themselves symbolically through dramatic productions of the Amistad and through other iconographic acts of memory. Iconography is often the quiet, yet effective, way to commemorate dated events. Far beyond official celebrations, iconographic representations, such as paintings and sculptures, continue the work of harmonizing national identification with the celebrated historic moment, thus making the historical past part of the present-day landscape.[22]

Indeed, the NPRC government in Freetown realized that the cultural icons displayed by young enthusiasts were driving the revolution. Fine artists, dramatists, sculptors, and musicians became the unofficial cheerleaders for the government. It was not long before the NPRC government accepted artists' requests that Sengbe Pieh grace the nation's currency. In addition, Sengbe Pieh's appearance on wall paintings in the city of Freetown and in many neighborhoods has made the Amistad event part of the household vocabulary. Even in other parts of the country—places like Bo, Kenema, and Makeni—murals of Sengbe Pieh reflect the growing national awareness. As Joseph Opala has acknowledged, this type of "patriotic art showcasing the nation's history and culture" is unprecedented in "a country with almost no tradition for patriotic imagery."[23]

The political revolution and the cultural awakening were so intertwined that each helped to fuel the other. The birth of the NPRC was, in many ways, the birth of a new cultural identity. Other cultural events helped to strengthen Strasser's political base. While Strasser was in the United States seeking medical treatment, he was one of the guests of honor at the 1992 Amistad Memorial dedication ceremony in New Haven,

Connecticut. Thus, because the Amistad event was enjoying greater recognition in the United States, so too did the NPRC regime.

Moreover, the street murals in Freetown provide evidence of the commingled significance of the Sengbe Pieh–NPRC cultural revolution. The content of the murals exceeds the official version in books on the subject by introducing an African-centered difference in their artistic interpretation of the Amistad narrative. While a few artists have generated portraits similar to that of Nathaniel Jocelyn's renowned depiction of Sengbe (Joseph Cinque) in New Haven, most Sierra Leonean artists have expanded the portraiture to include stories that delve into the historical past as well as into the future.[24] In a mural by Amadu Tarawalie, Sengbe Pieh is in the Nathaniel Jocelyn pose, but the "country cloth" has replaced the Roman toga.[25] He is holding a staff of a Mende chieftain, and in the background are jagged rocks rather than flowing hills. Not only is the picture bordered by the Sierra Leone flag colors (green, white, and blue) but also it is set within the larger frame of West African nation flags to represent ECOMOG, the military arm of the Economic Community of West African States, formed in the late 1980s.[26] Thus, the Amistad story is taken out of a Europeanized setting and placed within a Sierra Leone context. The mural is also a symbol of unity among West African nationals.

In a wall painting by Isah Kabbia, the whole of Africa is embraced by the Amistad narrative. Sengbe Pieh is presented as a Moses figure sent to deliver God's people from bondage. He beholds the tablets of the law from God. Light shines from the east into his face, whereas darkness—night—covers the west to which his back is turned. Africa is in the middle of the forces of darkness and light. The contrasting shades of color remind us of the classic struggle of the revolt, seemingly mimed in the Amistad schooner's journey east by day and west by night. Thus, the narrative in the painting not only demonstrates the people's awareness of their relations within a global network but also questions such relations of power.

In another mural by Kabbia, Sengbe Pieh is crowned "Black Ruler" of Africa. He no longer carries a cane, as in Jocelyn's painting, or a Mende staff (a symbol of both authority and peace), as in Tarawalie's mural. Sengbe now carries a spear; he is a man poised for war. In this narrative, "the law" or "the word" is transformed into an offensive weapon. Indeed the word is the sword, the artist reminds us, even as we recall Sengbe's much-adored rhetorical skills in the New Haven court trials. Sengbe's transposition in the three murals—from Mende native to West African in the first mural, to African in the second, and finally, to black ruler in the third mural—clearly demonstrates that black people everywhere can find meaning in the Amistad story. In becoming the voice of vindication against the global oppression of black people, Sengbe Pieh and the Amistad Africans are models for recovering lost identity and pride.

The popularity of the Amistad story in Sierra Leone is now a collective memory celebrated, and revitalized, by the people, because they are able to see a reflection of part of themselves in the struggles of Sengbe Pieh and the Amistad captives. Collective memory in this sense has become "a significant force in a dialectic of social change." [27] The Amistad incident, to which the people now have access, has been appropriated to express their present recognition of themselves as historical agents. It took the direct impact of the 1992 political upheaval, the audiovisual advantages of the theater, the iconography of wall paintings and sculptures, ballads aired over the radio and on street corners, together with *an interpretive exchange with the people's social interests and concerns* to elevate the Amistad event to its present status as the symbol of a new national consciousness.

For Sierra Leoneans, the centrality of the revolt in the Amistad story legitimizes their need to revise the neohistorical "amnesia" imposed on the nation by a series of corrupt and oppressive governments. In contrast to Spielberg's *Amistad,* in which the Africans were marginalized, portrayals of the Amistad story in Sierra Leone have raised the consciousness of the people such that they are now able to see themselves as historical agents capable of changing the oppressive circumstances around them. While the movie was ideologically nonthreatening, the Amistad narratives in Sierra Leone have instituted revolutionary activities at the grassroots level. [28]

The popularity of the Amistad as a revolutionary symbol in Sierra Leone could have accomplished much on behalf of the Strasser regime, but because the NPRC failed to identify fully with the people's pronounced sense of historical awareness, the government soon went the way of earlier corrupt governments. This time, however, Sierra Leoneans were more active in taking a stand for democracy. By 1996 they had negotiated their way to the ballot box. When the NPRC had a change of heart about democratic elections, the people insisted on continuing the process. International pressure also shamed the NPRC into allowing the electoral process to continue. The elections of March 1996 were the first truly democratic elections in some twenty-five years. [29] Ordinary citizens and officials at the voting booths bravely defended ballot boxes, even when government soldiers attempted to disrupt the elections by shooting into crowds and arresting civilians indiscriminately.[30]

Even then, the democratically elected SLPP government of Ahmed Tejan Kabba lasted barely a year before an unpopular and complicated coup took place in May 1997.[31] This latest military regime, the Armed Forces Revolutionary Council (AFRC), led by Major Johnny Paul Koroma, virtually held the entire population of Freetown hostage, because most Sierra Leoneans refused to recognize its authority or participate in its governance. Instead, the people turned to the Nigeria-led ECOMOG force that mounted months of military assault in an attempt to topple the AFRC. Both strategic military force and diplomatic negotiations resulted in the restoration of the embattled President Kabbah to office in March 1998. Kabbah's government can best be described as an administration in crisis. Distrustful of the military which has twice been forced to hand over power, Kabbah has relied both on ECOMOG forces and the homegrown *Kamajohs,* traditional Mende warriors, to stay in power.[32] The "irregular warfare" that has besieged the nation in the last four years has claimed 30,000 lives and has succeeded in wrecking the economy.[33]

Through all of these devastating events, however, the will of the people and their sense of nationhood have evolved. Rather than becoming cynical bystanders as in years past, they are actively combating antidemocratic forces at the price of their own lives. Opala summarizes the current situation in Sierra Leone by noting that the state (that is to say, the government) has collapsed but the nation (the people being governed) has not.[34]

Judging by events from the last few years, it is apparent that the raised consciousness of the Sierra Leonean people cannot now be reversed. The Amistad story has played a primary role in unveiling the cultural memory and the political consciousness of Sierra Leone's national identity. It has also informed people's interpretations of their present condition. The expression of the Amistad narrative as a continuing revolution is therefore emblematized in its dramatic return to a nation that had all but forgotten its own past. Sierra Leoneans have thus inadvertently called into question the representational practices of Spielberg's *Amistad* through the very different set of circumstances that living memories of the Amistad revolt have been able to effect in their lives.

Afterword

Attempts by scholars, activists, and artists to represent the contested, elided, and often unacknowledged historical past not only expose the deeply submerged problem of race relations between Africa and the West, but also bring us closer to transcending our cultural, social, and political differences. In Africa, the experiment of slavery throughout the nineteenth century and the systematic colonization of Africans by Europeans into the twentieth century plunged the continent into structural underdevelopment. Recently, President Bill Clinton's task force on race relations and his apologies to the people of Africa for American participation in the slave trade are attempts, at the institutional level, to confront denial, acknowledge complicity, and initiate dialogue. The present crisis of contradictory racial discourses in America has its parallels in the Amistad court trials.

The Amistad case was singular not just because its successful outcome was unprecedented but mainly because its legal victories did *not* foster a just pattern of development in other court trials involving race. On the one hand, the Amistad case drew wide support from the American public in Northern states and was the most celebrated case in the nineteenth century. On the other hand, it could not dislodge the deep racial sentiments among whites, nor could it destabilize entrenched legal policies that acknowledged the rights of the slaveholder.

Just as paradoxical is the re-emergence of the Amistad narrative at a time of major political setbacks for blacks in the United States—the rescindment of affirmative action policies, cutbacks in social programs, and challenges to school integration—and for Sierra Leoneans caught in the throes of a series of "civil wars." This is not mere coincidence. Although the Amistad image has been employed dynamically across and within racial boundaries, how it is interpreted depends on the varied meanings, engagements, and contextualizations each strata of society ascribes to it; thus, its status is ambivalent. For instance, some African Americans, believing the allegations that Sengbe Pieh was a slave trader, have understandably distanced themselves from the vibrant lessons of the Amistad revolt and view with suspicion efforts to commemorate the event. Despite the controversy, however, some whites and blacks have embraced the Amistad saga for the possibility of friendship that it literally and figuratively symbolizes.

For the Sierra Leonean people in particular, the Amistad story is not at all past; it is a present-day attempt to salvage national identity and personal dignity from a neocolonial history of oppression. In contrast, the Amistad symbol has proven to be both sweet and sour for Sierra Leonean politicians. The Amistad story does offer, however, a forum for fruitful dialogue about the painful history of slavery. The unique resolution of the Amistad trials in the United States has already initiated the possibility for racial cooperation in our increasingly multiracial, global world.

Scholars, activists, and artists can continue to redress this important historical caesura. Rather than limit this complicated historical process to a simplistic dichotomous portrayal of good and bad, we should embrace the story of slavery and the contradictions of freedom embodied in the Amistad narrative with vigor. Our desire for hasty solutions with which to seal the past will then be stymied by our willingness to excavate and process the past analytically and in the context of our present reality. For each of us, historical memory should reverberate in our personal, everyday choices.

The relevance of the Amistad story, then, finds us once more in the middle of a human tragedy still being played out. If the vicarious victory of the Amistad revolt somehow enlightens the dark historical past, it also confirms the powerful human belief that hope is still a bulwark against reality.

Notes

Chapter One. The Amistad Story in the American Context

1. I will henceforth refer to *La Amistad* in the adopted English equivalent, "the *Amistad*," and where the word "Amistad" is not a reference to the ship but rather is adjectival, it will remain without italics.

2. A. Jones's *From Slaves to Palm Kernels* offers a comprehensive history on the Gallinas region. It also vividly describes the slave trading post at Dombokoro, 49–51.

3. Laigo and Luiz were the slave dealers who bought most of the Amistad captives, according to Barber's report of his conversations with the captives in *Amistad Captives,* 9–15.

4. The account of the Amistad story narrated in this chapter and referred to elsewhere in this book is mainly referenced in *African Captives: Trial of the Prisoners of the "Amistad";* Barber, *Amistad Captives;* Adams, "Letterbook"; U.S. District Court records for Connecticut at the Federal Archives and Records Center, Waltham, Massachusetts; U.S. Congress, *House Executive Documents,* no. 185; archives of the American Missionary Association (AMA) at the Amistad Research Center (ARC); and other slavery pamphlets and newspapers.

5. An eyewitness to the illegal slave market in Lomboko and other West African coastal areas, Francis Bacon testified at the Amistad hearings that the "slave trade on that part of the coast [the Gallinas area] is the universal business of the country, and by far the most profitable, and all engaged in it who could raise the means. Extensive wars take place in Africa, for obtaining slaves from the vanquished. Different towns and villages make war upon each other for this purpose." See Barber, *Amistad Captives,* 21. See also Fyfe, *History of Sierra Leone* (London: Oxford University Press, 1962), parts 8 and 10; Oliver and Fage, *Short History of Africa* (New York: Penguin, 1988), 94–105; Davidson, *Africa in History,* 205–15.

6. Many missionary letters from the Mende mission in Kaw Mende, Sierra Leone, in the mid–nineteenth century spoke at length about the endless wars caused by slavery, often expressed as "war path" or "war road."

7. The notorious Don Pedro of Havana was a business partner with the House of Martinez, which owned most of the slave forts in the coastal areas of Sierra Leone. See Madden's deposition in U.S. District Court records for Connecticut, 20 November 1839, 133, 135 and the testimony of Grabeau, Monday, 7 October 1839, in *African Captives*, v; See also Barber, *Amistad Captives*, 3–6.

8. Madden's deposition confirmed the illegality of registering newly arrived Africans as *ladinos* in Cuba, U.S. District Court records for Connecticut, 20 November 1839, 133, 135. See also Baldwin, *Argument*, 31.

9. The *New London Gazette* of August 27, 1839, gives particulars in its report of the events surrounding the mutiny by the Africans and the capture by the U.S. brig *Washington*.

10. Testimony of Grabeau, Kimbo, Sengbe, and others, in *African Captives*. Although in the Amistad case Celestino provoked the Africans with threats of white cannibalism, there are numerous accounts that this belief was commonly held among many captives in Africa and the New World. See for example Bosman's account in *New and Accurate Descriptions*, (London, 1705), 363–65.

11. Sengbe (noted by Barber in *Amistad Captives* as "Sing-gbe") is the most accurate phonetic spelling of the Amistad leader's name. His family name was Pieh. In various newspapers covering the Amistad affair, he was called Cinquez, Cinqué, Cingue, Sinko, Jingua, Singbe, etc. Joseph Cinque, sometimes written as Cinqué or Cingue, has become the regular usage in America. However, in light of available information and our present awareness of the politics of naming, it is expedient to refer to him by the name he called himself rather than by Ruiz's contrived naming and its consequent Euro-American derivations.

12. See Barber, *Amistad Captives*, 4–5.

13. Testimonies of Ruiz and Montes onboard the *Washington*, 29 August 1839. Lieutenant Meade acted as interpreter for the Spaniards. Barber, *Amistad Captives*, 7.

14. As reported in the *New York Commercial Advertiser*, 20 November 1839, 2; See also Fordham's testimony in U.S. District Court records for Connecticut, 19 November 1839, 15.

15. See Barber, *Amistad Captives*, 5.

16. Janes to Leavitt, 30 August 1839, AMA, Box 197.

17. For example, in the 1833 Clinton Hall demonstration in New York City, a mob cried out for the blood of both Arthur Tappan and William Lloyd Garrison. See J. L. Thomas, *Liberator*, 168–69, 200–206; also Richards, *"Gentlemen of Property and Standing,"* 28, 29; also see Dillon, *Abolitionists*, 113–40; and Cain, ed., *William Lloyd Garrison*, 1–3.

18. Richards, *"Gentlemen of Property and Standing,"* 47–81.

19. See Fuller, *Prudence Crandall;* Foner and Pacheco, *Three Who Dared,* 5–46; Strane, *Whole-Souled Woman.*

20. On martyrdom of Reverend E. P. Lovejoy, see Trow, *Alton Trials* and Simon, *Lovejoy, Martyr to Freedom.*

21. Barber, *Amistad Captives,* iv–v.

22. Calderón to Forsyth, *House Executive Documents,* no. 185, 8–9.

23. *House Executive Documents,* no. 185, 8–9; emphasis in original.

24. Deposition by Robert Madden, U.S. District Court records for Connecticut, 20 November 1839, 133, 135. Also see Barber, *Amistad Captives,* 17. For an in-depth reading on Madden's life and travels see Madden, ed., *Memoirs.* Also see affidavit of one of the Africans, Bahoo, who confirmed the ethnicity of "Magru, Kenyee, and Kale," *African Captives,* 27.

25. Fox to Forsyth, *House Executive Documents,* no. 185, 27–28.

26. Sengbe's testimony, U.S. District Court records for Connecticut, 8 January 1840, 19–20.

27. In the nineteenth century, Connecticut had a rather ambiguous record on slavery and black civil rights. Although it was a free state, slavery was legally on the books until 1848; there were still a handful of legal slaves in the state in the 1830s. With regard to civil rights, it maintained the reactionary practice of separatism. "Indeed, of the New England states," notes Howard Jones, "Connecticut was perhaps the most hostile to the abolitionists," *Mutiny on the Amistad,* 99. For historical review see Morse, *Neglected Period.* See also Mitchell, "Slavery in Connecticut."

28. Newspaper accounts from New Haven and Hartford (cited in the *New York Commercial Advertiser,* 12 February 1840, 2) commented liberally on the suspicious vessel, the USS *Grampus.* The vessel had been deterred from its normal duties along the West African coast, where it served as part of the U.S. policy of commitment against the African slave trade, to berth in the New London harbor on an undeclared mission. The Hartford *Patriot and Democrat* cited the *Grampus* as an example of the federal government's ominous involvement in the Amistad case. The New Haven *Herald*'s equally open curiosity further fuelled the unsupported rumors. The *Grampus*'s clandestine mission was confirmed in a letter to the Secretary of the Navy by Secretary of State John Forsyth on 2 January 1840. Also see Giddings, *Amistad Claim,* 2.

29. Although the presence of the *Grampus* confirmed the government's collusion with Spain, abolitionists were prepared for any eventuality. See H. Jones, *Mutiny on the Amistad,* 199–200.

30. See the AMA collection for John Dougall's letter of 26 April 1841, at the ARC.

31. Years later, Justice Taney did in fact preside over the infamous Dred Scott trial. See Benton, *Dred Scott Case* and Fehrenbacher, *Dred Scott Case.*

32. See Giddings, *Amistad Claim,* 1–7.

33. Kali to Adams, 4 January 1841 (Adams, "Letterbook").

34. For arguments in the *Antelope* case, see Wheaton, *Reports of Cases Argued* 10, no. 66 (1825): 70–114; for a contextual account, see Noonan, *Antelope*. For references to the *Antelope* during the Amistad trial, see Baldwin's argument of 21 September 1839 in *Amistad Captives*, 39, and *Argument of JQA*, 116–34.

35. See Baldwin, *Argument*, 9.

36. *Argument of JQA*, 16–17.

37. Baldwin to Adams, 9 March 1841 (Adams, "Letterbook").

38. Tappan to Adams, 9 March 1841 (Adams, "Letterbook").

39. These contributions are somewhat reflected in bookkeeping records, receipts, and letters of support from various organizations and individuals that are on file in the AMA collection at the ARC.

40. Cable, *Black Odyssey*, 123.

41. See DeBoer, *Be Jubilant My Feet*, 82. DeBoer's path-breaking work on black abolitionism is grounded in the larger context of American abolitionism.

42. DeBoer, *Be Jubilant My Feet*, 104.

43. Owens, *Black Mutiny*, 309.

44. C. Martin, *Amistad Affair*, 219.

45. Kromer, *Amistad Revolt*, 80, 89.

46. Sengbe's testimony, U.S. District Court records for Connecticut, 8 January 1840, 19–20; and Barber, *Amistad Captives*, 9. There was a constant attempt by the prosecution to sabotage the words of the defense team and its clients; see, for example, *Emancipator*, 11 February 1841, in which "Cinquez" was said to be "stained with crime."

47. Barber, *Amistad Captives*, 9.

Chapter Two. Slave Revolts and the Production of Identity

1. For research on the social aspects of the self and intergroup relationships, see Singelis, "Measurement of . . . Self-Construals"; see also the following articles: Triandis, et al., "Individualism and Collectivism"; Markus, et al., "Role of the Self-Concept"; and Brewer and Gardner, "Who Is This 'We'?"

2. See Brewer and Gardner, "Who Is This 'We'?" 85.

3. Goffman, *Presentation of Self in Everyday Life*. See especially chapters 1 and 2.

4. According to Goffman, the "team" on stage intensively interacts with each other on the basis of a prepared text (*Presentation of Self in Everyday Life*, 149). For interdependence in the master/slave relationship, also see Genovese, *Roll Jordan Roll*, 146–49.

5. Genovese, *Roll Jordan Roll*, 77–105, 169. In a later study (*Encounters*), Goffman focuses on games as an expression of social interaction, 17–81.

6. In this chapter, I regard dramatic action as an act or event, whereas dramatic interaction is the continued impelling of events spawned by a dramatic act or event.

7. Davis, *Slave Power Conspiracy and the Paranoid Style,* 59 (emphasis added).

8. Genovese, *From Rebellion to Revolution,* 1–50.

9. Merk's comprehensive text, *Manifest Destiny and Mission in American History,* examines the United States's remapping of itself as a nation. In 1840 it was a divine obligation to expand northward, southward, and westward beyond the union's boundaries, so as to conquer the Gulf nations and to colonize the West Indies. In the debates that followed, the plans for expansion were either promoted or hindered relative to the debate on slavery and racial integration. See especially chapters 8 and 9. Also see Hietala, *Manifest Design,* chapters 1 and 8; Wienberg, *Manifest Destiny,* chapters 1 and 2.

10. For British exploitation of the French Revolution, see Saint-Méry, *Considérations,* 4–19; Edwards, *History Civil and Commercial,* 19–67; Garrett, *French Colonial Question,* 92–99. For debates on implications, see *Parliamentary History of England,* 27: 646–47; Murray, *West Indies and the Development of Colonial Government,* 4.

11. Kenrick, *Horrors of Slavery,* 38–40; Bourne, *Book and Slavery Irreconcilable,* 58–65, 114–18; Davis, *Problem of Slavery in the Age of Revolution,* chapter 7.

12. Edwards, *History Civil and Commercial,* 68–98.

13. See Jordan, *White over Black,* 399–402.

14. In *Violence in the Black Imagination,* a collection of nineteenth-century texts, Ronald Takaki illustrates the equation of the suicidal mission of slave revolts with freedom. Gilroy, in *Black Atlantic,* 63–68, analyzes death as a social statement of freedom, especially in reference to Douglass's *Heroic Slave.* Also see L. F. Goldstein, "Violence as an Instrument of Social Change," part 1.

15. See Trouillot's path-breaking essay, "From Planters' Journals to Academia," 86. This article reappears as "An Unthinkable History: The Haitian Revolution as a Non-event" in his major work, *Silencing the Past,* 70–107.

16. Trouillot, "From Planters' Journals to Academia," 93.

17. For a general history of the French revolution and its ties to Saint Domingue, see Stoddard, *French Revolution in San Domingo;* Davis, *Problem of Slavery in the Age of Revolution,* chapters 2 and 3; James, *Black Jacobins.*

18. Trouillot, "From Planters' Journals to Academia," 84–85.

19. Hobsbawm's *Age of Revolution* pays only lip service to the Haitian revolution, which is treated as a peripheral event, a colonial uprising, compared to the major revolutionary struggles in Europe and America. Davis's *Problem of Slavery in the Age of Revolution* attacks the paradox of institutional slavery in an era of revolutionary thinking. Davis presents Haiti as an important factor in Western de-

bates on slavery, but he does not focus on Haiti as an evolving revolution in its own right.

20. For history of Saint Domingue, see Ott, *Haitian Revolution;* Trouillot, *Silencing the Past;* Blackburn, *Overthrow of Colonial Slavery.*

21. Curtin, "Declaration of the Rights of Man in Saint-Domingue," 162.

22. In both historical and literary coverage, Toussaint's successful leadership of the revolt in Saint Domingue has received respectable attention, and the brief reflection here is not meant to diminish the significance of this record. For a history of Toussaint's rise and fall, see Tyson, ed., *Toussaint L'Ouverture;* Blackburn, *Overthrow of Colonial Slavery;* Nicholls, *Haiti in Caribbean Context.* For literary works on Toussaint, see Bell, *All Soul's Rising* (fiction); Glissant, *Monsieur Toussaint* (drama); James, *Black Jacobins* (drama); Lamartine, *Toussaint Louverture* (poetry).

23. Halasz, *Rattling Chains,* 75.

24. Coffin, *Slave Insurrections,* 10–13.

25. Genovese, *From Rebellion to Revolution,* 36. While creating a measure of autonomy in the Maroon communities, these treaties weakened resolve to go beyond the original context to that of independence and full nationhood (92).

26. Genovese, *From Rebellion to Revolution,* 36.

27. For an in-depth study of Gabriel Prosser's insurrection, see Egerton, *Gabriel's Rebellion. See* also Sidbury, *Ploughshares into Swords.*

28. Genovese, *From Rebellion to Revolution,* 92.

29. *Boston Gazette,* 6 October 1800; cited in Coffin, *Slave Insurrections,* 25–26.

30. Aptheker, *American Negro Slave Revolts,* 222. There are no references indicating that the escaped slaves were ever recaptured.

31. See Coffin, *Slave Insurrections,* 28; Aptheker, *American Negro Slave Revolts,* 29.

32. Sundquist, *Hammers of Creation,* 114.

33. Higginson, *Black Rebellion,* 82.

34. For an in-depth reading of Denmark Vesey's attempted insurrection, see L. J. Edwards, *Denmark Vesey;* Lofton, *Denmark Vesey's Revolt;* Starobin, ed., *Denmark Vesey.*

35. Hamilton, comp., *Account of the Late Intended Insurrection,* 9.

36. Higginson, *Black Rebellion,* 109.

37. Hamilton, *Account of the Late Intended Insurrection,* 6, 23.

38. Higginson, *Black Rebellion,* 121.

39. Hamilton, *Account of the Late Intended Insurrection,* 39.

40. Halasz, *Rattling Chains,* 133.

41. Edelman, *Symbolic Uses of Politics,* 5–6. Edelman's discussion of the function of remoteness in both referential and condensation symbols helped put in

context the symbolic potency of Saint Domingue in the political imaginary of American slave discourse.

42. For readings on Nat Turner, see Tragle, comp., *Nat Turner's Slave Revolt—1831;* Gray, *Confessions of Nat Turner.*

43. Gray, *Confessions of Nat Turner,* 54.

44. Halasz, *Rattling Chains,* 165, 173.

45. Higginson, *Black Rebellion,* 174, 176, 212–13.

46. John Blassingame, "Some Precursors of the *Amistad* Revolt," 27–29.

47. For example, the Kru from southeastern Liberia, referred to as "Krumen" in Sierra Leone, were usually professional seamen who often communicated between slave ships and traders on shore. They could easily have been one source of information on slave ship rebellions. See A. Jones, *From Slaves to Palm Kernels,* 45.

48. See for instance, Sengbe's dramatization of the horrors onboard the *Tecora* during his testimony, U.S. District Court records for Connecticut, 8 January 1840, 19–20.

49. See Channing, *Duty of the Free States.* Also see Sale, *Slumbering Volcano,* 120–45.

50. Herman Melville's "Benito Cereno" has been reviewed extensively by a number of scholars in Robert Buckholder, *Critical Essays on Herman Melville's "Benito Cereno."*

51. Delano, *Narrative of Voyages and Travels,* 318–31.

52. Karcher, "Riddle of the Sphinx," 200.

53. Melville's description of the *San Dominick,* as Karcher points out, is very similar to newspaper accounts of *La Amistad.* See Karcher, "Riddle of the Sphinx," 200; also see Barber, *Amistad Captives,* 3–5.

54. Sundquist, *Hammers of Creation,* 115.

55. Sundquist, *Hammers of Creation,* 94.

56. Melville, "Benito Cereno," 165.

57. Melville, "Benito Cereno," 214.

58. See Kaplan, "Herman Melville and the American National Sin: The Meaning of 'Benito Cereno,'" 45, 46; also see Sundquist, "*Benito Cereno* and New World Slavery," 156.

59. See Karcher, "Riddle of the Sphinx," 211.

60. Delano, *Narrative of Voyages and Travels,* 347.

61. Melville, "Benito Cereno," 237–38.

62. Critics who have examined Melville's text from this angle are Adler, "*Benito Cereno:* Slavery and Violence in Americas"; Schiffman, "Critical Problems in Melville's 'Benito Cereno'"; Karcher, *Shadow over the Promised Land,* 109–59. Karcher takes the same position in "Riddle of the Sphinx."

63. Melville, "Benito Cereno," 257.

64. See for instance, Katz, *Breaking the Chains,* 45–66; Coffin, *Slave Insurrections,* 10–11; Halasz, *Rattling Chains,* 28–29.

65. Higginson, *Black Rebellion,* 93–94.

66. Both northern and southern whites were sympathetic with the American Colonization society for diverse reasons. See Hinks, *To Awaken My Afflicted Brethren,* 202–10.

67. Hinks, To Awaken my Afflicted Brethren, 242.

Chapter Three. The Amistad Returnees and the Mende Mission

1. For history of the slave trade see Thomas, *Slave Trade;* Willis, ed., *Slaves and Slavery in Muslim Africa;* Manning, *Slavery and African Life;* Finkleman, ed., *Slave Trade and Migration;* Klein, *Middle Passage;* Davidson, *Africa in History.*

2. There were numerous antislavery voices on both sides of the Atlantic. Among these were Lloyd Garrison, Olaudah Equiano, Frederick Douglass, and William Wilberforce. Specifically, the Sierra Leone Company, an antislavery movement that was concerned about the increasing numbers of black poor in England, successfully voiced its position in the British parliament. For a comprehensive history of the company, see Fyfe, *History of Sierra Leone,* chapters 1–5. See also part 3 of Utting, *Story of Sierra Leone.*

3. The settler community had sided with the slave traders, who complained about the activities of the regent. A British ship thus destroyed one of King Jimmy's town. In retaliation, King Jimmy attacked British subjects—the settlers—by burning down their town.

4. See Olaudah, *Interesting Narrative and Other Writings,* 220–36, 325–51; Cuguano, *Thoughts and Sentiments on the Evil of Slavery,* 104–6; Fyfe, *History of Sierra Leone,* 13.

5. See Fyfe, *History of Sierra Leone,* 13–58.

6. On the impact of Islam, see Davidson, *Africa in History,* 125–39; Fyfe, *A Short History of Sierra Leone,* 14–16; Raboteau, *Slave Religion,* 5–6. On the early Christian effort, see Fyfe, *History of Sierra Leone,* 2–5; Raboteau, *Slave Religion,* 7–9. A Jesuit priest, Father Balthasar Barreira, had settled in Sierra Leone in 1605 and succeeded in baptizing several kings in the region. But because the people generally were not compelled by their kings to convert to Christianity, years of service by Barreira and other Jesuit priests who later came to the region resulted in very few conversions. French and Portugese capuchins were also known to traverse the West African coast in the seventeenth century.

7. The Aku community was generally the exception. Akus sent their children to Koranic schools and maintained their own Moslem religion. In other ways, Akus were fully integrated into the colonial culture.

8. See Cable, *Black Odyssey*, 148–49. Cable is one of very few American authors who analyzes documents from the Mende mission.

9. See Keller, et al., *Creation of Rights of Sovereignty through Symbolic Acts 1400–1800*. Mudimbe also takes this position in *Invention of Africa*, 44–97. Also see his discussion of the "politics of conversion" in *Idea of Africa*, 105–53. Also see Christopher, *Colonial Africa*, 64–87.

10. Mudimbe, *Invention of Africa*, 47. The contradictions of Christianity in the European enslavement of Africans in the New World also had its parallels in the oppression of native Americans and the rhetoric of Manifest Destiny that sanctioned the appropriation of their lands. See Axtell, *Invasion Within*. Also see Mulford, "Resisting Colonialism."

11. Cable, *Black Odyssey*, 148–49.

12. The main reference source for the letters is the Sierra Leone folder, Box 199, AMA archives at the ARC.

13. For example, Jones, *Mutiny on the Amistad;* Martin, *All We Want is Make Us Free;* Zeinert, *Amistad Slave Revolt*.

14. Owens, *Black Mutiny;* C. Martin, *Amistad Affair*.

15. See DeBoer, *Be Jubilant My Feet;* Beard, *A Crusade of Brotherhood: A History of the American Missionary Association*, 33–48.

16. For instance, a Mende scholar of history and linguistics, Konrad Tuchscherer (Boston University), shared with me his identification of a letter written by A. W. Bayfield to the British and Foreign Bible Society (London) dated April 10, 1917. Bayfield's letter records his visit to the mission and his encounter with an Amistad African who was about 100 years old at the time, "who remembers a great deal of what he saw in America." British and Foreign Bible Society Archives at Cambridge University, "W. African Languages," Box no. 1 (1916–1917). The letter indicates that the Africans remembered a great deal and spoke extensively about their experiences abroad.

17. Raymond to Amistad committee, 23 July 1846, Sierra Leone folder, Box 199, AMA archives ; emphasis added.

18. After 1882 the AMA handed over its program to the United Brethren in Christ (UBC) denomination in Sierra Leone to focus more efficiently on its work among minority groups in the United States.

19. Pieh to Lewis, 13 January 1842, Sierra Leone folder, Box 199, AMA archives. The letter was written onboard the *Gentleman*.

20. Raymond to Tappan, January 1842, Sierra Leone folder, Box 199, AMA archives.

21. Steele to Tappan, 1 February 1842, Sierra Leone folder, Box 199, AMA archives.

22. Raymond to Tappan, 21 December 1843, Sierra Leone folder, Box 199, AMA archives.

23. Steele, 21 December 1843, Sierra Leone folder, Box 199, AMA archives.

24. For an excellent examination of the slave wars in Mendeland, see Abraham, *Mende Government and Politics under Colonial Rule*, 1–30. Abraham reminds us that Mende warfare was not just about the slave trade; it also had its basis in legitimate political conflicts.

25. Raymond to Tappan(?), 9 October 1845, Sierra Leone folder, Box 199, AMA archives.

26. Raymond to Tappan, 9 February 1846, Sierra Leone folder, Box 199, AMA archives.

27. Raymond would later learn that Luiz, the dealer of Lomboko, was still a formidable force in the area. Raymond to Tappan, 9 December 1843, Sierra Leone folder, Box 199, AMA archives.

28. Amistad Executive committee, minutes on death of William Raymond, 14 March 1848, 6, Sierra Leone folder, Box 199, AMA archives.

29. Raymond to Amistad committee, 23 July 1846, Sierra Leone folder, Box 199, AMA archives. Also see Cable, *Black Odyssey*, 142.

30. Raymond to Tappan(?), 9 October 1845, Sierra Leone folder, Box 199, AMA archives.

31. Raymond to Tappan, 9 February 1846, Sierra Leone folder, Box 199, AMA archives.

32. See a related discussion of the effects of colonialism in the Third World in Bhabha, "The Other Question: The Stereotype and Colonial Discourse," 35.

33. See Osagie, "Amistad Affair and the Nation of Sierra Leone: The Dramatic Return of Memory," 161.

34. Abraham, *Mende Government and Politics under Colonial Rule*, 172–76.

35. Raymond to Tappan, 14 December 1846, Sierra Leone folder, Box 199, AMA archives.

36. In a letter dated July 23, 1846, Raymond explained some of the redemptions he transacted and also gave more insight into the principal slave economy of the country because he was well aware of the controversies he was generating in the United States.

37. James Will, a native merchant "who had supplied the mission with goods," sent a letter to the AMA on December 9, 1847, describing the nature of Raymond's death ("black vomit"). Kagne, one of the three Amistad girls, also died of yellow fever two weeks after Raymond's death.

38. Thompson was supposed to partner with another missionary, Brother Carter, a former schoolmate with whom he had reunited in New York months earlier, to run the mission house. Unfortunately, Carter, who had proceeded him, succumbed to sickness within eight days of Thompson's arrival in Sherbro country. Thompson arrived on July 22, 1848.

39. Thompson to Whipple, 10 August 1848, Sierra Leone folder, Box 199, AMA archives.

40. Thompson to Caulker, 3 December 1848, Sierra Leone folder, Box 199, AMA archives.

41. Thompson to Whipple, 30 January 1848, Sierra Leone folder, Box 199, AMA archives.

42. See DeBoer, *Be Jubilant my Feet,* 124–36. Her chapter on the Mende mission reviews the achievements of both Tucker and Root, 103–52.

43. Abraham, *Amistad Revolt,* 23.

44. DeBoer, *Be Jubilant My Feet,* 140.

45. *American Missionary,* 7, September 1853, 89.

46. *American Missionary,* 1, October 1846, 8.

47. Abraham, *Amistad Revolt,* 22.

Chapter Four. Sculpting History: African American Burdens of Memory

1. The $2.8 million replica of the slave ship *La Amistad* at Mystic Seaport was commissioned by the State of Connecticut.

2. Owens, *Black Mutiny,* viii.

3. For instance, C. Martin, *Amistad Affair,* and Cable, *Black Odyssey.*

4. Owens, *Black Mutiny,* 311.

5. Jones, *Mutiny on the Amistad,* 12.

6. Jones, "Mutiny on the *Amistad:* 'All We Want is Make Us Free,'" 21, 22.

7. See Cable, *Black Odyssey,* 37–38.

8. Dodson's play, *Amistad,* can be found in manuscript form in the James Weldon Johnson collection at Beneicke Library, Yale University.

9. "Twoness" and "second sight" carry the connotation of doubleness, or intuitive survival skills, in African Americans' relations with whites. See the introductory chapter in Du Bois, *Souls of Black Folk.*

10. I have in mind William Andrews's *To Tell a Free Story,* which examines the performative and oratorical modes of the slave narrative genre. In chapter 1, specifically, Andrews discusses various rhetorical strategies that escaped slaves employed not only to "write" themselves into history but also to create texts that manipulated the expectations of their white audiences.

11. Hay, *African American Theatre,* 15–26. Hay uses the inner life–outer life debate to schematize the differing positions of Alain Locke and Du Bois, respectively. Whereas the former emphasized the need for aesthetic authenticity in black drama, the inner life, the latter was consumed with the need to define theater as "a cultural tool for gaining political and economic rights" (21). See also Sanders, *Development of Black Theatre in America,* 1–18. Exploring theater models from

the 1920s through the 1960s, Sanders outlines the uncertain but progressive configuration of black identity through drama.

12. In essence, the debates on the place and purpose of black theater have been necessary in promoting strategies to enable its survival.

13. Morrison expresses this opinion in several filmed interviews as well as in her later novels, *Beloved, Jazz,* and *Paradise.* Her overarching theme is that African Americans can never circumvent, and must therefore come to terms with, their history. To deny the past is to deny one's identity, which proceeds from that past. See also her essay "Memory, Creation, and Writing," *Thought* 59 (1984): 385–90.

14. Loftus, *Memory: Surprising Insights into How We Remember and Why We Forget,* 67.

15. Gilroy, *Black Atlantic,* 189.

16. This position is implied in the theoretical construction of African and African American history in a text such as Asante's *Afrocentricity.*

17. Ronald Takaki's preface in his expanded edition of *Violence in the Black Imagination* succinctly summarizes African American responses to recent incidents of racial injustice.

18. Du Bois, "Krigwa Players Little Negro Theatre," 134.

19. In an attempt to capture the breadth of dramaturgical practices available to the black stage, I use the terms "drama" and "theater" interchangeably. Although theoretical distinctions have been made between these two mimetic modes, the cataloging of plays into subgenres is often impractical in terms of the modern stage. See Horn, "Ritual Drama and the Theatrical," 181–202; Soyinka, "From a Common Backcloth," 7–14.

20. Such artists include Alice Dunbar Nelson (1875–1935), Georgia Douglas Johnson (1886–1966), Willis Richardson (1889–1977), and Randolph Edmonds (1900–1983).

21. See Cockrell, *Demons of Disorder.*

22. Johnson, "Dilemma of the Negro Author," 477.

23. See Brown-Guillory, *Their Place on the Stage,* 19–20, 27.

24. For example, see plays by Willis Richardson, *The Flight of the Natives,* and Lorraine Hansberry, *The Drinking Gourd.*

25. William Branch's *In Splendid Error* is a good example.

26. Hill, "Revolutionary Tradition in Black Drama," 408.

27. Jones, "Community and Commentators," 69.

28. I use "performance" here in the sense that Joseph Roach uses it in his theorization of circum-atlantic performative memories in "Culture and Performance in the Circum-Atlantic World," 46.

29. Roach, "Culture and Performance in the Circum-Atlantic World," 46.

30. Owen Dodson was a formidable playwright, director, and poet. He was Professor of Drama at Howard University for over twenty-five years. For a comprehensive account of his life and work, see Hatch, *Sorrow is the Only Faithful One.*

31. Hatch, *Sorrow is the Only Faithful One,* 60.

32. Hatch, *Sorrow is the Only Faithful One,* 60.

33. It is difficult to discern how many scenes are in *Amistad.* Among Dodson's notes, an index card lists seven scenes and a dinner menu card lists eight. However, the *Amistad* script itself includes only five scenes. I nonetheless believe that several clues from the manuscript suggest eight scenes as Dodson's ultimate preference. The number of curtain falls in the play (he used these throughout the play as scene markers), the changed numbering system after a certain curtain fall in Scene five, and the different color ink used in the later sections of the manuscript all seem to confirm this.

34. See epigraph to Dodson's second draft of *Amistad,* Box 1, Folder 31, JWJ Collection, Beneicke Library, Yale University.

35. Dodson, *Amistad,* 2.

36. *New York Commercial Advertiser,* 10 January 1840, 19–20. Also see Jones, *Mutiny,* 123–24.

37. Dodson, *Amistad,* 12.

38. Dodson, *Amistad,* 36–37.

39. Dodson uses the "jungle star" imagery in his earlier play, *Divine Comedy,* in which Africa is recalled through a long history of ruptured memory:

Can we repeat
The legends of three hundred years
The fears
The terrors
The broken moons
The fallen jungle stars?
(347)

"Jungle star" seems to symbolize hope in the African past.

40. Paul Gilroy comments on death as an emancipating tool in *Black Atlantic,* 63.

41. Dodson, *Amistad,* 43.

42. Dodson, *Amistad,* 64.

43. Dodson, *Amistad,* 75.

44. Trouillot makes a clear distinction between Western ideas of revolt and revolution in historical representations; see "From Planters' Journals to Academia: The Haitian Revolution as Unthinkable History."

45. Dodson, "Who Has Seen The Wind? Playwrights and the Black Experience," 109.

46. The criticism levied by an unidentified critic (Box 1, Folder 31, JWJ Collection, Beneicke Library, Yale University) that "in general, the dramatic element of struggle seems to need strengthening in order not to be overshadowed by the lyric element" and that "the narrator needs to be freed from carrying too much of the burden of the plot in order to perform his true function an interpreter" seems unjustified. Dodson's lyricism is innovative; he is not at all overdependent on the plot for interpretation.

47. Cinque reads Psalm 124 from the King James Version of the Holy Bible.

48. Dodson, *Amistad*, scene 5. The manuscript pages are unnumbered at this point.

49. The main character of Dodson's *Divine Comedy*, the Apostle of Light, is based on Father Divine, an African American self-proclaimed prophet, who in his festive approach to religion creatively met the physical needs of those living in Harlem. For the story of Father Divine, see Weisbrot, *Father Divine and the Struggle for Racial Equality;* Watts, *God, Harlem U.S.A.;* Burham, *God Comes to America.*

50. For history of the Great Depression, see Norton, et al., *A People and A Nation,* 429–50. For effects of the Great Depression on American theater and drama, see Goldstein, *Political Stage,* especially chapter 9 on the Federal Theatre Project, 241–99.

51. Dodson's personal notes, Box 1, Folder 31, JWJ Collection, Beneicke Library, Yale University.

52. Dodson's biographer, James Hatch, considers this line of poetry the most memorable, and perhaps the most fitting, in Dodson's long, undulated history of failures and successes. See Hatch, *Sorrow is the Only Faithful One,* 298.

53. Despite the touted opportunities of the North, Du Bois and most of the "talented tenth" community had to go South in search of respectable jobs in black communities.

54. For a contemporary reading of the theater today, see Hill, ed., *Theater of Black Americans.* Also see Euba, *Archetypes, Imprecators, and Victims of Fate,* especially his diasporic reading of satire in "Drama of Epidemic," 121–61. Thorpe's play also reflects the aesthetic qualities of the postmodern theater. For a description of postmodern drama see Watt, *Post/Modern Drama: Reading the Contemporary Stage,* 1–13.

55. Thorpe examines both geopolitical and cross-racial collaborations in the economic network of slavery.

56. The concept of "in-between time" is borrowed from Homi Bhabha who uses the term to indicate the ambivalence that resides in the intersecting moments

or boundaries among cultures, races, locations, etc. See in particular his essay "Dissemination: Time, Narrative and the Margins of the Modern Nation" in *Location of Culture*. Another artist who, like Thorpe, uses the postmodern notion of "in-between time" is Charles Johnson, who deploys this complex strategy in his novels, *Oxherding Tale* and *Middle Passage*. Johnson's heroes survive through an uncanny ability to fit into different cultural spaces and times.

57. Expression borrowed from Gilroy, *Black Atlantic*, 198.

58. My analysis reflects a close reading of the manuscript and my impressions of performances of the play. The play was performed for two consecutive weeks in February and March 1997. *Chap Am So* is a two-act play requiring thirty-six character parts in its fifteen-scene format. The play was produced by Network of Cultural Centers of Color (NCCC) then housed at the Harry De Jur Playhouse in New York City and codirected by John Thorpe and Lorna Harris. *Chap Am So* was directed by Julius Spencer, a theater arts professor at the University of Sierra Leone who happened to have been a resident fellow at Boston University for the 1996–1997 academic year.

59. Thorpe makes a political choice in naming the Amistad hero "Sengbe" rather than "Joseph Cingue" (or any of its derivatives).

60. Thorpe, *Chap Am So*, 3.

61. Thorpe, *Chap Am So*, 3.

62. See Roach, "Culture and Performance in the Circum-Atlantic World," 47. Roach juxtaposes social memory (i.e., bodily knowledge [dance, performance, etc.] and other iconographic mediations of culture) against history (i.e., textual, archival knowledge), which seems to discredit the act of memory itself.

63. For a discussion of the perception of the "black mind" in Herman Melville's "Benito Cereno," see chapter 2.

64. Thorpe, *Chap Am So*, 13.

65. Thorpe, *Chap Am So*, 6.

66. See Jones, *From Slaves to Palm Kernels*, 43. Jones gives the names of white slave dealers who were operating in the Gallinas area between 1806 and 1849. Pedro Blanco (or Blango in *Chap Am So*) and Jozé Alvarez are included.

67. Thorpe, *Chap Am So*, 6.

68. Hegel expounds upon this point in *Hegel's Phenomenology of Spirit*, 111–19, 211–35. Many scholars have applied this discourse to master-slave relationships. For example, Davis's use of Hegel in his discussion of Toussaint L'Ouverture in *Problem of Slavery in the Age of Revolution* (39–40, 557–64) is particularly relevant to my reference to Hegel here.

69. Maggie Montesinos Sale has done an excellent study of black masculinity and the production of identity on American slave ship revolts, *Slumbering Volcano*. See my review of her work in *CLA Journal*.

70. Thorpe, *Chap Am So,* 6.

71. Alex Haley's position in *Roots* and Alain Locke's definition of historical consciousness in *The New Negro* parallel Thorpe's depiction here. Multiple positions and responses are characteristic of racial relations.

72. Testimony of Grabeau, Monday, 7 October 1839, in *African Captives,* v; also see Barber, *Amistad Captives,* 3–6.

73. Thorpe, *Chap Am So,* 15, 22.

74. For some examples of arbitrary laws and other tricks adopted to acquire slaves, see Jones, *From Slaves to Palm Kernel,* 45–50.

75. See Barber, *Amistad Captives,* 9–15.

76. See Genovese's reference to the practice of divide-and-rule in the slave-holding world, *Roll Jordan Roll,* 6

77. Thorpe, *Chap Am So,* 18.

78. A direct translation of "Chap am so" is "chopped," or "cut up," or "slaughtered like this" (the words must be followed by the action of killing). In a sense, "Chap am so" means fight back or resist the enemy.

79. This information is based on an interview with the president of the Amistad committee, Alfred Marder. The Amistad committee was formed in 1988 as a nonprofit organization. It currently has over one hundred members. In 1990 a special Amistad memorial committee was selected to oversee the Amistad project. The members were Barbara Hudson, consultant; Sylvia Boone, art historian; George Bellinger, president of the African American Historical Society; and Nathan Campbell, a journalist and advocate.

80. William Cinqué Henderson, Jr., expresses his ambivalence toward his middle name, by which he is generally known in family circles (see "Making a Name"). Another example is that of Donald David DeFreeze who as leader of the Symbionese Liberation Army (SLA), an antigovernment guerrilla group based in California, adopted the revolutionary title "Cingue Mtume" in 1974 as a form of protest. See Osagie, "*Amistad* Revolt Revisited." Also see Hearst, *Trial of Patty Hearst* and *Every Secret Thing.*

81. For example, in 1970, Random House published a collection of essays on black history and culture in a work titled *Amistad.* Henry Louis Gates and Kwame Anthony Appiah have also edited scholarly articles on artists, such as Alice Walker, Zora Neale Hurston, Richard Wright, Langston Hughes, and Toni Morrison, under the Amistad Literary Series (1993) distributed by Penguin.

82. The review here is based on a telephone interview with Ed Hamilton, which incidentally was conducted on his birthday.

83. See Bloch, "Washington Crossing the Delaware," 101.

84. Osagie, Interview with Ed Hamilton.

85. Chapter 2 discusses the changed circumstances of the African returnees to Sierra Leone.

86. Unlike artists such as Anish Kapoor who excel in the art of blankness or "resident narratives" (see Homi Bhabha's compelling essay on the valuable phenomenological lessons of emptiness, in *Anish Kapoor*, 27), Hamilton generally overdetermines the narrative content of his sculptures. Hamilton's later project approximating the narrative fullness of the 1992 Amistad monument is the African American Civil War Memorial in Washington, D.C., dedicated July 18, 1998.

87. Cable, *Black Odyssey*, 122–24; Barber, *Amistad Captives*, 77; Jones, *Mutiny on the Amistad*, 203; Wyatt-Brown, *Lewis Tappan and the Evangelical War against Slavery*, 217.

88. For Louisville history, see Wright, *History of Blacks in Kentucky: In Pursuit of Equality, 1890–1980*, volume 2.

Chapter Five. National Identity:
The Dramatic Return of Memory in Sierra Leone

1. See Schwartz, et al. "Recovery of Masada: A Study of Collective Memory," 148.

2. Schwartz, "Social Change and Collective Memory," 221.

3. Schwartz, et al. "Recovery of Masada," 149.

4. Maines, et al. "Sociological Import of G. H. Mead's Theory of the Past," 161.

5. Mead, *Philosophy of the Present*, 12, 95. Also see Halbwachs, *On Collective Memory*, 40; Mead, *Philosophy of the Act*, 81. These foundational texts on collective memory assert that the extent to which a society understands its past determines how that society constructs its present values.

6. See Clifton Johnson's contribution in Driskell's *Amistad II: Afro American Art*, 15.

7. Schwartz, "Social Change and Collective Memory," 222.

8. Sibthorpe, *History of Sierra Leone*, 125.

9. Alie, *New History of Sierra Leone*, 145–46.

10. The youth of Sierra Leone today remain the noticeable exception to the self-cynicism that plagued earlier generations. They have rejected the all-too-familiar portrait of Bai Bureh in a meditative and defeatist posture for a Bai Bureh that is a dynamic, conquering hero. Like Sengbe Pieh, Bai Bureh is one of the heroes represented in the ongoing cultural awakening. His portrait graces the one thousand Leone bank note.

11. Fanon, *Black Skins, White Masks*, 141.

12. Desouza George, *Broken Handcuff or Give Me Free*, 32.

13. Many Amistad Africans were caught in a clash of two cultures. They could not accept the missionaries' stringent rules, so antithetical to their own, and they were no longer wholly satisfied with their own traditions. Thus, they vacillated

between the mission and their hometowns. Some resolved this crisis by moving close to the mission.

14. On African drama and its context in the oral tradition, see Ogunba and Irele, *Theatre in Africa;* Etherton, *Development of African Drama;* Jeyifo, *Truthful Lie;* Soyinka, *Myth, Literature and the African World;* Okpewho, *African Oral Literature;* Conteh-Morgan, *Theatre and Drama in Francophone Africa.* On the dramatic in oral literature, see Schipper, *Beyond the Boundaries.* See also Bauman, *Verbal Art as Performance.*

15. According to Joseph Roach, performance includes the theatrical, but also "embraces a much wider range of human behaviors," "Culture and Performance in the Circum-Atlantic World," 46. See also Certeau, *Practice of Everyday Life,* 91–110.

16. Jeyifo, *Truthful Lie,* 105–18.

17. For a reading on theater for development studies, see Kamlongera, *Theatre for Development in Africa with Case Studies from Malawi and Zambia.*

18. Morrison, "Forum Theater in West Africa," 31.

19. Mlama, "Women's Participation in 'Communication for Development': The Popular Alternative in Africa," 43.

20. This workshop was a 1986 UNICEF project. Mlama, "Women's Participation in 'Communication for Development': The Popular Alternative in Africa," 45.

21. Freetong Players Theatre Group Publication, *Telem Newsletter* (July 1994), 3.

22. Haffner, *Amistad Kata Kata,* and Raymond Desouza George, *Broken Handcuff or Give Me Free.* Both are unpublished scripts.

23. Osagie, Interview with Charlie Haffner.

24. Haffner, *Amistad Kata Kata,* 1–2.

25. Williams, "Towards a Theory of Cultural Production in Africa," 11.

26. Haffner, *Amistad Kata Kata,* 3.

27. Haffner, *Amistad Kata Kata,* 16, 17.

28. This derogatory, even sexist, reference to Joseph Momoh was based on the people's critique of his leadership as lacking firm, principled qualities. Momoh's administration was one of inaction, indecision, and indiscipline. It did not help matters that Momoh's rounded, rather chubby figure, which never evinced the portrait of an active soldier, not only drew much laughter from the people but also caused them to suspect that Siaka Stevens was still running the country from behind the scenes.

29. See Kabba, et al., *Sierra Leonean Heroes.*

30. Cartwright, *Political Leadership in Sierra Leone,* 226. On the dilemmas of independence and subsequent unenviable political practices, see Collier, *Sierra Leone: Experiment in Democracy in an African Nation,* 96–125.

31. "Unity, freedom, justice" are inscribed in the Sierra Leone coat of arms but are as yet unrealized. Until recently, this developing nation has been politically divided along ethnic lines. Continued looting of the national treasury, and the government's consequent moral degeneration, has denied the people any true sense of freedom and justice.

32. Opala, *Ecstatic Renovations!*, 10.

33. Opala, *Ecstatic Renovations!*, 14.

34. The play was finally completed in 1994. Following a performance in Freetown, the Aureol Players toured Edmonton, Victoria, and Vancouver, Canada, that same year. Like some of the earlier forerunners of performance culture—such as playwright Amadu Maddy, who predates Desouza George's generation; Dele Charley and John Kolosa Kargbo, who were both formidable playwrights and directors; and the playwright Shefumi Garber, who eventually left Sierra Leone for better prospects in the West—Desouza George has contributed to the development of culture in Sierra Leone.

35. Osagie, Interview with Raymond Desouza George.

36. Desouza George, *Broken Handcuff*, 2.

37. Kali to Adams, 4 January 1841 (Adams, "Letterbook").

38. Desouza George, *Broken Handcuff*, 31.

Chapter Six. Hollywood Images, African Memories:
Spielberg's *Amistad* and Sierra Leone Culture and Politics

1. See Rosten, *Hollywood: The Movie Colony, the Movie Makers.*

2. On the need for alternative visions, see Gabriel, *Third Cinema in the Third World;* also see Solanas and Getino, "Towards a Third Cinema," in Nichols, ed., *Movies and Methods,* 44–64. Also see M. T. Martin, ed., *Cinemas of the Black Diaspora,* especially 1–21. For revisions of Hollywood images, see Bakari and Cham, eds., *African Experiences of Cinema,* especially parts 2 and 4; M. T. Martin, ed., *Cinemas of the Black Diaspora;* Barlet, *Les Cinémas d'Afrique Noire;* Diawara, *African Cinema;* and Ukadike, *Black African Cinema.*

3. Gabriel, *Third Cinema in the Third World,* 3.

4. Works that contest Hollywood's hegemonic position have been quite numerous since the 1970s. See for example, Cripps, *Slow Fade to Black.* For more current writings, see Morley and Chen, eds., *Stuart Hall, Critical Dialogues in Cultural Studies;* see especially Julien and Mercer, "De Margin and De Centre," 450–64. Also see Cripps, *Making Movies Black;* Rosenbaum, *Movies as Politics;* Bogle, *Toms, Coons, Mulattoes, Mammies and Bucks.*

5. Powers, et al., in *Hollywood's America,* compare patterns of representation of whites and minorities in Hollywood films (see 172–87). Using violence as an indicator of positive or negative representation, the authors conclude that whites

are presented as more likely to resort to violence than blacks. This well-controlled representation of minorities, the authors admit, does not in fact reflect the varied, real-life experiences of blacks and other minorities (187).

6. See Lemisch's review of the film *Amistad*, "Black Agency in the *Amistad* Uprising." According to Lemisch, the nonideological position of Spielberg's narrative reintroduces "archaic themes" from the conservative fifties (57). Eric Foner also argues that *Amistad* tells us more about the nineties, a decade bereft of strong ideological politics, than about the political temper of the mid–nineteenth century ("Hollywood Invades the Classroom," A13).

7. The idea here is borrowed from Homi Bhabha's "The Other Question: The Stereotype and Colonial Discourse," in which he reads colonial discourse not in terms of the simple representation of images as either positive or negative, but as the intervention of "the *processes of subjectification* made possible and (plausible) through stereotypical discourse" (18). A revised version of Bhabha's essay appears in *Location of Culture*, 66–84.

8. See Chow's first chapter, "Seeing Modern China," 3–33, in *Woman and Chinese Modernity*, for an understanding of the relationships of power involved in the seemingly innocent act of watching a movie.

9. Schneider, "Advising Spielberg: A Career Studying the Amistad Rebellion," A12.

10. See Gans, "Hollywood Entertainment: Commerce or Ideology?" Also see Hall, et al., eds., "Encoding/decoding," in *Culture, Media, Language*, 128–38. Using V. N. Volosinov's analysis of class struggle through language in *Marxism and the Philosophy of Language*, Hall discusses the intervention of ideologies at the connotative level of the sign, 133.

11. Debbie Allen was, together with Spielberg, a coproducer of the movie *Amistad*. She is credited with selling the idea of the movie to Spielberg's Dream-Works.

12. Many who have been sympathetic to Spielberg have been so more from gratitude than from serious evaluations of the movie. This seems to confirm film critics' views that Spielberg's making a movie about black people is in itself satisfying. However, such rudimentary reactions will continue to forestall efforts either to examine such films with a critical eye or to challenge film makers to approach black themes with greater maturity. See Julien and Mercer, "De Margin and de Centre," 454–55.

13. The case was finally settled in a civil lawsuit in 1998.

14. See websites such as cnn.com/showbiz and the Internet Movie Database, December 1997–January 1998.

15. See Stulov, "Alexs D. Pate: 'The Slave is Just a Term,'" 116.

16. Lemisch, "Black Agency in the *Amistad* Uprising," 66.

17. Bhabha uses Paul Abbot's critique of recognition and visibility as a platform to discuss the ambivalent status of the stereotype in "Other Question," 31–32.

18. Chow, *Woman and Chinese Modernity,* 31.

19. Conversation in Spielberg's *Amistad.*

20. Foner, "Hollywood Invades the Classroom," A13.

21. Fontenot, "Black Misery, White Guilt and *Amistad,*" 10.

22. On the significance of iconography in the collective memory of a people, see Warner, *Living and the Dead;* Kammen's chapter, "Revolutionary Iconography in National Tradition," in *Season of Youth;* and B. Schwartz, "Social Context of Commemoration."

23. Opala, *Ecstatic Renovations!* 6.

24. Amateur photographer Tim Waites worked in Freetown from 1991 to 1993 and documented the street murals discussed here. He was a member of the Volunteers Overseas program in England.

25. An attire made entirely using traditional materials and technology.

26. Mural was painted by Amadou Tarawalie.

27. Schwartz, et al., "Recovery of Masada," 160.

28. For instance, the late President Siaka Stevens so feared the revolutionary potential of national symbols that he discouraged them. Instead, he built a cult of personality around himself during his unpopular administration.

29. For a comprehensive survey of the political history of post-independence Sierra Leone, see Cox, *Civil-Military Relations in Sierra Leone;* also see Collier, *Sierra Leone: Experiment in Democracy in an African Nation.*

30. See Opala, "Sierra Leone: The Politics of State Collapse," 15.

31. Ahmed Tejan Kabbah's democratically elected government was ousted by the Armed Forces Revolutionary Council in May 1997.

32. The *Kamajohs,* a native militia group, has been the only native group able to successfully resist both the military and the rebel forces. Supported militarily by the Nigerian-led ECOMOG forces, they are known to combine indigenous warrior tactics, traditional medicine, and unparalleled discipline in their defense of Mendeland.

33. The civil war in Sierra Leone has been described as "irregular warfare," probably because of the facelessness of the war (due to its seemingly endless disputes and factions) and the fact that paid mercenaries from the Ukraine, South Africa, and elsewhere have fought on all sides, thereby enlarging the conflict beyond its regional significance. Thus, political as well as material factors—namely, the exploitation of the diamond-rich sections of the country—have complicated the national crisis.

34. Opala, "Sierra Leone: The Politics of State Collapse," 22. Opala made a similar statement in July 1997 in an interview on *Fresh Air with Terry Gross,* titled "Escaping a Nation in Chaos."

Works Cited

Abraham, Arthur. *The Amistad Revolt*. Freetown: USIS, 1987.

——. *Mende Government and Politics under Colonial Rule: A Historical Study of Political Change in Sierra Leone, 1890–1937*. Freetown: Sierra Leone University Press, 1978.

——. "Sengbe Pieh." *Dictionary of African Biography*. 2: 141–44. Algonac, Mich.: Reference Publications, Inc., 1979.

Adams, John Quincy. "Letterbook 1839–1845." *The Adams Papers*. Boston: Massachusetts Historical Society, 1954.

Adler, Joyce S. "*Benito Cereno*: Slavery and Violence in the Americas." In *Critical Essays on Herman Melville's "Benito Cereno,"* 76–93. Edited by Robert Burkholder. New York: G.K. Hall, 1992.

The African Captives: Trial of the Prisoners of the "Amistad" on the Writ of Habeas Corpus before the Circuit Court of the United States for the District of Connecticut, at Hartford, Judges Thompson and Judson, September Term, 1839. New York: American Antislavery Society, 1839.

Alie, Joe. *A New History of Sierra Leone*. New York: St. Martin's Press, 1990.

American Missionary. In *Historical Summary of the American Missionary Association*. Edited by C. L. Woodworth. Boston, MA, 1878.

Andrews, William L. *To Tell a Free Story: The First Century of Afro-American Autobiography, 1760–1865*. Chicago: University of Illinois Press, 1986.

Aptheker, Herbert. *American Negro Slave Revolts*. New York: Columbia University Press, 1943.

Argument of John Quincy Adams before the Supreme Court of the United States. New York: S. W. Benedict, 1841.

Asante, Molefi Kete. *Afrocentricity*. Trenton, N.J.: Africa World Press, 1992.

Axtell, James. *The Invasion Within: The Contest of Cultures in Colonial North America*. New York: Oxford University Press, 1985.

Bakari, Imruh, and Mbye B. Cham, ed. *African Experiences of Cinema*. London: British Film Institute, 1996.

Baldwin, Roger Sherman. *Argument of Roger S. Baldwin, of New Haven, before the Supreme Court of the United States, in the case of the United States, Appellants, vs. Cinque, and others, Africans of the Amistad*. New York: S. W. Benedict, 1841.

Barber, John W. *A History of the Amistad Captives*. New Haven, Conn.: E. L. & J. W. Barber, 1840.

Barlet, Olivier. *Les Cinémas d'Afrique Noire: Le Regard en Question*. Paris: L'Harmattan, 1996.

Bauman, Richard. *Verbal Art as Performance*. Prospect Heights, Illinois: Waveland Press, 1984.

Beard, Augustus F. *A Crusade of Brotherhood: A History of the American Missionary Association*. Boston: Pilgrim Press, 1909.

Bell, Madison. *All Soul's Rising*. New York: Pantheon, 1995.

Benton, Thomas Hart. *Historical and Legal Examination of the Decision of the Supreme Court . . . in the Dred Scott Case*. New York: D. Appleton, 1857.

Bhabha, Homi K. *Anish Kapoor: With Essays by Homi K. Bhabha and Pier Luigi Tazzi*. Berkeley: University of California Press, 1998.

———. *The Location of Culture*. New York: Routledge, 1994.

———. "The Other Question: The Stereotype and Colonial Discourse." *Screen* 24, no. 6 (November–December 1983): 18–36.

Blackburn, Robin. *The Overthrow of Colonial Slavery, 1776–1848*. New York: Verso, 1988.

Blassingame, John W. "Some Precursors of the *Amistad* Revolt." In *The Amistad Incident: Four Perspectives*, 26–35. Middletown, Conn: Humanities Council, 1992.

Bloch, Maurice E. "Washington Crossing the Delaware." *The Paintings of George Caleb Bingham: A Catalogue Raisonné*. Columbia: University of Missouri Press, 1986.

Bogle, Donald. *Toms, Coons, Mulattoes, Mammies and Bucks: An Interpretive History of Blacks in American Films*. 3d ed. New York: Continuum, 1994.

Bontemps, Arna. *Black Thunder*. New York: MacMillan, 1936.

Bosman, William. *New and Accurate Descriptions of the Coast of Guinea*. London, 1705.

Bourne, George. *The Book and Slavery Irreconcilable*. Philadelphia, 1816.

Branch, William. *In Splendid Error*. In *Black Theater USA: Forty-Five Plays by Black Americans, 1847–1974*, 588–617. Edited by James V. Hatch and Ted Shine. New York: The Free Press, 1974.

Brewer, Marilynn B., and Wendi Gardner. "Who Is This 'We'? Levels of Collective Identity and Self Representations." *Journal of Personality and Social Psychology* 71, no. 1 (1996): 83–93.

Brown-Guillory, Elizabeth. *Their Place on the Stage: Black Women Playwrights in America.* New York: Praeger, 1988.

Buckholder, Robert E., ed. *Critical Essays on Herman Melville's "Benito Cereno."* New York: G. K. Hall & Co, 1992.

Burham, Kenneth. *God Comes to America: Father Divine and the Peace Mission Movement.* Boston: Lambeth Press, 1979.

Cable, Mary. *Black Odyssey.* New York: Viking Press, 1971.

Cain, William E., ed. *William Lloyd Garrison and the Fight against Slavery.* New York: St. Martin's Press, 1995.

Cartwright, John R. *Political Leadership in Sierra Leone.* Toronto: University of Toronto Press, 1978.

Certeau, Michel de. *The Practice of Everyday Life.* Translated by Stephen F. Rendall. Berkeley: University of California Press, 1984.

Channing, William Ellery. *The Duty of the Free States; or Remarks Suggested by the Case of the Creole.* Boston: W. Crosby & Co., 1842.

Chase-Riboud, Barbara. *Echo of Lions.* New York: William Morrow & Co., 1989.

Chow, Rey. *Woman and Chinese Modernity: The Politics of Reading between East and West.* Minneapolis: University of Minnesota Press, 1991.

Christopher, A. J. *Colonial Africa.* Totowa, New Jersey: Barnes and Noble, 1984.

Cockrell, Dale. *Demons of Disorder: Early Blackface Minstrels and Their World.* New York: Cambridge University Press, 1997.

Coffin, Joshua. *An Account of Some of the Principal Slave Insurrections.* New York: Antislavery Society, 1860. Reprinted in *Slave Insurrections: Selected Documents.* Westport, Conn.: Negro Universities Press, 1970.

Collier, Gershon. *Sierra Leone: Experiment in Democracy in an African Nation.* New York: New York University Press, 1970.

Conteh-Morgan, John. *Theatre and Drama in Francophone Africa: A Critical Introduction.* Cambridge: Cambridge University Press, 1994.

Cox, Thomas S. *Civil-Military Relations in Sierra Leone: A Case Study of African Soldiers in Politics.* Cambridge, Mass.: Harvard University Press, 1976.

Cripps, Thomas. *Making Movies Black: The Hollywood Message Movie from World War II to the Civil Rights Era.* New York: Oxford University Press, 1993.

———. *Slow Fade to Black: The Negro in American Film, 1900–1942.* New York: Oxford University Press, 1977.

Cugoano, Quobna Ottobah. *Thoughts and Sentiments on the Evil of Slavery and Other Writings.* Edited by Vincent Carretta. New York: Penguin Books, 1999.

Curtin, Philip D. "The Declaration of the Rights of Man in Saint Domingue, 1788–1791." *Hispanic American Historical Review* 30, no. 2 (May 1950): 157–75.

Dahl, Mary B. *Free Souls*. Boston: Houghton Mifflin, 1969.

Davis, David Brion. *The Problem of Slavery in the Age of Revolution 1770–1823*. Ithaca, N.Y.: Cornell University Press, 1975.

———. *The Slave Power Conspiracy and the Paranoid Style*. Baton Rouge: Louisiana State University Press, 1969.

Davidson, Basil. *Africa in History: Themes and Outlines*. New York: Macmillan, 1991.

DeBoer, Clara Merritt. *Be Jubilant My Feet: African American Abolitionists in the American Missionary Association 1839–1861*. New York: Garland Publishing, 1994.

Delano, Amasa. *A Narrative of Voyages and Travels in the Northern and Southern Hemispheres*. Boston: E. G. House, 1817. Reprint, New York: Praeger, 1970.

Desouza George, Raymond. "The Broken Handcuff or Give Me Free," Freetown, Sierra Leone, 1994. Unpublished.

Diawara, Manthia. *African Cinema: Politics & Culture*. Bloomington: Indiana University Press, 1992.

Dillon, Merton L. *The Abolitionists: The Growth of a Dissenting Minority*. DeKalb: Northern Illinois University Press, 1974.

Dodson, Owen. "Amistad." Second Holograph. Box 1, Folder 30. Owen Dodson Collection. Beneicke Rare Book Library, Yale University. Unpublished.

———. *Divine Comedy*. In *Black Theater USA: Forty-Five Plays by Black Americans, 1847–1974*, 322–49. Edited by James V. Hatch and Ted Shine. New York: The Free Press, 1974.

———. "Who Has Seen the Wind? Playwrights and the Black Experience." *Black American Literature Forum* 11 (Fall 1977): 108–16.

———. Notes to Amistad. Second Holograph. Box 1, Folder 31. Owen Dodson Collection. Beneicke Rare Book Library, Yale University. Unpublished.

Douglass, Frederick. "The Heroic Slave." In *The Oxford Frederick Douglass Reader*, 131–63. Edited by William L. Andrews. New York: Oxford University Press, 1996.

———. "What to the Slave Is the Fourth of July?" In *The Oxford Frederick Douglass Reader*, 108–30. Edited by William L. Andrews. New York: Oxford University Press, 1996.

Driskell, David C. *Amistad II: Afro-American Art*. New York: United Church Board for Homeland Ministries, 1975.

Du Bois, W. E. B. "Krigwa Players Little Negro Theatre." *Crisis* 32 (July 1926): 134–36.

———. *The Souls of Black Folk*. 1903. New York: NAL. 1969.

Edelman, Murray. *The Symbolic Uses of Politics*. Urbana: University of Illinois Press, 1964.

Edwards, Bryan. *The History Civil and Commercial, of the British Colonies in the West Indies.* Vol. 2. Philadelphia, 1806.

Edwards, Lillie J. *Denmark Vesey.* New York: Chelsea House, 1990.

Egerton, Douglas R. *Gabriel's Rebellion: The Virginia Slave Conspiracies of 1800 and 1802.* Chapel Hill: University of North Carolina Press, 1993.

Etherton, Michael. *The Development of African Drama.* New York: Africana Publishing Co, 1982.

Euba, Femi. *Archetypes, Imprecators, and Victims of Fate: Origins and Developments of Satire in Black Drama.* New York: Greenwood Press, 1989.

Fage, J. D. "Slavery and the Slave Trade in the Context of West African History." *Journal of African History* 10 (1969): 393–404.

Fanon, Frantz. *Black Skin, White Masks.* 1952. London: Pluto Press, 1986.

Fehrenbacher, Don E. *The Dred Scott Case, Its Significance in American Law and Politics.* New York: Oxford University Press, 1978.

Fick, Carolyn. *The Making of Haiti: The Saint Domingue Revolution from Below.* Knoxville: University of Tennessee Press, 1990.

Finkleman, Paul, ed. *Slave Trade and Migration: Domestic & Foreign.* Volume 2. New York: Garland Publishing, 1989.

Foner, Eric. "Hollywood Invades the Classroom." *New York Times,* 20 December 1997, A13.

Foner, Philip S., and Josephine F. Pacheco, *Three Who Dared: Prudence, Crandall, Margaret Douglass, Myrtilla Miner—Champions of Antebellum Black Education.* Westport, Conn.: Greenwood, 1984.

Fontenot, Chester. "Black Misery, White Guilt and *Amistad.*" *Melus.* Forthcoming.

Fuller, Edmund. *Prudence Crandall: An Incident of Racism in Nineteenth Century Connecticut.* Middletown, Conn.: Wesleyan University Press, 1971.

Fyfe, Christopher. *A History of Sierra Leone.* London: Oxford University Press, 1962.

———. *A Short History of Sierra Leone.* London: Longman, 1979.

Gabriel, Teshome H. *Third Cinema in the Third World.* Ann Arbor, Mich.: UMI Research Press, 1982.

Gans, Herbert J. "Hollywood Entertainment: Commerce or Ideology?" *Social Science Quarterly* 74, no. 1 (1993): 150–53.

Garrett, Mitchell B. *The French Colonial Question, 1789–1791.* Ann Arbor: George Wahr, 1916.

Genovese, Eugene D. *From Rebellion to Revolution: Afro-American Slave Revolts in the Making of the Modern World.* Baton Rouge: Louisiana State University Press, 1979.

———. *Roll Jordan Roll: The World the Slaves Made.* New York: Pantheon Books, 1974.

Giddings, Joshua Reed. *Amistad Claim. History of the Case . . . Speech of Mr. Giddings of Ohio in the House of Representatives.* 21 December 1853. n.p.

Gilroy, Paul. *The Black Atlantic: Modernity and Double Consciousness.* Cambridge, Mass.: Harvard University Press, 1993.

Glissant, Edouard. *Monsieur Toussaint.* Translated by Joseph G. Foster and Barbara A. Franklin. Washington D.C.: Three Continents, 1981.

Goffman, Erving. *The Presentation of Self in Everyday Life.* New York: Doubleday Anchor Books, 1959.

———. *Encounters: Two Studies in the Sociology of Interaction.* New York: Bobbs-Merrill Co., 1961.

Goldstein, L. F. "Violence as an Instrument of Social Change: The Views of Frederick Douglass (1817–1895)." *Journal of Negro History* 61, no. 1 (January 1976): 61–72.

Goldstein, Malcolm. *The Political Stage: American Drama and Theater of the Great Depression.* New York: Oxford University Press, 1974.

Gray, Thomas R. *The Confessions of Nat Turner.* Baltimore: Thomas Gray, 1831. Reprinted in *The Confessions of Nat Turner and Related Documents.* Edited by Kenneth Greenberg. New York: Bedford Books of St Martin's Press, 1996.

Haffner, Charlie. "*Amistad* Kata Kata: Play Celebrating Sengbe Pieh the Hero of the *Amistad* Revolt," Freetown, Sierra Leone, 1988. Unpublished.

Halasz, Nicholas. *The Rattling Chains: Slave Unrest and Revolt in the Antebellum South.* New York: David McKay Company, 1966.

Halbwachs, Maurice. *On Collective Memory.* 1941. Edited and translated by Lewis Coser. Chicago: University of Chicago Press, 1992.

Hall, Stuart, et al., eds. *Culture, Media, Language.* London: Unwin Hyman, 1980.

Hamilton, J., comp. *An Account of the Late Intended Insurrection among a Portion of the Blacks of This City, Charleston, S.C.* Charleston: A. E. Miller, 1822. Reprinted in *Slave Insurrections: Selected Documents.* Westport, Conn.: Negro Universities Press. 1970.

Hansberry, Lorraine. *The Drinking Gourd.* In *Black Theater USA: Forty-Five Plays by Black Americans, 1847–1974,* 714–36. Edited by James V. Hatch and Ted Shine. New York: The Free Press, 1974.

Hatch, James V. *Sorrow Is the Only Faithful One: The Life of Owen Dodson.* Urbana and Chicago: University of Illinois Press, 1993.

Hay, Samuel A. *African American Theatre: An Historical and Critical Analysis.* New York: Cambridge University Press, 1994.

Hayden, Robert. "Middle Passage." In *Collected Poems,* 48–54. Edited by Frederick Glaysher. New York: Liveright Publishing Corp., 1985.

Hearst, Patty. *Trial of Patty Hearst.* San Francisco: The Great Fidelity Press, 1976.

———. *Every Secret Thing.* New York: Doubleday, 1982.

Hegel, G. W. F. *Hegel's Phenomenology of Spirit*. Translated by A. V. Miller. New York: Oxford University Press, 1977.

Henderson, Cinqué. "Making a Name: A Personal *Amistad* Voyage." *The New Republic*, 22 December 1997, 16–18.

Hietala, Thomas R. *Manifest Design: Anxious Aggrandizement in Late Jacksonian America*. Ithaca, N.Y.: Cornell University Press, 1985.

Higginson, Thomas Wentworth. *Black Rebellion*. New York: Arno Press and *The New York Times*, 1969.

Hill, Errol, ed. *Theater of Black Americans: A Collection of Critical Essays*. New York: Applause Theatre Book Publishers, 1987.

———. "The Revolutionary Tradition in Black Drama." *Theatre Journal* (December 1986): 408–26.

Hinks, Peter P. *To Awaken My Afflicted Brethren: David Walker and the Problem of Antebellum Slave Resistance*. University Park: Pennsylvania State University Press, 1997.

Hobsbawn, Eric J. *The Age of Revolution, 1789–1848*. New York: New American Library, 1962.

Horn, Andrew. "Ritual Drama and the Theatrical: The Case of Bori Spirit Mediumship." In *Drama and Theatre in Nigeria: A Critical Source Book*, 181–202. Edited by Yemi Ogunbiyi. Lagos: Nigeria Magazine, 1981.

James, C. L. R. *The Black Jacobins: Toussaint L'Ouverture and the San Domingo Revolution*. 2d rev. ed. New York: Vintage Books, 1963.

Jeyifo, Biodun. *The Truthful Lie: Essays in a Sociology of African Drama*. London: New Beacon, 1985.

Johnson, Charles. *Middle Passage*. New York: Penguin, 1990.

———. *Oxherding Tale*. Bloomington: Indiana University Press, 1982.

Johnson, James Weldon. "The Dilemma of the Negro Author." *American Mercury* 15 (December 1928): 477–81.

Jones, Adam. *From Slaves to Palm Kernels: A History of the Galinhas Country (West Africa) 1730–1890*. Wiesbaden: Franz Steiner Verlag, 1983.

Jones, Howard. *Mutiny on the Amistad*. New York: Oxford University Press, 1987.

———. "Mutiny on the *Amistad*: 'All We Want is Make us Free.'" In *The Amistad Incident: Four Perspectives*, 7–25. Middletown: Connecticut Humanities Council, 1992.

Jones, Rhett S. "Community and Commentators: Black Theatre and Its Critics." *Black American Literature Forum* 14, no. 2 (Summer 1980): 69–76.

Jordan, Winthrop. *White over Black: American Attitudes toward the Negro, 1550–1812*. Chapel Hill: University of North Carolina Press, 1968.

Julien, Isaac and Kobena Mercer. "De Margin and De Centre." In *Stuart Hall, Critical Dialogues in Cultural Studies*, 450–64. Edited by David Morley and Kuan Hsing Chen. London and New York: Routledge, 1996.

Kabba, Muctaru, et al. *Sierra Leonean Heroes: Fifty Great Men and Women Who Helped to Build our Nation*. London: Commonwealth Printers, 1988.

Kamlongera, Christopher. *Theatre for Development in Africa with Case Studies from Malawi and Zambia*. Bonn, Germany: Education, Science, and Documentation Centre, 1988.

Kammen, Michael. *A Season of Youth: The American Revolution and the Historical Imagination*. New York: Knopf, 1978.

Kaplan, Sidney. "Herman Melville and the American National Sin: The Meaning of "Benito Cereno." In *Critical Essays on Herman Melville's "Benito Cereno,"* 37–47. Edited by Robert Burkholder. New York: G. K. Hall, 1992.

Karcher Carolyn. "The Riddle of the Sphinx: Melville's 'Benito Cereno' and the *Amistad* Case." In *Critical Essays on Herman Melville's "Benito Cereno,"* 196–229. Edited by Robert Buckholder. New York: G. K. Hall & Co., 1992.

———. *Shadow over the Promised Land: Slavery, Race, and Violence in Melville's America*. Baton Rouge: Louisiana State University Press, 1980.

Katz, William Loren. *Breaking the Chains: African American Slave Resistance*. New York: Atheneum, 1990.

Keller, Arthur S. *Creation of Rights of Sovereignty through Symbolic Acts 1400–1800*. New York: Columbia University Press, 1938.

Kenrick, John. *Horrors of Slavery*. Cambridge, Mass.: Hilliard & Metcalf, 1817.

Klein, Herbert S. *The Middle Passage: Comparative Studies in the Atlantic Slave Trade*. Princeton, N.J.: Princeton University Press, 1978.

Kohn, Bernice. *The Amistad Mutiny*. New York: McCall, 1971.

Kromer, Helen. *The Amistad Revolt, 1839: The Slave Uprising aboard the Spanish Schooner*. New York: Franklin Watts, 1973.

Lamartine, Alphonse Marie Louise de. *Toussaint Louverture: Poème dramatique en cinq actes et en vers*. Edited by George Raffalovich. New York: The Century Co., 1931.

Lemisch, Jesse. "Black Agency in the *Amistad* Uprising: Or, You've Taken Our Cinque and Gone." *Souls: A Critical Journal of Black Politics, Culture, and Society* 1, no. 1 (Winter 1999): 57–70.

Lofton, John. *Denmark Vesey's Revolt: The Slave Plot That Lit a Fuse to Fort Sumter*. Kent, Ohio: Kent State University Press, 1983.

Loftus, Elizabeth. *Memory: Surprising Insights into How We Remember and Why We Forget*. Reading, Mass.: Addison-Wesley, 1980.

Madden, Thomas M., ed. *The Memoirs (Chiefly Autobiographical) from 1798 to 1886 of Richard Robert Madden*. London: Ward & Downey, 1891.

Maines, David R., et al. "The Sociological Import of G. H. Mead's Theory of the Past." *American Sociological Review* 48 (April 1983): 161–73.

Manning, Patrick. *Slavery and African Life: Occidental, Oriental, and African Slave Trades*. New York: Cambridge University Press, 1990.

Markus, H., et al. "Role of the Self-Concept in the Perception of Others." *Journal of Personality and Social Psychology* 49 (1985): 1494–512.

Martin, B. Edmon. *All We Want is Make Us Free: La Amistad and the Reform Abolitionists.* Boston: University Press of America, 1986.

Martin, Christopher. *The Amistad Affair.* New York: Abelard- Schuman, 1970.

Martin, Michael T., ed. *Cinemas of the Black Diaspora: Diversity, Dependence, and Oppositionality.* Detroit: Wayne State University Press, 1995.

Martineau, Harriet. *The Hour and the Man.* London: E. Moxon, 1841.

McPherson, James. *The Struggle for Equality: Abolitionists and the Negro in the Civil War and Reconstruction.* Princeton, N.J.: Princeton University Press, 1964.

Mead, George Herbert. *The Philosophy of the Act.* Chicago: University of Chicago Press, 1938.

———. *The Philosophy of the Present.* Chicago: Open Court Publishing, 1932.

Melville, Herman. "Benito Cereno." 1855. In *Billy Budd and Other Stories.* New York: Penguin Classics, 1986.

Merk, Frederick. *Manifest Destiny and Mission in American History.* New York: Alfred Knopf, 1963.

Mitchell, Sydney K. "Slavery in Connecticut and Especially in New Haven" MSS 48. Box 2. Folder B-2, 1. Whitney Library, New Haven Colony Historical Society. 1949.

Mlama, Penina Muhando. "Women's Participation in 'Communication for Development': The Popular Alternative in Africa." *Research in African Literatures* 22, no. 3 (1991): 41–53.

Morley, David, and Kuan-Hsing Chen, eds. *Stuart Hall, Critical Dialogues in Cultural Studies.* London and New York: Routledge, 1996.

Morrison, Joy F. "Forum Theater in West Africa." *Research in African Literature* 22, no. 3 (Fall 1991): 29–40.

Morrison, Toni. "Memory, Creation, and Writing." *Thought* 59 (1984): 385–90.

Morse, Jarvis M. *A Neglected Period of Connecticut's History, 1818–1850.* New Haven, Conn.: Yale University Press, 1933.

Mudimbe, V. Y. *The Idea of Africa.* Bloomington: Indiana University Press, 1994.

———. *The Invention of Africa: Gnosis, Philosophy, and the Order of Knowledge.* Bloomington: Indiana University Press, 1988.

Mulford, Carla. "Resisting Colonialism." In *Teaching the Literatures of Early America,* 75–94. Edited by Carla Mulford. New York: MLA, 1999.

Murray, D. J. *The West Indies and the Development of Colonial Government, 1801–1834.* Oxford: Clarendon Press, 1965.

Nicholls, David. *Haiti in Caribbean Context: Ethnicity, Economy and Revolt.* New York: St. Martins Press, 1985.

Niles, Blair. *East by Day.* New York: Farrar & Rinehart, 1941.

Noonan, John T., Jr., *The Antelope: The Ordeal of the Recaptured Africans in the Administrations of James Monroe and John Quincy Adams*. Berkeley: University of California Press, 1977.

Norton, Mary Beth. *A People and a Nation: A History of the United States*. Brief/3d ed. Boston: Houghton Mifflin, 1991.

Ogunba, Oyin, and Abiola Irele. *Theatre in Africa*. Ibadan, Nigeria: University of Ibadan Press, 1978.

Okpewho, Isidore. *African Oral Literature*. Bloomington, Indiana: Indiana University Press, 1992.

Olaudah, Equiano. *The Interesting Narrative & Other Writings*. London, 1789. Edited by Vincent Carretta. New York: Penguin, 1995.

Oliver, Roland, and J. D. Fage. *A Short History of Africa*. New York: Penguin, 1988.

Opala, Joseph A. *"Ecstatic Renovations!" Street Art Celebrating Sierra Leone's 1992 Revolution*. Freetown: Ro-Marong Industries, Ltd., 1994. Also in *African Affairs: The Journal of the Royal African Society* 93, no. 371 (April 1994): 195–218.

———. "Escaping a Nation in Chaos." *Fresh Air with Terry Gross*. National Public Radio. WHYY Philadelphia, 8 July 1997.

———. "Sierra Leone: The Politics of State Collapse." Paper prepared for presentation at the conference on Irregular Warfare in Liberia and Sierra Leone, SAIC, Denver, Colorado, 30 July–1 August 1998.

Osagie, Iyunolu. "The *Amistad* Affair and the Nation of Sierra Leone: The Dramatic Return of Memory." In *Contemporary Literature in the African Diaspora*, 159–65. Edited by Olga Barrios and Bernard Bell. Leon, Spain: University of Salamanca, 1997.

———. Interview with Charlie Haffner. Freetown, Sierra Leone, 18 April 1994.

———. Interview with Raymond Desouza George. Freetown, Sierra Leone, 29 April 1994.

———. Telephone Interview with Ed Hamilton. 14 February 1996.

———. Interview with Alfred Marder. New Haven, Conn., 12 June 1996.

———. "The *Amistad* Revolt Revisited in Sierra Leone." In *Culture(s) in Contention: Difference and Complementarity*, 138–56. Edited by Hugh Silverman. Chicago: Northwestern University Press, 1999.

———. Review of *The Slumbering Volcano: American Slave Ship Revolts and the Production of Rebellious Masculinity*, by Maggie Montesinos Sale. *CLA Journal* 42, no. 1 (September 1998): 124–28.

Ott, Thomas O. *The Haitian Revolution 1789–1804*. Knoxville: The University of Tennessee Press, 1973.

Owens, William A. *Black Mutiny: The Revolt on the Schooner Amistad*. Philadelphia: Pilgrim Press, 1953.

The Parliamentary History of England. Volume 27. London: T. C. Hansard, 1816.

Pate, Alexs. *Amistad: Based on the Screenplay by David Franzoni and Steven Zaillian.* New York: Penguin, 1997.

Pesci, David. *Amistad.* New York: Marlowe & Co., 1997.

Powers, Stephen, David Rotham, and Stanley Rotham. *Hollywood's America: Social and Political Themes in Motion Pictures.* Boulder, Colo.: Westview Press, 1996.

Raboteau, Albert J. *Slave Religion: The "Invisible Institution" in the Antebellum South.* New York: Oxford University Press, 1978.

Richards, Leonard L. *"Gentlemen of Property and Standing," Anti-Abolition Mobs in Jacksonian America.* New York: Oxford University Press, 1970.

Richardson, Willis. *The Flight of the Natives.* In *Plays of Negro Life.* Edited by Alain Locke and Montgomery Gregory. New York: Harper, 1927.

Roach, Joseph. "Culture and Performance in the Circuum-Atlantic World." In *Performativity and Performance,* 45–63. Edited by Andrew Parker and Eve K. Sedgwick. New York: Routledge, 1995.

Rosenbaum, Jonathan. *Movies as Politics.* Berkeley: University of California Press, 1997.

Rosten, Leo. *Hollywood: The Movie Colony, the Movie Makers.* New York: Harcourt, Brace, and Comp., 1941.

Saint-Méry, Moreau de. *Considérations présentées aux vrais amis de repos et du bonheur de la France, à l'occasion des nouveaux mouvemens de quelques soi-disant Amis-des-Noirs.* Paris, 1791.

Sale, Maggie Montesinos. *The Slumbering Volcano: American Slave Ship Revolts and the Production of Rebellious Masculinity.* Durham, N.C.: Duke University Press, 1997.

Sanders, Leslie. *The Development of Black Theater in America: From Shadows to Selves.* Baton Rouge: Louisiana State University Press, 1988.

Schiffman, Joseph. "Critical Problems in Melville's "Benito Cereno." In *Critical Essays on Herman Melville's "Benito Cereno,"* 29–36. Edited by Robert Burkholder. New York: G.K. Hall, 1992.

Schipper, Mineke. *Beyond the Boundaries: African Literature and Literary Theory.* London: Allison & Busby, 1989.

Schneider, Alison. "Advising Spielberg: A Career Studying the *Amistad* Rebellion." *The Chronicle of Higher Education,* 9 January 1998, A12.

Schwartz, Barry. "Social Change and Collective Memory: The Democratization of George Washington." *American Sociological Review* 56 (April 1991): 221–36.

———. "The Social Context of Communication: A Study in Collective Memory." *Social Forces* 61, no. 2 (December 1982): 374–402.

Schwartz, Barry, Yael Zerubavel, and Bernice M. Barnett. "The Recovery of Masada: A Study in Collective Memory." *The Sociological Quarterly* 27, no. 2 (1986): 147–64.

Sibthorpe, A. B. C. *The History of Sierra Leone.* 4th ed. London: Frank Cass and Co., 1970.

Sidbury, James. *Ploughshares into Swords: Race, Rebellion, and Identity in Gabriel's Virginia, 1730–1810.* New York: Cambridge University Press, 1997.

Silverman, Hugh, ed. *Culture(s) in Contention: Difference and Complementarity.* Chicago: Northwestern University Press, 1999.

Simon, Paul. *Lovejoy, Martyr to Freedom.* St. Louis, Mo.: Concordia, 1964.

Singelis, Theodore M. "The Measurement of Independent and Interdependent Self-Construals." *Personality and Social Psychology Bulletin* 20, no. 5 (October 1994): 580–91.

Slave Insurrections: Selected Documents. Westport, Conn.: Negro Universities Press. 1970.

Solanas, Fernando and Octavio Getino. "Towards a Third Cinema." in *Movies and Methods,* 44–64. Edited by Bill Nichols. Los Angeles and Berkeley: University of California Press, 1976.

Soyinka, Wole. "From a Common Backcloth." In *Art, Dialogue, and Outrage: Essays on Literature and Culture,* 7–14. New York: Pantheon, 1988.

Starobin, Robert S., ed. *Denmark Vesey: The Slave Conspiracy of 1822.* Englewood Cliffs, N.J.: Prentice Hall, 1970.

Sterne, Emma Gelders. *The Long Black Schooner: The Voyage of the Amistad.* Chicago: Follett, 1953.

Stoddard, Theodore Lothrop. *The French Revolution in San Domingo.* Boston: n.p., 1914.

Strane, Susan. *A Whole-Souled Woman: Prudence Crandall and the Education of Black Women.* New York: W. W. Norton & Co., 1990.

Stulov, Yuri. "Alexs D. Pate: 'The Slave is Just a Term.'" *Belarusian Association for American Studies* (1998): 113–18.

Sundquist, Eric J. *The Hammers of Creation: Folk Culture in Modern African-American Fiction.* Athens and London: University of Georgia Press, 1992.

———. "*Benito Cereno* and New World Slavery." In *Critical Essays on Herman Melville's "Benito Cereno,"* 146–67. Edited by Robert Buckholder. New York: G. K. Hall & Co., 1992.

Takaki, Ronald T. *Violence in the Black Imagination.* New York: Oxford University Press, 1993.

Telem Newsletter. Freetown: Freetong Players Theatre Group Publication (July 1994): 1–4.

Thomas, Hugh. *The Slave Trade: The Story of the Atlantic Slave Trade, 1440–1870.* New York: Simon & Schuster, 1997.

Thomas, John L. *The Liberator: William Lloyd Garrison, A Biography.* Boston: Little, Brown and Co., 1963.

Thorpe, John. *Chap Am So: A Historical Drama.* New York: Network of Cultural Centers of Color, 1996.

Tragle, Henry Irving, comp. *Nat Turner's Slave Revolt—1831.* New York: Grossman, 1972.

Triandis, Harry C., et al. "Individualism and Collectivism: Cross-cultural Perspectives on Self-Ingroup Relationships." *Journal of Personality and Social Psychology* 54, no. 2 (February 1988): 323–38.

Trouillot, Michel-Rolph. "From Planters' Journals to Academia: The Haitian Revolution as Unthinkable History." *Journal of Caribbean History* 25, nos. 1 and 2 (1991): 81–99.

———. *Silencing the Past: Power and the Production of History.* Boston, Mass.: Beacon Press. 1995.

Trow, John F. *The Alton Trials of Winthrop S. Gilman . . . for a Riot Committed in Alton.* New York: J. F. Trow, 1838.

Tyson, George F., Jr., ed. *Toussaint L'Ouverture.* Englewood Cliffs, N.J.: Prentice Hall, 1973.

Ukadike, Nwachukwu Frank. *Black African Cinema.* Berkeley: University of California Press, 1994.

U.S. Congress. *House Executive Documents,* no. 185. 26th Congress, 1st Session. 1840.

Utting, Francis A. J. *The Story of Sierra Leone.* 1931. New York: Books for Libraries Press, 1971.

Volosinov, V. N. *Marxism and the Philosophy of Language.* Translated by Ladislav Matejka and I. R. Titunik. New York: Seminar Press, 1973.

Walker, David. *Walker's Appeal in Four Articles: Together with a Preamble, to the Coloured Citizens of the World.* Third edition. Boston: David Walker, 1830.

Warner, W. Lloyd. *The Living and the Dead: A Study of the Symbolic Life of Americans.* New Haven: Yale University Press, 1959.

Watt, Stephen. *Post/Modern Drama: Reading the Contemporary Stage.* Ann Arbor: University of Michigan Press, 1998.

Watts, Jill. *God, Harlem U.S.A.: The Father Divine Story.* Berkeley: University of California Press, 1992.

Weisbrot, Robert. *Father Divine and the Struggle for Racial Equality.* Urbana: University of Illinois Press, 1983.

Wheaton, Henry. *Report of Cases Argued and Adjudged in the Supreme Court of the United States, 1816–1827.* 12 vols. Philadelphia, 1883.

Wienberg, Albert K. *Manifest Destiny: A Study of Nationalist Expansionism in American History.* Gloucester, Mass.: Peter Smith, 1958.

Williams, Adebayo. "Towards a Theory of Cultural Production in Africa." *Research in African Literature* 22, no. 2 (Summer 1991): 5–20.

Willis, John Ralph, ed. *Slaves and Slavery in Muslim Africa.* London: Totowa, N. J. F. Cass, 1985.

Wright, George C. *A History of Blacks in Kentucky: In Pursuit of Equality, 1890–1980.* Volume 2. Frankfort: Kentucky Historical Society, 1992.

Wyatt-Brown, Bertram. *Lewis Tappan and the Evangelical War against Slavery.* Cleveland: The Press of Case Western Reserve University, 1969.

Zeinert, Karen. *The Amistad Slave Revolt and American Abolition.* North Haven, Conn.: Shoe String Press, 1997.

Index

Abolition of slavery, 32; American
abolitionists and, 8–12, 22
Adams, John Quincy, 14, 15–17, 19,
126; in *Amistad* (movie), 123, 128;
in Desouza George's play, 116, 117;
in Dodson's play, 80
Africa, 3, 5, 53
Afrocentrism, 73
All People's Congress (APC), 111
Allen, Debbie, 122, 124–25, 158
(n. 11)
Alvarez, 87, 88
American Colonization Society, 37,
51, 146 (n. 66)
American dream, 82
American Missionary Association
(AMA), 18, 19, 20, 65; missionaries
of, 55–57, 66
Amistad case, 136, 141 (n. 28); in
Dodson's play, 77–83, 151 (n. 33);
impact of, 66–68; in movie, 21, 80,
116, 120, 135, 158 (n. 11); revolt,
112, 137; ship, 5, 6, 71
Amistad committee: nineteenth cen-
tury, 17, 18; twentieth century, 91,
154 (n. 79)

Amistad Kata Kata, 105–10
Antelope (*Ramirez*), 15–17, 142
(n. 34)
Antislavery, 19, 51, 54, 146 (n. 2)
Antonio, 5, 7, 13; in Thorpe's play,
89
Argaiz, Cavallero Pedro Alcántara, 12
Armed Forces Revolutionary Council
(AFRC), 135
Aureol Players, 157 (n. 34)

Bacon, Leonard, 11
Bahoo, 141 (n. 24)
Bai Bureh, 100–102, 113; portrait of,
155 (n. 10)
Baldwin, Roger Sherman, 9, 12, 15,
17; in *Amistad* (movie), 121, 125,
128; in Dodson's play, 80
Barber, John W., 19, 23
Barracoon, 4
Bas-relief, 92
Blanco, Pedro, 4; in Thorpe's play
(Blango), 87
Bowery (theater), 72
Bozales, 4, 7, 12
British Council, 106

Broken Handcuff, The, 113–18
Brown, John, 75
Burnah, in Desouza George's play, 116

Calderón de la Barca, Angel, 9–10, 12
Calendar, Ebenezer, 113
Canada, 13, 19, 157 (n. 34)
Cannibalism, 5, 78, 126, 140 (n. 10)
Caribbean, 4, 27, 34
Carter, 148 (n. 38)
Catawba Indians, 37
Caulker, 66
Celestino, 5, 78, 89
Centennial celebration, 72, 76
Chap Am So, 83–91
Charley, Dele, 157 (n. 34)
Chase-Riboud, Barbara, 124
Christ figure, 79, 80
Christianity, 55, 79, 80, 146 (n. 6), 147 (n. 10)
Cinque, Joseph. *See* Sengbe
Civil Rights, 90, 96, 97; in Connecticut, 141 (n. 27); movement, 83
Civil war: American, 20; in Sierra Leone, 61–64, 66, 130, 136, 155 (n. 86)
Clarkson (British Governor), 113
Clarkson, Thomas, 54
Collective amnesia, 102
Collective memory. *See* Memory
Colonialism, 56, 64–65, 66, 68, 114, 148 (n. 32); colonial past, 73; colonial rule, 100, 113; education, 100
Colonization, of Africa, 81, 82, 136
Connecticut, 95, 141 (n. 27)
Covey (Govie), James, 11, 63, 64, 90
Creole brig, 45, 52

Cuba, 10
Culloden Point, 6

Davis, David Brion, 26
Day, George, 11
DeBoer, Clara Merrit, 22
Delano, Amasa, 86
Desouza George, Raymond, 102, 113–14, 116–18
Dessalines, Jean Jacques, 31, 34
Dodson, Owen, 76–83, 97
Dombokoro (Lombokoro, Lomboko), 3, 4, 89, 139 (n. 2)
Double consciousness, 72, 73, 94; double-voiced black drama, 74
Dougall, John, 13
Douglass, Frederick, 51, 52, 75, 128
DreamWorks, 21, 124, 130, 158 (n. 11)
Dred Scott case, 141 (n. 31)
Du Bois, W. E. B., 74, 149 (n. 11)

Echo of Lions, 124
ECOMOG, 133, 135, 159 (n. 32)
Emancipator, 8, 19
England, 31; black poor in, 54, 146 (n. 2); position of, on slavery, 11
Enlightenment, 30, 31

Farmington, 13, 18
Female Emancipation Society, 17
Ferrer, Ramon, 5
Ferry, John, 9
Foone, 18, 95
Fordham, Peletiah, 6, 7, 140 (n. 14)
Forsyth, John, 10, 12, 13
Fourah Bay College, 114
Fox, Henry, 12
Freeman, Morgan, 121, 128, 129
Freetong Players, 104, 106, 110

Freetown, 54; City Hall, 112; destroyed, 55
French: attack on Freetown, 55; Jacobins, 30, 33, 37; Revolution, 26–32, 46, 143; Société des Amis des Noirs, 32
Fuliwa (George Brown), 12, 63–64

Gag rule, 9, 129
Gallinas, 3, 139 (nn. 2, 5), 153 (n. 66)
Garber, Shefumi, 157 (n. 34)
Garrison, Lloyd, 8, 140 (n. 17)
Gedney, Lieutenant, 6, 7, 13, 80
Gentleman, 18, 58, 59
Gibbs, Josiah Willard, 9, 11
Gilpin, Henry, 14–16
Goffman, Erving, 25–26
Grabeau (Grabo), 5, 12; in Desouza George's play, 116
Grampus, 13; Adams's critique of, 15–17
Great Depression, 72, 81, 82
Green, Edward Henry, 67
Green, Henry, 6, 7, 13
Grundy, Felix, 12
Guinea, 4, 44

Haffner, Charlie, 105–6, 109
Haiti. See Saint Domingue
Haitian Revolution, 28, 31–35, 75; as peripheral, 143 (n. 19)
Hamilton, Ed, 91–97, 116
Havana, 4, 5; slave market, 7, 11
Hay, Samuel, 149 (n. 11)
Holabird, William, 7, 12, 13; in Amistad (movie), 125
Hollywood, 119–21, 123, 124, 126, 130
Hopkins, Anthony, 123

Hounsou, Djimon, 123, 125, 127
Hut tax, 100

Iconography, 132, 134, 159 (n. 22)
Identity, 24, 38, 132, 150 (nn. 11, 13); collective, 24, 25; national, 26, 111, 112, 135, 137; politics of, 52, 76
Insurrection, American, 36. See also Slave revolts
Intertribal wars, 3
Islam, 55; the Aku community, 146 (n. 7)

Jacobins, 26–32, 46, 143
Jamaica, 34, 63
Janes, Dwight, 8
Jim Crow South, 82
Jimmy (King), 54, 146 (n. 3)
Joadson, 121, 128, 129
Jocelyn, Nathaniel, 92, 133
Jocelyn, Simeon, 8
Judson, Andrew, 7, 9, 11, 13, 17, 117

Kabba, Ahmed Tejan, 135
Kagne, 11, 148 (n. 37)
Kali (Kale), 11, 14, 65
Kamajohs, 135, 159 (n. 32)
Kargbo, John Kolosa, 157 (n. 34)
Kaw Mende, 62, 66, 98, 102, 140 (n. 6)
Kinna (Johnson), 14, 58, 64
Kissicummah, 63, 66
Koroma, Johnny Paul, 135
Krio, 101
Kru, 145 (n. 47)

La Amistad, 5, 6, 71
Ladinos, 4, 7, 140 (n. 8)
Laigo, 3, 4

Leavitt, Joshua, 8, 13
Lee, Spike, 122
Liberator, 8
Liberia, 3, 4
Louisville, Ky., 92, 95
L'Ouverture, Toussaint, 31, 33, 34, 41
Lovejoy, Elijah, 8
Ludlow, Henry, 11
Luiz, 3, 4

Macaulay, Zachary, 54
Madden, Richard R., 11, 12
Maddy, Amadu, 157 (n. 34)
Mammy Yoko, 113
Mani, 60, 84, 85, 91, 102
Manifest Destiny, 27, 143 (n. 9), 147 (n. 10)
Marder, Alfred, 154 (n. 79)
Margai, Albert, 111
Margai, Milton, 111, 113, 115
Margru (Sarah Kinson), 11, 67, 86
Maroons, 34–54, 144 (n. 25)
Martin, Christopher, 21, 22–23
Martinez, House of, 140 (n. 7)
McConaughey, Matthew, 121
Mead, G. H., 110
Meade, Lieutenant, 7, 140 (n. 13)
Melodrama, 72
Melville, Herman, 20, 46–50, 86
Memory: public, 50, 71, 123; collective, 72, 76, 85, 98, 99, 101, 108, 134; cultural, 50, 91; as death, 78; of history, 83, 137; national, 102, 103; revisionist, 73; social, 153 (n. 62)
Mende language, 9, 67, 68, 127
Mende mission, 19, 98, 99, 140 (n. 6), 147 (n. 16), 156 (n. 13)
Mercenaries, 159 (n. 33)
Middle Passage, 12, 45, 85, 86, 89, 91, 95–96, 103, 116, 125

Mirabeau, Comte de, 32
Modernity, 83
Momoh, Joseph, 111, 156 (n. 28)
Monroe (Governor of Virginia), 37
Montauk Point, 77
Montes, Pedro, 4, 12, 77, 79; in Desouza George's play, 116
Murals, 76, 132, 133–34
Mystic seaport, 71

Naimbana, 54
National Provisional Revolutionary Council (NPRC), 112, 113, 134
Network of Cultural Centers of Color (NCCC), 153 (n. 58)
New Haven, 95, 110, 132
New London, Conn., 7
Noble savage ideology, 127
Nova Scotians, 54, 55

Oberlin College, 67
Ogé, Vincent, 32, 33
Opala, Joseph, 106, 110, 112, 113, 135
Oral tradition, 99, 103, 107; orality, 108, 109, 110
Owens, William, 21, 22–23, 71

Patriotism, 111
Peculiar institution, 28, 46, 51
Performance: of culture, 72, 103; dramatic, 76, 84
Perseverance, 47
Pieh, Sengbe. *See* Sengbe
Pinckney treaty of 1795, 10, 15
Portuguese: slave dealers, 3; slave ships, 15
Prisoners of war, 3
Pro-slavery, 9, 19, 28
Prosser, Gabriel, 27, 35–38, 50
Puerto Príncipe, 4, 5

Quasi-historical genre, 71
Queen Victoria, 12

Raymond, Elizabeth, 18, 55, 61
Raymond, William, 18, 55, 58–65; death of, 65, 148 (n. 37)
Rebellion, 25, 26, 145 (n. 47). See also Slave revolts
Redemption, 65, 148 (n. 36)
Rigaud, André, 33, 34
Root, Barnabas, 66, 67
Ruiz, Jose, 4, 12, 77, 79; in Desouza George's play, 116

Sa (James Pratt), 63–64
Saint Domingue: American slave stories in, 39, 44; debates on slavery in, 27, 28; slave resistance/revolt in, 27, 29–35, 44, 46, 50; as symbol of slave revolts, 41; and white fear, 27, 29, 40
San Dominick, 46, 47, 86
Savery Library, 76
Sedwick, Theodore, 9
Senegambia, 3
Sengbe, 5, 88, 91; in Amistad memorial, 91–97; and courtroom trial, 12; in Dodson's play, 77; in Kaw Mende, 62; letter of, to Lewis Tappan, 58–59; and missionaries, 59–62; name derivation, 140 (n. 11); as national symbol, 112; and revolt on Amistad schooner, 5–7; and slave trade (rumors), 23, 63, 137, 142 (n. 46)
Sharp, Granville, 54
Sierra Leone, 3, 4
Sierra Leone Company, 54, 55, 56, 146 (n. 2)
Sierra Leone's People's Party (SLPP), 111

Sisiwuru, 63
Slave revolts, 10, 24, 27, 43–45, 143 (n. 14), 153 (n. 69). See also Rebellion
Slave trade, 53, 96, 141 (n. 28), 148 (n. 24); abolition of, 55; and African traders, 87; cessation of, 66; and European traders, 4, 139 (n. 3), 146 (n. 3), 148 (n. 27), 153 (n. 66); suppression of, 4, 11, 44, 55
So ko ma (Henry Cowles), 64
Spain, 27; treaty of 1795, 10; treaty of 1817, 4, 12
Spencer, Julius, 153 (n. 58)
Spielberg, Steven, 21, 116, 120, 135, 158 (n. 12)
Staples, Seth, 9
Steele, James, 18, 55, 59, 60
Stevens, Siaka, 111, 156 (n. 28), 159 (n. 28)
Story, Justice Joseph, 117
Strasser, Valentine, 112, 132
Symbionese Liberation Army (SLA), 154 (n. 80)

Talladega College, 76, 77
Taney, Roger B., 13, 141 (n. 31)
Tappan, Arthur, 8, 140 (n. 17)
Tappan, Lewis, 8, 13, 17, 59, 60
Tecora, 4, 5, 85, 86, 116, 125
Teme, 11, 65
Temne, 55, 100, 101
Theater: black revolutionary, 75–76; as cultural tool, 149 (n. 11); for development, 104
Thompson, George, 65–66, 148 (n. 38)
Thompson, Smith, 9
Thorpe, John C., 83–87, 89–91, 97

Townsend, Amos, 11
Triptych, 93, 96
Tryal, 46, 47
Tucker, Harry, 62
Tucker, Thomas, 67, 68
Turner, Nat, 42–43, 50

United States, 27; treaty with Spain, 10
University of Sierra Leone, 114

Van Buren, Martin, 7, 9, 13
Van Gibbs, Thomas, 68
Vesey, Denmark, 39–42, 50

Walker, David, 51, 128
War path (road), 3, 140 (n. 6)
Washington (brig), 6–7, 140 (n. 9)
Wilberforce, William, 54
Wilcox, Norris, 23
Will, James, 148 (n. 37)
Wilson, Henry, 18, 55, 61, 63
Wilson, Tamar, 18, 55, 61, 63
Winfrey, Oprah, 124
Woodruff, Hale Aspacio, 76
World War II, 81, 83

Yoruba Travelling Theater (Nigeria), 104